FROM
SEVEN TO SEVENTY

Memories of a Painter and a Yankee

By Edward Simmons

With an Interruption by
OLIVER HERFORD

FULLY ILLUSTRATED

Publishers
HARPER & BROTHERS
NEW YORK AND LONDON

FROM SEVEN TO SEVENTY

Copyright, 1922
By Harper & Brothers
Printed in the U. S. A.

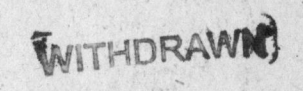

¶ The intimate reminiscences of a great American artist, the painter of murals in the Congressional Library and in many public buildings all over the country, whose mind travels back to walks, talks, and adventures with famous people he knew—Emerson, Thoreau, Charles Sumner, John Brown, and many others of literary New England or the wild West.

¶ His rich, full life in America, as well as his contacts with Whistler, Rosa Bonheur, Abbott Thayer, Paul Verlaine, and the great people of Europe are recorded with a wealth of serious and humorous anecdote and in a flowing, picturesque style that makes them as easy reading as fiction.

From Seven to Seventy

EDWARD SIMMONS : IN 1893

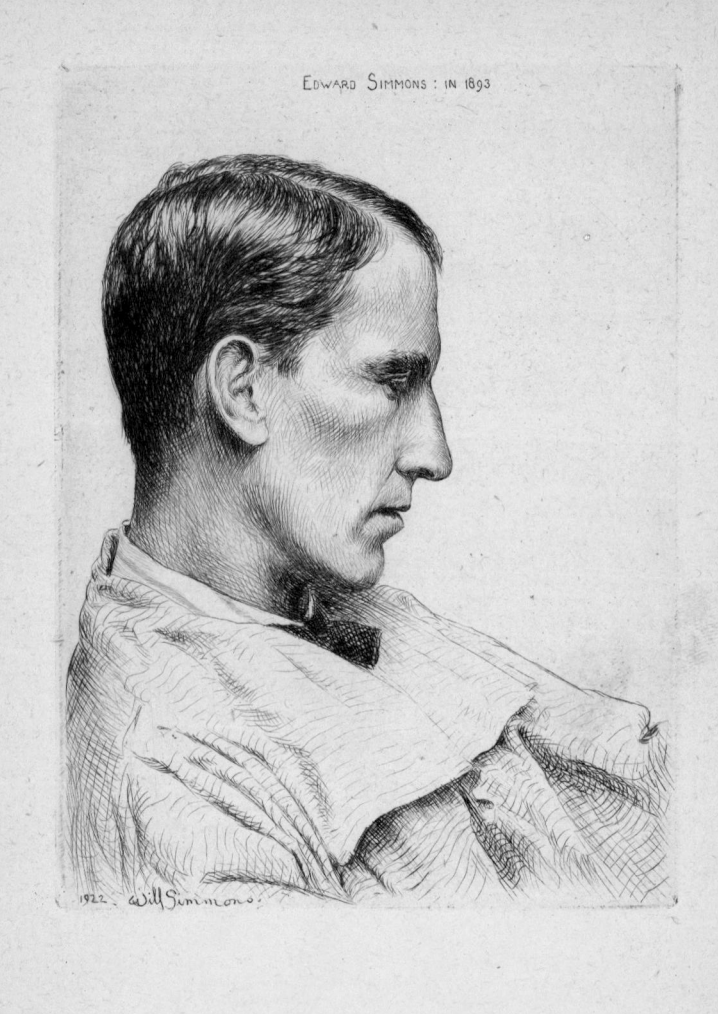

CONTENTS

CHAP.		PAGE
	INTERRUPTION	ix
	INTRODUCTION.—A YANKEE HERITAGE	xiii
I.	MAKING MY EARLY HISTORY.—CONCORD, MASSACHUSETTS	1
II.	FINDING MY WINGS.—HARVARD COLLEGE	24
III.	IN SEARCH OF A CAREER.—OUT WEST	43
IV.	ON BEING A TENDERFOOT.—NORTH OF CALIFORNIA . .	76
V.	ADVENTURES IN ÆSTHETICISM.—PARIS AND STUDENT DAYS	117
VI.	THE MIDDLE AGES.—BRITTANY; SPAIN	141
VII.	FROM BRETON TO BRITON.—ST. IVES, CORNWALL; LONDON	162
VIII.	SUMMER ADVENTURINGS.—I. CARRIÈRE ST. DENISE. II. BARBIZON. III. MONTREUIL. IV. GREZ. V. STUTTGART	184
IX.	FIRST DECORATIONS	202
X.	DEMOCRACY AND THE FINE ARTS	219
XI.	STANFORD WHITE	237
XII.	FINE ARTS IN RELATION TO "A NUMBER OF THINGS" . .	256
XIII.	THE PLAYERS	279
XIV.	AMERICAN HUMOR	303
XV.	PAINT AND PAINTERS	321
XVI.	IN RETROSPECT	342

ILLUSTRATIONS

PORTRAIT OF THE AUTHOR	*Frontispiece*	
Etching by Will Simmons, from a photograph by Benjamin Kimball		
THE OLD MANSE AT CONCORD	*Facing p.*	2
SARAH ALDEN (BRADFORD) RIPLEY	"	10
EDWARD SIMMONS AT THE AGE OF SEVEN . . .	"	16
MARY EMERSON (RIPLEY) SIMMONS	"	22
"THE CARPENTER'S SON"	"	178
"JUSTICE"	"	212
"THE THREE FATES"	"	218
"MELPOMENE"	"	236
"JANUARY"	"	258
"THE RETURN OF THE FLAGS"	"	272
"CLEANSING THE SOIL OF THE BAD ELEMENTS" . .	"	330
EDWARD SIMMONS AT THE AGE OF SEVENTY . . .	"	340

Interruption

IF some curious reader, chancing upon this foreword to the narrative of the life of Edward Simmons, should require my reason for calling it an Interruption instead of an Introduction, I might reply with the obvious evasion that so distinguished a painter as Edward Simmons needs no introduction.

The recipient of medals innumerable, and the most flattering mention in every European capital, surely should need no introduction even in his own country, many of whose public buildings and galleries are enriched by examples of his work in decoration, portraiture, or genre.

But this, as I have said, would be an evasion and not my true reason for calling my preface an interruption, and since the curiosity that can drive a reader to the perusal of matter that is essentially deterrent, wholly superfluous, and probably dull must be of a persistence that will brook no gainsay, I will make a virtue of compulsion and narrate for that reader's private enlightenment a story of a very personal nature concerning Mr. Simmons, the telling of which I had rather hoped to avoid.

The story, in so far as it is related to the title of this preface, speaks for itself, and since it bears upon a personal characteristic of the painter, inherited, I am told, from generations of oratorical forebears, a characteristic which also speaks for itself, I must ask the reader to regard it as strictly confidential and to allow it to go no further.

Interruption

Picture then, Curious Reader, a Boston dinner party at which Mr. Edward Simmons as guest of honor is exercising without let or hindrance the lingual accomplishment bequeathed to him by generations of eloquent forebears, and demonstrating to a fresh audience that the supposed "lost art of conversation" was not so much lost as cornered.

A dinner party, however, even a Boston dinner party, has in addition to its social and intellectual side a practical, alimentary aspect not to be ignored by anyone, particularly an artist. And since the act of obtaining nourishment employs the function of swallowing, and the function of swallowing cannot be successfully synchronized with that of speech, there were of necessity occasional brief pauses in the flow of oratory.

It was at the moment of one of these unavoidable pauses that a lady (to be remembered, as was the "clergyman" who interrupted Dr. Johnson, only by her temerity) seized the opportunity to get a word in edgewise.

Now the traffic laws that regulate the respective movements of the human pharynx and larynx are as inexorable as those that govern our public highways, and at the same instant that the lady opened her mouth to speak, the Edwardian larynx resumed its right of way.

"Oh, pardon me, Mr. Simmons, I interrupted you," was all she could manage to gasp.

"Madam," replied Simmons, with the Chesterfieldian smile the gift of which many an Academician would give all his decorations to possess—"madam, no one can *speak* without interrupting me!"

Interruption

And that is why I have chosen to call my impertinent preface to a narrative which for human interest can (to my thinking) be compared only to that of Benvenuto Cellini, an— But pardon me, Mr. Simmons, I am interrupting you!

OLIVER HERFORD.

Introduction
A Yankee Heritage

FOR years I have wanted to make two cartoons—the first, dated 1800, to be simply a lovely woman holding a baby, and called, "New England with Her Child America." In the second, dated 1900, the mother, New England, is grown old and, clad in a poke bonnet and mitts, is sitting in a carriage with her son, America, who is now a bearded man smoking a black cigar. He is driving, the horse is running away, and she is trying to grab the reins. He yells:

"Ma, if you don't stop that there will be trouble!"

I was born in the middle of the last century, when this bearded man was still a youth, and I have watched his struggles throughout the years, until, without his mother's realizing it, he has slipped quietly from home to go out and mingle with the rest of the world, leaving her, a toothless and old grandma, to sit by the fire and dream that she is still the young mother of the cartoon.

My ancestors were the Pilgrims, that first group of adventurers who embarked upon the *Mayflower* in search of a far-off land where they might worship in peace. They had not the qualities of the Puritans who came later. The Pilgrims were the impractical dreamers, and in one year were lectured by their backers because they spent too much time in prayer and too little in trade. The blood of nineteen different people who made that voyage flows in my veins and, try as hard as I may, I have never been able to find that this pure

From Seven to Seventy

English lineage had been broken during the first hundred years in America and certainly not for centuries before that in the old country.

From them has come to me a want of deference, bred in them by a hatred of kings; a lack of rhythm—the nasal twang began by a desire to ridicule the Mother Church and ended by becoming a virtue; and an intense hatred of restraint in any form.

From my father I must have received whatever artistic leanings I possess, although I believe them to be only a form of Yankee handicraftsmanship. He was a better carpenter than a preacher, and his sketch book is filled with careful copies of many old masters which he saw abroad. I owe a deep debt to some one for curbing his imagination in one instance, however, for he wrote to an intimate friend on the day of my birth: "I have waited to reply to your letter that I might announce the name we had chosen for the bouncing boy whose voice I can now hear upstairs. But, since this year they have seen fit to take from us Daniel Webster and the Duke of Wellington, I think I shall name him Duke Webster."

My father died before I was old enough to know him, but I got quite a vivid picture of his side of the family from a distant relative whom I met by accident one day. He said: "The Simmonses have always been a long-legged set of lazy galoots. We have had great success with the other sex. We have been able to do one thing a little better than other folks and stick to it until we have about a thousand dollars—then we sit down and loaf until it is gone."

Mother was different. When she was a girl she had

Introduction

a serious talk with her dad, telling him it was foolish for her to study piano or music of any kind.

"What is your ambition?" he asked.

"To scrub a kitchen floor better than anyone else," she replied; and he succumbed, his New England nature realizing that, after all, it might be well to have one practical person in the family. Mother's thrifty streak came in very useful, for a young widow with four lusty children to feed did not have an easy time in those days. The sun never rose upon her asleep and her small economies were ever her own pride and the butt of our selfish derision. After her day's work was over, it was my delight—little brute that I was— to lie in bed and listen to her voice, reading to me from some story of delicious adventure. When her head drooped and the book fell from her hands, I, still wide awake, would whine and finally yell, until she pulled herself together and went on. Mother's day was an endless round of doing something for others.

From the land where these first American ancestors of mine settled so long ago, I get the shape of my body and the contour of my face. I look more like an Iroquois Indian than an Englishman. Some historian has remarked that the change in the Yankee is due to intermarriage with the redskins. Imagine the spectacle of a staid Governor Bradford wedded to an Indian squaw! Two hundred years of the same climate, the same food, and the same life produced the same type, that's all.

From Seven to Seventy

"Mon verre n'est pas grand
Mais je bois dans mon verre."
ALFRED DE MUSSET

Chapter I: Making My Early History
Concord, Massachusetts

THERE may have been much distinction in living in Concord, Massachusetts, in the 'fifties, but to me, as a boy, the whole town was only a delightful playground and the people who lived there merely "home folks." To be sure, I invested some of the great ones with halos of romance. This was not because I knew anything about their literary or artistic attainments, but rather because of the lack of heroic characters in the town. Had there been a Jesse James or a Charlie Chaplin anywhere round, I should probably have woven my dreams of adventure about them. But the jail was always singularly empty, and the movies had not been invented. I was forced, therefore, to pin my youthful imaginings upon a Hawthorne, an Emerson, or a Thoreau! I have always felt I was greatly cheated.

I lived in the Old Manse, from which Hawthorne plucked his mosses. It was built in 1760 by the Rev. William Emerson, the grandfather of Ralph Waldo, and was a delightful house for a boy to grow up in. There was a long hallway running from east to west, and from the stairway a line of grisly divines, framed in black, looked down. They were mostly ancestors, and they gave a terrible air of austerity to the interior; but below and above were many redeeming features.

One was the swing shelf in the basement, always covered with fascinating goodies. Here on Saturday night one might cut with one's jackknife a hunk of juicy meat roasted ready for Sunday's dinner, and wash it down with cream from the shining pan of milk next to it. Here were preserves, jellies, cakes, and pies just cooling from the oven; while over in the corner barrels of apples were stored away for winter consumption. I shall never forget the delights of the swing shelf.

The Old Manse was built in the manner of the eighteenth century—entirely of wood, the oaken timbers being held together with oaken plugs. We boys found it quite easy to draw these from place, and we used them for tholepins in our dory. Fortunately, the grown-ups got on to us or I believe the house would have eventually collapsed.

There was a gabled roof with chimneys at both ends, and, of course, all sorts of wonderful nooks and crannies to hide away in. It was up in this attic that my grandmother Ripley was found by a caller rocking a cradle with her foot and holding a book in her hand which she was intently reading. It was written in Sanskrit! She apologized because she needed a dictionary to read this language. This was not so of Latin and Greek, as she read them fluently; but she used to say, "I cannot *think* in Sanskrit."

She whom the name, "Peasant Princess," fits better than any other, was the wife of Emerson's father's half-brother, and therefore older than Emerson. He used to spend a great deal of his time with her at the Old Manse, and she had much to do with influencing his life. One can see this from his letters as a boy.

My grandmother's sitting room was the delight of

THE OLD MANSE AT CONCORD

At the window — Edward Simmons's mother; under the umbrella — his sister Elizabeth; Standing — his first cousin, Sarah Alden (Thayer) Ames; Seated — one of his cousins of the Bradford branch

my life. There was a broad chimney shelf, and low down on the left-hand side a framed bit of handwriting, an invitation to Lieutenant Bradford to dine with General Washington. Over that was a big hornet's nest, a stuffed owl, and, strangest of all, a copy of the "Beatrice Cenci" and Titian's "Tribute Money," brought back from Italy by my father. I always thought, as a child, that the head of Christ was a family portrait and that the Jew with the tribute money was a tradesman. Why the tradesman was giving one of us money instead of *vice versa*, I did not know.

Here in this room I used to dream until most likely interrupted by some caller upon grandmother. Then I would retire to the corner and listen to their conversation about antislavery, human freedom, states' rights, etc.—understanding not a word, but fascinated by the fervor of the speakers. I have seen gathered together in this parlor Emerson, Frank Sanborn, Charles Sumner, and John Brown, the last short and squat, his great beard upon his breast, and spreading his coat tails before the fire like a pouter pigeon.

Something that occurred years later, when I was a student at Harvard, made me appreciate my grandmother more than ever. Prof. Asa Gray, a man of seventy, and the first botanist of the world at that time, met me in the Yard one day and stopping me said:

"I understand that your name is Simmons and that you are the grandson of Mary Bradford Ripley?"

I replied that I was.

He took off his skull cap and bowed low to the ground, saying, "Allow me to do honor to the offspring of one of the ablest botanists I have ever known."

I remember her looks well. Her features were very marked and her nose big and straight. Her hair was then white and she had blue-gray eyes. There is a photograph of her sitting under a grape arbor, looking very absent-minded, with the little finger of her left hand hooked in the corner of her mouth—a habit of my sister and both of my boys!

Grandfather's salary as a Unitarian clergyman was the munificent sum of six hundred dollars a year, and on this my grandmother managed to bring up a large family of children—doing all the cooking and sewing herself—marry off three of the girls, and send the two boys through college. "As big as Sam Ripley" was the saying throughout the countryside, and, although he was lusty and hail, my grandfather died when he was in his prime—in fact, before I was born. The circumstances of his death, which I heard when a youngster, made a deep impression upon me.

It was the day before Thanksgiving. The Old Manse was full of guests and relatives when he took his daughter Elizabeth and, filling his buggy with goodies, drove out to distribute them to his poor parishioners. The last gift delivered, they turned upon the road home, he remarking that the Widow Hall would certainly enjoy the two chickens he had left her. It was a rainy, bleak November night and Lizzie, snuggling into the robes, almost went to sleep, when, looking down, she noticed the reins were slipping. She spoke to him, but he did not answer. Even then she could not realize what the matter was, until, reaching to gather in the lines, she felt his hand cold beneath hers. He was already dead.

I often used to think of that drive—the tragedy of the young girl guiding the horse over miles of muddy road in a blinding rain, and the arrival at the brightly lighted house, full of laughter and merriment, with the sad burden by her side. How did she tell them? Did she call from the road, or did she leave him there and go into the house? How *could* one tell what to do under such circumstances? Perhaps the joyous crowd ran out to meet her and there was a great hush—they never told me that part. But I liked to believe that it was my grandmother Ripley, who, all alone, was watching from the doorway, and knowing intuitively that something was wrong, took the whole situation into her strong, capable hands.

Like all boys, I was intensely interested in birds and animals. One day I was playing in the grass in front of the Old Manse, when I suddenly looked up to see a short man with a blond beard leaning over me.

"What have you there, Eddie?"

"A great crested flycatcher's egg," I replied.

This was a very rare find.

He wanted me to give it to him, but I would not. Then he proposed a swap.

"If you will give it to me, I will show you a live fox," he said. This was too much to resist. We made a rendezvous for the next Sunday.

Although descended from a line of parsons, I had already learned that Sunday was, for me, merely a holiday, and it was evidently the same for him. This man was Henry D. Thoreau.

Accordingly, the following Sabbath I trudged down to his place at Walden Pond, and he, who had "no walks to throw away on company," proceeded to devote his entire afternoon to a boy of ten. After going a long way through the woods, we both got down on our bellies and crawled for miles, it seemed to me, through sand and shrubbery. But Mr. Fox refused to show himself—and worse luck than all, I never got my egg back! I have always had a grudge against Thoreau for this.

Concord was a town utterly without crime. There was no gazing into the jail windows to catch a glimpse of the hideous offenders against the law. I never really heard of but one prisoner in my life, and he was so mild that he hardly made an impression. During my time this man was the only inhabitant of the jail and, technically, he did not belong there. A number of years before he had been imprisoned for some offense, and, after being released, returned and begged to be taken in again, as he was lonely and had gotten used to the place. So, one could see him 'most any summer evening sitting out on the steps of the jail. He was a great pet of the Emerson family, and was hired to play the violin for all the dances.

One of my memories of the Old Manse is that of the Thursday-afternoon visits of Ellery Channing, the poet. I never saw anything written by him until I left the town. He was always asked to supper and always stayed, becoming thereby a part of the mental furniture of the place. He was old, fattish, disorderly, absent-minded, and to me so unæsthetic, that I *knew* he could not be a good poet. I don't believe he was. A humbler than Thoreau, who practically occupied the same position in the estimation of the Emersons. I remember

Making My Early History

with what was then for me horror, but now extreme sympathy, that years before, his wife had left him because she had insisted upon his having a carpet in his study. This he kept patiently removing until, returning from a camping trip, he found it firmly nailed to the floor; so he pulled it up, tore it in strips, and hurled it out of the window, thereby ruining the carpet and both their tempers.

Another frequent caller upon our family was Charles Sumner. I remember him most vividly upon one occasion. He had come in for luncheon. Mother, who left the intellectual part of the life to others and always said, "I find philosophers have just as hearty an appetite as other people—especially for pie," was in the kitchen, making this delectable dish. I was playing upon the sitting-room floor. Suddenly I felt a hand upon my head.

"My boy," he said, "when you grow up you'll find out two things. One is that all men have mothers, but I don't think you will ever meet any other man who has ever had a mother like yours."

My father died when I was three years old and I had always taken mother more or less for granted, and I thought him very silly at the time.

I once asked mother how she came to be married. My father, who had almost been tarred and feathered in the South for his antislavery sermons, had fled North and finally became the fashionable young preacher of Boston. Mother was one of five sisters, and said she was astounded when he asked her to marry him, as she always supposed it was Lizzie he wanted—Lizzie being the intellectual one. It was that way with mother. Brought up in an intellectual atmosphere where learning was considered the only thing of account, she was always surprised when anyone showed a preference for her—a woman who would rather scrub a kitchen floor than write an essay!

Mother's democratic tendencies spread in every direction. There was a pew in church that was supposed to be reserved for the poor. "No one in the poorhouse is any poorer than we are," said mother, and marched us into it every Sunday. The Old Manse pew was farther up the aisle, and, besides, one had to pay for that.

Although she was such a housewife, she had a great independence of thought. A woman had come to Concord, with no husband, and given birth to a child. This, for New England at that time, was a terrible scandal. The boy was my age and went to school. All the other boys whispered behind his back as if he had been in jail, although by this time his mother was properly married to a young farmer up on Barret's Hill. No one ever spoke to her in church or bowed. My mother, very quietly, every summer, put on her best clothes and walked the mile or more up the hill to call.

To me Hawthorne always typified the haughty Southerner. I did not know what haughty Southerners were like, but I had heard them talked about and supposed they were very superior creatures—an idea my worthy relatives would have promptly squelched had they known it. Hawthorne was a hero to me, and whenever I read a romance, such as *Ivanhoe* or the "Iliad," I pictured the conqueror as tall, broad, dark, and spare, with a dark mustache. This was the way Hawthorne looked to me.

I would never have dared speak to him, and do not remember having seen him at the house; but, of course, the Old Manse was filled with memories of his presence.

I remember staring for hours at a time at the words he wrote on the window of the dining room, and wondering how he did it. It read:

"On this day my daughter Una was born, while the trees are all glass chandeliers."

What a sentence for a boy to dream about! It is still there, and there are many other windows with his name only.

I had never seen any diamond rings; none of my womenfolk wore rings, and it seemed strange to me how anyone could write on a pane of glass!

Hawthorne, contrary to public opinion, did not own the Old Manse, but only rented it from the Ripleys. In fact, he lived there only a year or more. It was a great disillusion to find later that the grown-ups of my family did not consider him a great hero, and in fact thought his writing on the windows a horrible defacement of the house—especially as they had had some difficulty in collecting the rent.

My most vivid memory of Hawthorne is during the time I was attending the intermediate school. In front of the building was the town square, separated from the school by an iron fence. Here we boys used to play baseball, and upon going home, I, forgetful as always, would invariably leave behind my dinner pail or my jacket. I was invariably sent back to fetch it.

By this time the shadows had begun to fall, and

very often I saw Hawthorne and his wife pass by, arm in arm, she in white and he dark—dark as the coming night. They spoke in low tones and seemed to be oblivious of any passers-by. I was told that he went out only at night, and this made him all the more romantic to me. The truth was that he was very shy, and so, in the daytime, went only into the woods in back of his house. He was a great lover of children, but so fearful of meeting them that he concealed himself in a hollow tree in order to see the festival that the school gave once a year.

Mr. Channing told me that once he was rowing with Hawthorne on the Assabet River, the north branch of the Concord. He remarked that the reflection of the hemlocks in the water was unusual.

"Which is the reflection?" said Hawthorne, pointing first to the hemlocks and then to the picture in the water. This seems to me to be very characteristic of Hawthorne's method of thought.

Concord was an historical spot, and in the summer was overrun with tourists, who, not content with viewing the scene of the "shot heard round the world," etc., would invade the Old Manse. These gangs were allowed to go all over the house in which Hawthorne once lived, much to the discomfort and derision of the occupants. One day, when I was still quite a young man, there was a party of people upstairs nosing around, and my uncle Gore (Judge Ripley) and I were in the sitting room. My sister had brought in, not long before, a long, draggly bit of Spanish moss and put it on the chimney shelf. While the tourists were upstairs, my uncle rose and, taking the moss, went to

SARAH ALDEN (BRADFORD) RIPLEY
Grandmother of Edward Simmons
(From a pencil drawing by Edward Simmons)

the front door, where, climbing upon a chair, he hung it. It trailed down three or four feet. When the party came down and started to go out, the moss was evidently in the way. Lifting it up so that the door would open without catching it, my uncle bowed and with his best manner as chief justice of the Minnesota Supreme Court, remarked:

"The moss—of which he wrote!"

Every jaw fell; their eyes rolled upward and in dead silence they marched to their carryall.

A little old woman with mitts and poke bonnet appeared at the Emerson house one day and begged for a piece of "your dear father's clothing."

"I am making a rag carpet of poets' garments," she said.

She was refused.

"Is that field yours?" she asked, pointing across the way. She was told it was.

"Do you mind if I trespass? You see, I am also making a collection of crickets from poets' homes."

I should like to have seen the crickets stuck up in a row on their pins, but I fancy the rag carpet would have been more amusing. Imagine walking on Mr. Longfellow's red flannel shirt!

Every remembrance of my boyhood seems permeated with the Civil War. It is hard for me to remember when it began or when it ended. We were always having holidays at school, either for a victory or for a defeat. The flag was constantly up or at half mast at the town pump, giving us the idea of "goin' fishin' or somethin'."

There comes before my mind a ghastly figure (bearded) in a box in the church. A dead man! The first I had ever seen! He had been shot in the South.

One day under the red dogwood bush in the Southeast corner of our place, I found the cap and jacket of a conscript. After escaping, he had evidently changed there. I pictured him "shot at dawn" if caught, so I never told.

I have heard that the Old Manse was an underground station for slaves, but I never saw any evidence of it myself. I remember that Frank Sanborn stayed at our house for awhile when he escaped from the Southern people, who tried to carry him away out of the jurisdiction of Massachusetts. If there were negroes there, I should have known as much about it as I did about childbirth—always being sent away on the latter occasions. In fact, I had never seen but one negro in my life. He was an escaped slave, very old, who took care of our garden, cow, etc. He limped badly from rheumatism, and my uncle Charles had given him some liniment. One day I heard my uncle ask:

"John, did you really try that liniment?"

"Oh, yes sah!" said John.

"Did it do you any good?"

John assured him that it did, but uncle Charles was not quite convinced that he was telling the truth, so he persisted:

"Did it turn your knee black, John?"

"No blackah dan it was befo', sah."

Suddenly, I realized that John's legs were the same color as his face!

It seemed to me that every day after school I was

nailed by my grandmother and a bunch of old women and made to sing war songs. I can see them now, sitting round in a circle, pulling lint and crying (for invariably some one they cared for had just died) and listening to me bellow:

Say, darkies, hab you seen de massa wif de muschaf on his face
Go long de road sometime dis mornin' like he gwine to leab de place?
He seen de smoke way up de ribber whar de Lincum gunboats lay
An' he took his hat an' lef' very sudden, like he gwine t' run away.

"Oh, de massa run, ha! ha! De darkies stay, ho! ho!
For it mus' be now de Kingdom's comin';
It's de year ob jubilo!"

I tried to enlist at the age of ten as a drummer boy. I was told I would be taken when I had learned to beat a tattoo on a drum. Delighted, I ran home to tell the news, only to find that the orderly had been sent up the back street to tell my mother, and instead of being received as a hero I was severely reprimanded. This only increased my disgust with the war.

One of the most picturesque figures of Concord in those days was A. Bronson Alcott. I knew him well as a friend of the family, but on looking back I visualize him in two places. He was very long, slab sided and lean, and what you would call pasty faced, with hair that fell to his shoulders. I can see him sitting in his abominable rustic chairs—with a disease that happens to trees making lumps all over them. He made this furniture himself and used to be very proud of it, but I used to run by like mad for fear of being asked to go in and sit on one of those benches, which I felt might make lumps all over *me*.

The other picture is Mr. Alcott sitting beside our teacher, a woman, at school. It was one of those first afternoons of spring when all outdoors is calling to boyhood and you can think of a thousand interesting things to do. But this strange creature took up a whole afternoon in reading Bunyan to us! Needless to say, I have sidestepped Bunyan ever since.

They tell a story of Mr. Alcott being accosted, in his youth, by a farmer in Bellows Falls, who asked:

"What do you do for a living, Mr. Alcott?"

"I write."

"Hell! What?"

"Thoughts."

"What for?"

"For posterity."

Exit farmer.

I have always thought that if the good Bronson had lived in the twentieth century he would almost certainly have belonged to that colony which inhabits the district west of Washington Square.

Louisa looked very much like her father—pasty and lean, with a very large nose. To me, as a child, she seemed a very unattractive and a most unkissable person, probably because she was quite a masculine type. Her sister May was very different. She was tall and good-looking, with lots of beautiful blond hair. She painted, and later went to Paris to study. It seemed to me she was always lying in a hammock, being rocked and read to by my brother or Julian Hawthorne. Louisa may have been impressed with this picture, as May is the Amy of *Little Women*, and these two boys are supposed to be a composite

Making My Early History

hero. I have been told I was the little boy who rolled downstairs in his nightgown, in the story of the Pickwick Club entertainment, but do not remember the actual occurrence.

Louisa was evidently quite awkward, and in many ways not house broke; also absent-minded and careless, as is the traditional author. It seems that her manners at table were commented upon once too often by other members of her family. She decided not to stand it. So one morning she managed to be the first at breakfast, and when the remainder of the family turned up in the dining room they were greeted with a strange sight. Louisa had pinned the New York *Tribune* around her head and was wearing it like a great helmet. The pages reached the table and completely covered her plate. Only her hands were visible. At intervals they would come out, take something, and retire behind the paper again. For weeks she kept this up and no amount of pleading would stop her, until there was a general abject apology from the whole family.

None of the second generation appreciated the Concord atmosphere. Louisa tells of her astonishment, when grown, to learn that no society was so fine or intellectual as that of her childhood.

The saddest results of this strangely intellectual atmosphere was the number of spinsters it produced. The Misses Blood were always a curious sight to me. Their house, way up in the woods, was chair to chair and bureau to bureau, completely around the rooms, with priceless old Colonial furniture, but their economies were a revelation. Every Sunday they would stop in front of the Old Manse at the foot of the avenue and, retiring into a niche in the trees, put on their shoes and stockings, which they had carried during the three-mile walk. They always stayed for second service, and one of my amusements, when the sermon was dull, was to watch them begin their lunch, which generally consisted of Bent's water crackers. In and out, in and out went the hard, round objects, in their attempts to bite with their one or two remaining back teeth. The sight almost hypnotized me.

Their death, which occurred after I was grown up, was one of the unspoken tragedies of life. One day a farmer passed and noticed there was no smoke coming from their chimney. He went in and found one of the sisters dead at the bottom of the cellar stairs, having fallen down and broken her leg. The other sister, who had become paralyzed and deaf, was sitting in a chair upstairs, also dead. The one had not been able to move after her fall, and the other could not hear her cries. Both had died from starvation.

I was brought up as a young duke—without the estates!—and I was never allowed to earn money. I recall being severely reprimanded by my mother and made to walk back three miles to return a nickel a man had given me for running an errand. I was told I should have been glad to do it for nothing. I remember my surprise, years later, when I was in Europe, to hear that Americans were "commercial." The desire for great material gain was either astonishingly developed in one generation, or did it, as I suspect, creep in a little as the emigration from the Old World increased? Certainly there was none of it in that truly American town of Concord, Massachusetts.

EDWARD SIMMONS
At the age of seven

Making My Early History

In Concord it was no disgrace to be poor—nearly everyone was—and until I was nearly grown I never had a new suit of clothes. My brother's and my breeches were made from the old army uniforms, the cloth having a wearing quality that was almost like iron and would pull a nail out of anything rather than tear. We were called "Blue Legs" until we were quite grown up.

My cousins, the Emersons, represented affluence, in my childish mind. Their house was a square wooden one, set among trees, mostly pines and chestnuts. There was a solemn, gravelike quality to it. I remember going down alone on errands, and always had a feeling of awe upon approaching it. I think this was because the trees were so close to the house that the grass would not grow and everything was damp around it. The door was always open, and Mr. Emerson generally came into the hall when anyone approached. This was a wonderful relief to me, as I was terrified by the women and servants. The inside gave me the impression of wealth and spaciousness. It may have been the reflection of the talk I heard at home, but it seemed very impressive and august.

No amount of grown-up talk could make me fear Mr. Emerson, however, or feel the slighest embarrassment in his presence. He seemed, like my grandmother, to be a perfect example of serenity. He received me as an equal and entertained me as if I were a young prince. He had reached that extreme height of simplicity where he could be interesting to a boy, and, while I preferred him to any of the others, I was quite sure he did not count for as much.

Mr. Emerson's study was to the right of the hall. There was a large fireplace, and what were to me magnificent red-velvet chairs on either side. There must have been hangings of the same material, as I got the feeling of crimson everywhere. From the floor to the ceiling, the walls were lined with books—books that had been read and reread until the bindings were very much worn.

Of my early memories of Mr. Emerson, two are most vivid. The first in his garden, where he often took me, walking slowly about and telling me of each flower and plant as if it were a particular friend. I never read his *Days* that I do not visualize him in his "pleached garden," showing me his pear trees.

The second memory is of Thanksgiving time. Every year on this day there was a gathering of the clan at the Emersons. There were the Thayers, Jacksons, Emersons, Simmonses, Bradfords, and Ripleys, but no others. The dinner was the traditional New England affair, the table heaped with food; and the conversation consisted of the usual family gossip. I remember there was always a discussion among the women as to whether one said Mr. Emerson or Cousin Waldo.

As soon as dessert was served and the nuts and fruit brought on, there was a little ceremony that was invariably performed. Mr. Emerson would look down from the head of the table and, pretending not so see me, say:

"Where is that little boy who likes figs?"

This was my cue to march up to him, and, taking me on his knee, he would pop into my mouth, one by

Making My Early History

one, these delightful and expensive fruits, until I could not contain another one. Of course, my mother protested all the time, but he paid not the slightest attention.

After dinner, in the evening, we played all sorts of games such as dumb crambo, and then everyone had to perform. It was a pet theory of Mr. Emerson's that everyone should learn self-expression, and he demanded a recitation from the children of four and five up to those of the marriageable age. There was absolutely no way to get out of this.

Despite the protests of the women, Mr. Emerson would have his after-dinner cigar. In fact, he almost always got his way, although he was never dictatorial. Sometimes it was with a gentle remark. When his wife asked him if she could have a spiritualistic meeting in the front parlor, he answered her with Hotspur's words:

"Certainly, for well I know thou willst not utter what thou dost not know and so far will I trust thee, gentle Kate!"

On another occasion, when Aunt Mary was visiting the family, he happened to be in Boston. Aunt Mary slept in her coffin. She was very small, so purchased it before her death to be sure she had the right size and would not rattle! Mr. Emerson wrote to his wife in Concord, telling her he was going to bring some notables home for a visit, and begged her to persuade Aunt Mary not to wear her shroud at breakfast.

Emerson's sense of honor and justice were two of his most important qualities. The farmers used to come to him to settle their legal quarrels. Whatever difference of religious opinion the community held, they refused to allow him to be criticized in any way. When the Rev. Grindell Reynolds—an excellent but limited divine—got up in the Unitarian church and referred to the street upon which Emerson lived as "Atheist Lane," the congregation rose in a body and filed out.

Another instance of his very highly developed sense of justice is the case of General Loring, who was supposed to be a traitor to the antislavery movement. The lesser minds raved and swore they would never speak to him again. Whittier wrote a poem about him. Emerson gave no tongue, but one evening after a Lyceum lecture in Salem he saw the general in line with those who wished to congratulate and shake hands with him. Speaking very distinctly so that everyone about could hear, he said, taking the proffered hand:

"General Loring, if what I hear of you be true—I shake hands with you under protest."

The last time I saw Mr. Emerson was in 1879. I was in my twenty-seventh year, had just returned from California, and was spending some time in Concord before going abroad. Charles H. Davis, the painter, was visiting me at the Old Manse, and we both went over and supped with him. He seemed much older, but was still that example of perfect serenity I had known as a boy. His memory was beginning to fail him, which made him a bit querulous, but his daughter Ellen supplied it whenever she could. For example, he forgot that he had ever seen Tom Taylor's tribute, or apology, to Lincoln, in *Punch*—in spite of the fact that it is included in the Parnassus—and read it to us, at my request, with astonishment and delight. He read beautifully, and his voice retained all of its old hypnotic quality.

While his memory failed in the detail of names and places, he still retained, in most cases, his fascinating mode of expression, and the process of thought was still there. He said the night Davis and I were there— "Last week, it was the day . . . the day that . . . who was it was here? Ellen, can you remember? Oh! It was our religious friend." He referred to Whittier.

He asked, upon going out for a walk, "Where is that thing everybody borrows and no one ever returns." He meant an umbrella and had forgotten the name.

This story was told me by my mother. They knew (the women) that Emerson's opinion of Longfellow was the same as theirs—the Bromides—and that the two men, of course, loved and admired each other—which they did not. Of course, Mr. Emerson must go to the funeral of the poet. Accordingly, the poor man was pulled up, himself more dead than alive, and brought down to Cambridge. He sat at the church, seemingly unconscious of the *raison d'être* of it all. Then he rose (holding on to his coat tails was not effective) and joined the procession about the body.

On crossing the Cambridge Common later, he suddenly stopped, faced around toward the church, and then looking at them, said:

"I do not remember the name of our friend we have just buried, but he had a beautiful soul."

In some people the loss of memory can be a blessed thing.

I cannot write a biography, and my opinion is of no value, but Emerson was one of the supermen I have met. He seemed to glorify everything with which he came into contact. Like all great men, he was surrounded with a lot of worshipers, most of them inferiors, and, as Henry James says, these Concord figures were not so interesting in themselves as that Emerson thought them so. He was the kind of man who "rendered the commonplace sacred."

He was always a teacher or a preacher, whether he remained in the Church or not. He spoke of Shakespeare as "our man" and Homer as the "old man," showing that by training his mind he stood with one mental foot on Homer and the other, with us, on Shakespeare. He could have been a great lyricist, but, as Henry Adams remarks, there is no rhythm in New England; the climate will not permit it. Emerson was ashamed of his love of beauty, rhythm, and lyricism, as being not quite true to New England. Like Renan, he blossomed the more fully when surrounded by beautiful women. He married two. To me he seems a very shrewd Yankee. Look at the depth of his thought in "Lovers, preserve your strangeness."

It was because he talked to a great number of his own ilk that he penetrated America's thought so easily. I agree with Matthew Arnold that Emerson was the first essayist of the nineteenth century.

The Concord literati are gone, the town has completely changed, but the Old Manse is still there, holding many secrets. Not the least interesting of these was uncovered in about '81, when the house was torn up to put a bow window in the corner of the southeast

MARY EMERSON (RIPLEY) SIMMONS
Mother of Edward Simmons
From a portrait by Edward Simmons

Making My Early History

parlor. The wall paper, undoubtedly hideous in color when placed there, had mellowed to a lovely Whistlerian tone. This, of course, had to be removed. To the astonishment of everyone, it was discovered that the pattern had been printed upon the back of French newspapers of the period of the Revolution. (This economy in paper will be understood by our experience in the last war.) There were editions with the speeches of Mirabeau and many other of the patriots of the time. Think of Frank Sanborn, my uncle George Bradford, and Mr. Emerson, to say nothing of my grandmother Ripley and John Brown, gathered about the fireplace in this room, discussing the problems of the Civil War, while from the walls cried out to them Mirabeau, Robespierre, and Danton:

"CON-CITOYENS!—CON-CITOYENS!"

Chapter II: Finding My Wings
Harvard College

WHEN I passed the examination for Harvard I had a French turned-up nose, two spindle legs, and weighed only 114 pounds. Everyone called me a "barrel on straws," until I cried myself to sleep night after night for fear I was going to be a little runt.

I developed very late and very quickly; I did not shave until I was eighteen years old, yet only one year later I measured six feet in height and weighed 165 pounds.

My mind was as undeveloped as my body, and my proudest brag was that I knew the name of everyone who lived in Concord, Massachusetts, and that I hadn't an enemy in the world.

I had no taste whatever—if I had been crushed under the tongue, I would have given out nothing. I was proud of the first nicknames they gave me, most of them being "Wimba," "Wambat," "Winnie"—all of them being derived from that flattering title, "Wamba, son of Witless." I was proud, also, of being able to make a louder noise than anyone else, due to my training in the public school, where we were taught to go to the back of the room and shout one another down.

It never occurred to me to refuse to go to college. I went because I was told to, and had no particular desires about it one way or another. My expenses of something under nine hundred dollars each year were furnished me by my family and again I never gave a thought as to where or how they were obtained. Money, I was taught, I should not work for, but gifts were to be freely taken—probably this was due in some measure to the inherited ideas of parsons, who are always supported. I could easily have led my class, but I saw no reason for excelling. I was considered a pretty second-rate person at home; they didn't expect anything from me, and to win, for my own sake, things I had been surrounded with *ad nauseam* as a child, held no attraction for me. In fact, I had not really learned to care for books as such, and college opened up nothing new to me except in the line of English and botany. My power of judgment was poor, as I had not been required to use it before. I was conditioned in algebra, in which I was expert, because I devoted nearly all of the time allotted to it in the examination to Greek composition, and could not finish the answers to the questions in algebra on time.

Holworthy Hall, the old Colonial building, was as full of inconviences then as it is to-day, but the rooms were just as much sought after. The old-fashioned grates; the window seats whose yearly coats of paint formed a covering over an inch thick, of a lovely ivory color; the leaky plumbing and general disrepair—gave an interesting atmosphere, and the traditions hung round about as thick as the cobwebs on the walls. My suite, a sitting room and two bedrooms, was given me by Professor Cutler for my service rendered the parietal committee who governed the private acts of the students. In this capacity I was called the "Last of the Parietals," as the next year the summonses were sent through the mails. I do not remember much about my duties except that I had to report to the committee every morning to see if there were any papers to be served that day. The freshmen and sophs generally took the summons kindly enough, but the upper classmen were sometimes rather disdainful of the messenger, and I remember only once being treated in an undignified manner. I had to order a senior who had disregarded the rule about snowballing to appear before the committee. He was very rude to me, seemed to blame me personally, and at last tried to kick me down the stairs. I told my chum about it that night.

"Who was the chap?" he asked.

"I think his name is Cabot Lodge," I replied.

"Oh, you must be mistaken!" he laughed. "I know Cabot Lodge, and *he* would never have the nerve to kick you downstairs."

The pranks of those days took the same forms as they do to-day—lawlessness, vandalism, and kicks against authority in general. The Commons, where we boarded for the munificent sum of five dollars a week, was run by the students; and sometimes they showed a surprising lack of originalty (or was it extravagance?) in the choice of food. I couldn't stand the meals from the first; but when we had mutton every day for a week the whole crowd struck and, rising at a signal and holding our plates in our right hands, we deposited the contents on the floor, singing:

> "Oh, Lord of love, look from above
> Upon this leg of mutton;
> Once it was sweet and fit to eat,
> But now, good God, it is rotten!"

Any jokes on the authorities were allowed to pass if put over in the right way. Old Doctor Peabody, who was the clergyman in the chapel when the pulpit was not occupied by a visiting preacher, was given a class in ethics to teach. It was considered the thing to worry this large, plain, worthy divine whenever we could, and putting asafetida down the radiator, causing a nauseous stink to permeate the room, was the act of some student's fertile brain. If the intention was to bother the doctor, however, this act failed of its purpose, as he took pains to announce to all the class that he was entirely lacking in a sense of smell.

The old doctor led prayers each morning, and it was a tradition of the college that if the bell failed to ring we could plead ignorance of the time and not appear. Alas! the man whose duty it was to call chapel was far too reliable for that to happen. He had been ringing the bell for years and had grown old and white in the service—incidentally, he was beloved of all of us, and our friend.

One morning, however, there was great silence. Nobody went to prayers, and as the bell did not even ring for classes, of course we stayed away. It seems that some brave student had climbed up on to the metal rod that joined the roofs of Hollis and Harvard Halls and, managing in some way to haul up a bucket of water, turned the bell over, fastening the clapper to a beam, and filled it with the liquid. When the bell ringer pulled the rope, nothing happened. The water had frozen and it was some four hours before he managed to thaw it out.

Sometimes the pranks took the form of really

righteous criticism. Outside the college boundaries, and in the town, was a huge statue of a soldier, a memorial of the Civil War. He was clothed in a uniform and trappings, including an overcoat with cape, but, incongruous to us, he wore no hat. A student passing a shop saw an enormous gold hat—it must have been three feet in width—placed outside as an advertisement. The next morning, to the amusement of the townspeople, the soldier appeared no longer bareheaded, but wore a chapeau that came way down over his ears, completely covering his face. The police tried to get it down, with no result except a great slipping and sliding on the sides of the monument. We boys formed a cordon around it and did all we could to impede the recovery of the trophy. At last the fire department had to be called out with hook and ladder, and amid much good-natured joshing brought down the hat, which we promptly pounced upon and bore away. The police would not be satisfied until we told them how it got there. A student, who was a Texan, threw a lasso over the statue's head, and one of the boys climbed up hand over hand. We never heard anything from the sculptor, so our criticism must have gone home.

Even President Eliot was not free from gibes and witticisms. He is a tall man and has a large red birthmark on one side of his face which, instead of disfiguring him, really adds much distinction to his looks. Of course, this was the cause of the origin of many nicknames. I remember the visit of Duke Alexis of Russia, the uncle of the late Tsar. Doctor Eliot, in showing him the college, brought him to my

room. Of course, I was excited, and after they left I
watched them from the window until they disappeared
from sight. The duke was the most magnificent
male I ever saw—six foot two or three, blond beard,
dazzling uniform of white; he represented the ideal
type of warrior. Beside him was our president, lean,
sharp faced, almost as tall, walking with not quite so
military a tread, but holding his own in a remarkable
fashion. The students who had come out to watch
them drew back—you can always trust them to behave,
if necessary—but a crowd of "townies" followed on
behind. Then two little "micks" with shirt tails
flying, detached themselves from the crowd and one
yelled to the other:

"Say, Tommie, which is the juke—the feller in
white or the feller with the red face?"

One day a grinning boy presented himself at my
door and asked if I would take him for a roommate.
I had two bedrooms and was glad to have a companion.
We became the heads of the sign-stealing crowd.
The police commissioner of Cambridge had announced
that he would jail the next offender in this line, and
this was enough to set us madly at it. We stole business
signs and street signs, tore the name plates off doors,
wagons, and horse cars. My roommate's father was
horrified to see on the outside of our door, when he
visited us on Class Day, the sign, "H. H. Crocker and
Co.," which had been missing from his place of business
for four years. When I came home from Europe in
'91, my mother asked me to throw away some trophies.
Among them were eighteen signs of ground glass
upon which was printed in black "Harvard Street,"

and a policeman's badge which I had been very proud of getting in a fight.

I always hated to lie; but at that time was content if I kept to the letter of the truth and disregarded the spirit. I was afraid of flunking a certain examination, and knew I could pass if I only had more time to work up the subject. Thinking up every kind of excuse, I finally decided that only a physical disability would let me off. Consequently, I did something that required more courage for one who has always been afraid of physical pain than it is easy to imagine. Making a deep gash in my thumb, I told the professor I couldn't hold a pen, as I had "cut myself with a razor"—which was perfectly true. Of course, he let me off.

Out of our poverty and desire for a good time grew some interesting things. A crowd of us who cared for cheap vaudeville went in weekly, on Mondays, to the Howard Athenæum, incidentally the smuttiest and most improper show I have ever seen anywhere—and this in Boston! We pledged ourselves to spend only fifty cents on the evening's entertainment, and this sum was generally divided as follows——ten cents for car fare, thirty-five cents for a standee ticket, and five cents for a beer, making it necessary to walk back if we failed to beat our way on the street car.

Whenever anyone had what we called a "find"—earned something or had a check outside his allowance—we allowed him to treat, never otherwise. The feed generally consisted of a barrel of beer and several dozen oysters which we put in the coals of the fireplace, and, as they popped open, threw in salt and pepper, and then squeezed their noses together when they were ready to serve.

From this we began dining together once a month, and somehow came to be known as "The Ring." There were James Duane Lowell (nephew of the poet), Ned Higginson, Ned Walker, Frank Childs Faulkner, Waldo Reed, and others I can't recall; but although many sought to join us, we never increased our number, and I think therein lay our success. We met each time in a different member's room, the host of the occasion providing two roast chickens and bread and butter. The others contributed something strictly limited to a dollar in price, which usually turned out to be a bottle of whisky. Each one of us could bring in his chum as a guest, and as we sat around the table, our bellies full and the alcohol sending a glow over our beings, the songs and stories that passed around that board would have been epoch making, could we have preserved them.

Indeed, a desire to keep some of them did crop up, and it was here, at one of these dinners, that the Harvard *Crimson* was born. We called it the *Magenta* then, as the Civil War was too recent for cochineal to be cheap, and crimson was not to be had. The *Advocate* was the college paper of those days, and we decided it was much too stuffy and needed a rival.

I was entirely too crazy to be allowed an editorship, so had to be content with sundry contributions. I remember being received at home with freezing looks after publishing my first—and last—"poetry," a translation of one of the Odes of Anacreon. The family objected to:

> When I drink wine, etc.
> In my *curving arm* I hold a maiden.

No one at home referred to it. The art of it had no appeal to them whatsoever, and they were ashamed of me. If I had had any Swinburnean tendency, or like Keats, who gave out eighteen-year-old slush of appalling indecency, I would have been squelched.

Another group of us—August Belmont, Herbert Wadsworth, etc., who cared for paintings—started the Art Club. There was money in this crowd, and I was taken in only because they thought I could draw and could be useful. This was the first indication of a desire for the fine arts in the college. I was much disappointed when I got back from Europe in '91 to find that all the first books, records, and lists of members that I, as secretary, had started, had been either lost or destroyed. But the club had increased in outward show, even if it had lost its traditions, and had housed itself quite fittingly.

A club to which I did not belong and one of which the membership was kept strictly secret was the Med. Fac. It was supposed to have originated as a take-off on the medical faculty and to it were ascribed all the very foolish pranks that were committed around the yard. The authorities could never get hold of them, and I do not believe any one of them was ever punished, although some of their antics were dangerous to human life and only the pleas of youth could have excused them. One man placed a stick of dynamite down the sewer, fortunately resulting in no harm; and in my own case a skyrocket suddenly went off between my legs one dark night. This made me think my chum was a member of the crowd, but, of course, I never could prove it. It is said that the Med. Fac. once sent a letter to the Tsar of Russia announcing his election to the organization. He, thinking to add one more honor to his already numerous ones, took the invitation *au serieux* and sent them a present of a very beautiful set of surgical instruments.

There are one or two pleasing incidents or traditions of Harvard that I like to remember—things that help one to a greater appreciation of humanity in general. One was told me by my uncle by marriage. When he was a student in the college he was given fifty dollars by an old "grad" who like him had struggled through poverty to get his education, and told to buy himself an overcoat, the man saying:

"It isn't I who give it to you, but a former graduate who gave it to me; and when you get out in the world and make good on your own, you are asked to pass it on."

No one knew the identity of the first donor and only one person will know whether it is going on to-day; but I do hope that some mischance has not occurred to break the chain—the recipient being too unsuccessful, or dying before he could return it.

Another pleasing occurrence of a quite different character happened during Commencement. At this time the authorities chose certain men, who had distinguished themselves during their course, and gave them "parts." I remember Fenollosa of my class, who afterward became the Imperial Commissioner of Arts for the Japanese government, was one of these selected, and delivered an essay on Leibnitz. The students always held fake Commencement and caricatured the parts. A boy can be disrespectful or irreverent, and a thing is generally no good if he does not make fun of it; but every now and then something hits him and he is serious. One of the students, Frank Low, had made himself so beloved by his fellows that they did not guy him, and I shall never forget how his mock part ran:

>Frank to all,
>Low in his own esteem.

I wonder if this is not the kind of a mock part that America would write for Theodore Roosevelt?

Arthur Bartlett Maurice, a Princeton graduate, once contradicted my statement that Harvard played the first game of intercollegiate football in America, claiming that honor for his own college. As Mr. Maurice is a much younger man than I, and must have it on hearsay, I am going to doubt his knowledge. Besides, I like my own story better. It was in my sophomore year, in 1872. Previous to this time, my class had started what later developed into the modern college yell. Each class had a cheer, generally ending with the usual, "Hip, hip, hurrah!" But, we being very personal, decided to give ours in a different way. So we would begin the following slowly, gradually increasing the speed and making it staccato at the end:

>Whoop her up for '74
>Whoop her up, whoop her up,
>Whoop her up for '74
>Whoop her up, whoop her up,
>Whoop her up for '74
>Whoop her up, whoop her up,
>Whoop her up for '74—
>Rah! Rah! Rah!

Hurrah became "rah," and in order that the men should keep together, one of us would beat time, which I believe was the origin of the "yell leader."

Returning from the athletic field one day, Harry Grant, Coe Taylor (captain of the baseball team), a man named Herrick, Harry Morse, myself, and others saw a crowd of Cambridgeport boys—hoodlums—kicking a football about. We took it away from them and started kicking it ourselves. Some one suggested that it would be fun to have a real football—this was a round rubber one—so we all subscribed and sent into Boston for an egg-shaped one made of leather. To our consternation, we found we could not handle it at all. However, we were interested; some one found a book of rules and gradually we learned the game.

Then it was a question of finding a team to play against. No college in America knew the game at the time, so we sent a challenge to McGill in Canada, and to our surprise we beat them to death. They came down for a return match, and we beat them again. Swiftness of foot was of more importance than strength then, and I was allowed to be one of the team, but could not go to Canada, as everyone paid his own expenses and I did not have the money.

I did not realize that our amateur attempts had amounted to anything, and when I came to America in 1891 I asked a young woman I met about the Harvard baseball scores. She seemed rather vague on the subject and, looking at me as if I were an antediluvian, said:

"Oh, baseball is old-fashioned. Football is the thing."

There is a tradition in Harvard that, although football was not actually born until 1872, the first seeds were planted long before the Civil War. The sophomores and freshmen—always enemies—used to take this round rubber ball out on the field as an excuse for a fight. By 1859 this resulted in so many minor accidents, that finally, when one boy's leg was broken, the authorities stopped it altogether.

One evening after this rule was enforced, a queer gathering of people proceeded to the Delta (athletic field). It had the air of a mediæval funeral procession with its priests carrying tall candles, chanting solemnly, and preceding a small bier borne by draped figures and followed by mourners of every description, weeping and wailing their sorrow at the departure of a loved one. In this case the dear departed was a football, red in color and looking suspiciously like a large toy balloon, which rested lightly in its casket. With all the ceremony of a real funeral, it was solemnly interred.

Three nights after, a very different procession went forth along the same way. There was a clash of cymbals, bright lights, music, gayly decorated banners, and maidens dancing joyously. Again they proceeded to the burial ground where, after curious incantations had been performed over the grave—to the astonishment of everyone who saw it—the soul of the football detached itself from its resting place and rose grandly and sedately to the heavens!

It seems to me that we cannot overestimate the importance of eating and drinking, for out of these desires of the human body have come most of the clever ideas of the world. Conviviality stimulates the brain, and, while the viands may be of ever so simple a quality, the atmosphere in which they are partaken means everything to sensitive genius. From a general

Finding My Wings

poverty of purse, if not of mind, sprang the Stomach Club of Paris, and likewise, if I may compare them, the Hasty Pudding Club of Harvard. It began when two or three clever men found it necessary to economize, and they made up their minds to live on that delectable New England dish—cornmeal mush. Probably, having only one kind of food to cook, they became proficient in the art, for in my day it was certainly good to eat. The three or four men had developed into a large number, and the meetings came to have a very different purpose from that of the economy of food; but never had they varied in any degree from their first idea, and not a single dish was added to their fare of—hasty pudding.

A certain quality of cohesion is necessary to make a crowd of fellows stick together through so many years, so gradually, a number of tests came into being, and a novice must pass these before becoming a full-fledged member. As these tests vary in every case, but all are based on great principles of truth, honor, and manhood, I am not giving away the secrets of the organization if I tell a few of the amusing incidents of my initiation into the Hasty Pudding Club.

For two weeks before his final acceptance, the candidate is required to *run* everywhere he goes, and he must not speak a single word to anyone except the member appointed to be his keeper. I had faithfully kept this rule of silence—hard as it was for me—when one night at dinner I tried to attract the waitress's attention, with no result.

"Speak to her just this once. I won't tell," said Ned Higginson, who was my keeper.

I argued I mustn't, but he assured me it would be

all right, so I did. When it came to the final reckoning and he was asked if I had kept the rules, he told on me. I don't believe I was ever so righteously angry in my life. Disregarding the fact that it was a formal party and I was in evening clothes, I turned and would have knocked him down had they not held me. Then I heard laughs and cries of:

"Yes, he's the kind of a man we want."

You must be the type who trusts your friends by doing (while blindfolded) anything that he swears on his honor he has done before you, but if it is proven that that friend has deliberately gone back on you, you must show that you resent it. For example, my anger at Ned was pardoned; but a son of one of the generals in the Civil War went through all the requirements until he refused to put on some article of clothing which seemed to him filthy (his eyes being bandaged), in spite of the fact that all of the others swore they had gone through the same experience without harm. He never became a member of the Hasty Pudding Club.

One of the requirements is an essay which is taken very seriously by the patient neophyte, but is really of no importance. Mine, on the subject of "Public Insane Asylums *vs.* Private Mad Houses," was never read, for the reason that it was stolen by a ring within the club who called themselves "Owls of the Night" and thought it very funny to reduce the size of the new man's head by destroying his work whenever possible. I was sure I had hidden my essay where no one would find it—in the bottom of the spittoon, covered with layers of newspapers, then melted candle grease, and lastly, the remaining space filled with water and cigar

Finding My Wings

butts. But my roommate told; and I had to lie, when asked for it, so as not to go back on the gang.

One of the most interesting possessions of the club was the Crocodile Book, or the record kept by the secretary since the beginning. At the end of one of the chapters was a charming drawing by Washington Allston, of a fat boy gobbling mush from a pot. I used to stare at this and wonder about the man who did it. Alas! when I went back, some twenty years later, there was no trace of the drawing and no one could be found who had ever heard of it.

These acts of vandalism are found more often among the educated classes than otherwise. I often think of the clergyman who was found with a hammer in his hand, having just knocked a piece off a tomb in Westminster Abbey, which dated back to the days of Edward the Confessor—the only one that had never been cracked or harmed! The judge very wisely did not punish him, but left him to the tender mercies of the newspaper reporters. He is still running. We have not the right to destroy the labor of some one else. The beautiful things of Greece, the wisdom of Rome, music of Germany, and the Cathedrals of France and Italy have been inherited from the past, and if we deface them we are defacing our own property.

I have my small triumphs. One occurred in the Hasty Pudding Club. When I went back for a visit after coming home from Europe, I was shown a fine building, positively shaming the rooms we had had in Stoughton Hall. I went in with a somewhat bewildered manner, feeling like a stranger in a strange land. Then something struck my eye. Where had I seen it before?

There at the end of a hall was a drawing—a playbill for a performance of "The Rivals"—of two cocks, one black and the other of the yellow barnyard type, fighting over a little white hen. Looking in the corner, I saw it was signed with my name!

It is better than money, family, or friends when a whole generation embraces you. My personality was not there; neither is that of the man who made the Venus di Milo—but *she's* there. There are contests as to who wrote the plays we ascribe to Shakespeare, but there are no contests over Hamlet. It's great to see that what you have tried to do has been kept.

There is a poem by Arthur Macy (probably not published) about a Common Councilman who in walking down the street and, happening to look up at the Boston Public building, sees a shield and upon it the design by Saint-Gaudens, of two little naked boys. It runs something like this:

> What nameless horror meets his modest eyes?
> . . . .
> There, reared aloft in perfect equipoise,
> Two very small, unexpurgated boys.

Hurrying down to the meeting hall, he has the Council pass a bill that after this "boys shall be born in pants." The only difference in the opinion of my rival fraternity at college—namely, the Alpha Delta Phis—would have been that they should be born clothed; but after talking it over, they would have decided it should be in "trousers." This substitution of a good old Anglo-Saxon word for one of Latin slang would have been due to the influence of our beloved Professor Child, whom we all called "Stubby."

"Stubby" Child represented a natural revolt against Bostonianism—the practice of putting pantalettes on piano legs. To him his language was a faith or a religion, and I know that all America would speak and write much worse English to-day were it not for the disciples that this man scattered throughout the country. The secret of his influence was that he *cared*, and therefore he produced a result. He was unimportant to look at, had no voice to speak of, and exercised no hypnotism, but he managed to imbue us all with a permanent love of our own language. I am sure he would as soon have thought of using a foreign word in place of an Anglo-Saxon word or its derivative, as he would of dishonoring his own mother. His influence was more powerful, because it was subtle, and although he does not seem to be well known, I have met men in many parts of the world who immediately fell on my neck when I said I had been the the pupil of "Stubby" Child.

My grandmother said, "The law of love is higher than the law of truth," and I think she was right, for love is unalterable and truth changes. Christ's statements may not be true to us to-day; Einstein with his "relativity" may have upset Newton's theory of gravity; but these men remain just as great as they ever were, for in them we see their passionate love for what they thought to be true.

Somehow, I can never think of Harvard that I don't see "Stubby" Child, with that row of yellow curls around his head like a halo, hurling a copy of Chaucer's *Canterbury Tales* out of the window and shouting to the class:

"This man is an Oxford graduate and, according to England, is a scholar, and yet he has substituted the nauseating adjectives 'gay' and 'blithesome' in that immortal description of the Friar in the line which runs:

"As *hoot* he was and *lecherous* as a sparwe."

Chapter III: In Search of a Career
Out West

HARVARD had taught me this—that I did not know a thing—not even the meaning of human life. Somehow I think a college education is of benefit to two classes of people only—those who desire to acquire a social position and those who want to get training in a certain subject. I have not the battle instinct and could never see any use in competition. If I had not come of good people I might have wanted to fight to get with good people, and that is about all college can give. I can remember getting only one real thrill to go out in the world and do something, and that was after a sort of valedictory talk by old Doctor Grey. I had always cared for the out of doors and it appears I stood well in botany. When the venerable professor told us that it takes fifty years to make a nutmeg orchard, and that a million dollars was waiting anyone who would walk into Boston with him the next day and prove to certain capitalists that he could tell the difference between the male and female nutmeg, my commercial instinct was aroused and a gleam of ambition came to me for the first time. I resolved to find out about the male and the female nutmeg.

There was no way to learn anything about beauty in Harvard—no instruction in it and no honors for it. Taking their cue from the Pligrim Fathers and, since then, the Church, they did not believe in the value of any of the senses of the body, but only in the quality of the human mind and the power to ratiocinate. Any expression or feeling for beauty, except that made by sacred music, was common, vulgar, and to be repressed. If Harvard could manage to produce one Corot, one Beethoven, or one Michael Angelo, her name would be known longer in future ages than it will be for all the small imitation Shakespeares she has sent out over the country. Even Mr. Emerson, in my opinion, was half ashamed of his lyrical gift; and the elder Story, the sculptor, is more honored in Boston for a law book he wrote, before thirty, than for any of his statues.

One day in Mr. Story's studio, in Europe, was a group of American business men who always made it more or less one of their loafing places. Of course, they had all been well bred enough to wander around and see what the old man had been working at lately, but it was not long before they were settled down over their cigars, discussing the business of stocks and bonds—what they were all thinking about and all they really cared about. Story stood it as long as he could, walking nervously up and down in silence. Finally he whirled, saying:

"Gentlemen, gentlemen, gentlemen, Phidias built the Parthenon. Who in hell were the stockholders?"

After my graduation, it was a question of a career. I had spent four years to find out that I did not know anything, and was to spend three more to find out what I wanted to do. All my ancestors had lived by talk. I had inherited the "gift of gab," but there seemed to be no market for it in my generation. It had turned from the pulpit to the stage and novels, in order to get an audience. Rhetoric and fiery oratory is not an

In Search of a Career

honest way to teach, as it hypnotizes the listeners. Reading a speech coolly the next morning in the newspaper is the only fair way to judge it. My father felt this and changed his preaching into a dry, matter-of-fact style, not caring to influence by his personality. He immediately lost his audience.

Groping for an occupation, I went to New York and, with a half-formulated idea to become an architect, called on Russel Sturgis. He was a blond-headed young man, about thirty-five, and seemed to me to be quite old and efficient. Looking at me very keenly, he said:

"Do you know anthing about the bearing power of bricks?"

"No."

"Do you care anything?"

"No."

"Have you any rich relatives to back you?"

"No."

"You don't want to be an architect. You want to be a painter."

This quite astonished me, for I rather thought I did, although I had never formulated the desire in my mind. Besides, to be a painter was not an occupation— but rather on par with a strolling player, a tinker, or a mountebank. Mr. Sturgis told me that my ideas were all wrong and that the painters of the day were real people and, furthermore, making a lot of money. Of course, I could not start in then, but resolved to hold the thought in the back of my mind. In the meantime, my New England coat was feeling so tight as almost to burst the seams if I did not get out of it. I wanted to get away from something. I knew not what. But freedom lay away from home, so, starting out with two hundred and fifty dollars, I went as far as I dared, which was Cincinnati, Ohio.

There was a Boston colony in Cincinnati and I landed among friends, keeping the plunge from being as bad as it might have been. I remember nothing of the trip out except the foundries of Pittsburgh. This wonderful display of great columns of fire, shooting up to the sky, seemed to represent, as I had never seen it before, the Spirit of Flame. Upon arrival, I was seized by Jim Perkins and not allowed to spend a night in a hotel. His brother was married to a relative of close friends of ours on Milton Hill near Boston, and this was enough introduction for him to take me into his home. Afterward, I lived with Chap Dwight, whose mother had been an intimate friend of my father's, and it was here that I got my first taste of a European influence. He was a wealthy bachelor and lived like one, but had very cosmopolitan ideas of life—a new change for me.

My first job was an agent for an oil firm which had its main office in Pittsburgh. It may have been the only one I could get, but I rather imagine that my droolings and dreamings over the wondrous flames of the foundries of Pittsburgh invested the work (in my mind) with romance and took away (in the minds of my relatives) the sting of my having to be called a salesman. The first month I made one sale. Overjoyed at getting an order for a thousand barrels of oil, I signed a contract to deliver them at a certain time f. o. b.—Cincinnati. Harvard College had taught me many things, but had neglected to give me any idea whatever of those letters, "f. o. b." My salary was fifty dollars a month, the freight was sixty, so I quit at the end of the month, owing my boss ten dollars.

I considered the matter closed and that I had learned a good lesson; but, unfortunately, I had had a large amount of business stationery printed. Thinking my young cousins could use it to draw on and desiring never to see it again, I sent it home. But I had reckoned without my dear mother's sense of economy. For years I was forced to receive letters from her with

EDWARD SIMMONS
Agent —— Oil Co.

at the head of the page.

After this not very profitable occupation I turned my attention to tutoring, fitting a boy for West Point, and another for the Yale Scientific School. The former was the son of an ignorant Irishman and had got a limited amount of information at the Jesuit school. I taught him geography, history of the country and states, of which he knew nothing, and I made him learn the Declaration of Independence and simple mathematics. He went in with flying colors.

I found that my business career did not interfere in any way with my social life in Cincinnati. I was still anxious to be an artist and was painting in my bedroom every night. The city was, even at that time, beginning to be an art center for the Middle West. Nicholas Longworth, grandfather of the husband of Miss Alice Roosevelt, had shown a particular aptitude for making money and a better one for spending it the right way. As a young man he had climbed the hills of the town and, looking from them across the water, decided it would be impossible for the city to extend in but one way. Accordingly, he put his savings into land, always keeping one lap ahead of the spread of population. Caring for beautiful things, he began to encourage the fine arts, and it was at his home that I saw my very first collection of oil paintings. Concord was the home of the steel engraving, and the copies of oils that my father had brought back with him from Europe and hung up in the Old Manse swore at everything else in the house. The Longworth collection was mostly German pictures—by Koeck-Koeck, Meyer von Bremen, and two by Lessing of the life of Huss, the martyr, which were evidently worthless, but so aroused my decorative instinct that I remembered them for years after.

Wandering up the main street of Cincinnati one evening, I saw a name plate on a doorway—one I had never heard—and after it the magic word "Artist." I was thrilled. There was actually some one in this town living and having his being and spending his time painting. I used to pass back and forth before this sign, which was at the bottom of a stairway, like a dentist's or a photographer's; and finally, one evening just at dusk, I got the courage to go up. Knocking timidly on the door, I was greeted with loud roars of "Come in." The dingy room was a holy of holies to me—I had never seen an artist's studio before. In the far corner was a man in a khaki apron, using the blackest of soft soap to wash what were, in my eyes, enormous brushes. Heretofore, my own experiments in oil painting had been made with the usual small brushes and a tin box used by maiden ladies. The bigness and boldness of this establishment took my breath away.

When I got the courage to look about I saw that, besides this big Norse viking with the tumbled hair, there was a sculptor in the corner, modeling—think of the daring!—a figure in the nude! I must have presented a ridiculous figure, for there was a laugh behind my back, and, turning, I saw a woman almost naked, sitting on a stool! They asked me why I had wanted to come in, and I told them I tried to paint, but that I had never seen a studio before. I looked with wonder at the big canvases on the wall, and even then realized that here was a sense of color altogether different from that of the German artists, and that the capacity for brushwork was a marvel—for this painter was none other than Frank Duveneck, who had just returned from Munich.

When I went up to West Walnut Hills and told them that I had found a real artist in Cincinnati, I was laughed at in a very pitying way; but later on, when this same Duveneck gave a showing of his work in Boston and was hailed as the "new American Velásquez," I felt a great satisfaction, although I was no longer in Cincinnati and could not enjoy my triumph.

After an experience as a casket maker's assistant, where I was expected to board with him and sleep in the manufactory, and eventually—great stress was laid on this—become a partner in the business, I decided to accept an offer my cousins had made me to go farther west and become a clerk in a department store they had started in San Francisco. I had previously received a proposition to become a salesman of cheap jewelry, for, so this man told me, my line of talk would be a sure-fire success for making sales to "servant girls at the back door."

My ticket as far as Chicago was given me by Chap Dwight, who was connected with railways, and for the rest of the way I paid for a first-class fare and no Pullman—in those days it was possible to sit up in the smoker. This I did as far as Cheyenne, where my troubles began. I was told that the train would stop for an hour, so I alighted to take a look about the town and get some dinner. The only thing that aroused my interest was a sign marked "Simmons" over a doorway with steps leading down to it and quite evidently a dive. There were two baize doors above which shone bright lights, with reams of smoke rising above the heads of men. I went down and started to push open the door, but just at that moment loud voices were raised inside and something whizzed by my head. I looked up, and, not six inches from my outstretched hand was a clean bullethole through the door. I never opened it.

Trying not to hurry, I made my way back to my train and started to get aboard, searching in every pocket for my ticket. It was gone. I begged clemency from the conductor and tried to make him remember that I had got on at Chicago, but I had no berth, and there were too many deadbeats trying to get to California in those days for him to have any pity whatsoever for me. In desperation, I spoke to the baggageman. He advised me to go as far as my money would take me and then telegraph home for more. Anything was better

In Search of a Career

than being left at midnight in this city of careless bullets. Out to Rawlins, Wyoming, was as far as my pocketbook would take me, and I would have two dollars and fifty cents left for a bed and telegram.

Imagine a town eight thousand feet above the sea, freezing cold, again the middle of the night. How I got off the train and over to the hotel, where shown the only light, I do not know. I do know, however, that I put a chair under the handle of the door, candle and matches and my pistol beside the bed, before I went to sleep. Daylight showed no improvement, but only took away the air of dark mystery and bared to the eye a bleakness indescribable. To have been told that there was no telegraph office would not have surprised me a bit, but to learn that it was "not a money order station" was almost worse. Sitting on a stone in front of the hotel, I tried to think out my problem. The temperature was twenty or thirty below zero, nothing grew in the ground, and all the ice and snow was blown away by the terrible winds as soon as it fell. That morning two men had been found frozen stiff within a hundred yards of the hotel. They had not seen the light, which was on the other side of the house, and had simply lain down and decided to stop. To see the dead bodies of these men who had given in a hundred yards from safety was one of the greatest lessons I ever learned—NEVER STOP!

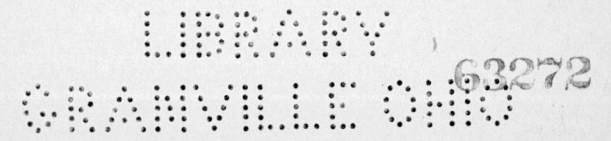

I soon became acquainted with the population, which consisted of mine host and his Chinese cook, the storekeeper and sheriff, two hundred men in the roundhouse, and two women who earned their living in a questionable manner at night and spent the daylight hours sewing and mending for the workmen. Although these women were undoubtedly under thirty, they looked aged and worn, and their hands were calloused from the needle. Every vestige of attraction had departed long ago, and I wondered how they could be so kindly and cheerful amid such surroundings of hopelessness.

At last I formulated a plan and, going to the storekeeper, who was sure to have cash on hand, I asked him if he ever lent money and at what per cent? He said, "yes," but what security could I give? Two or three hundred tramps passed through the town every day, and my word that it would be sent to him was no good whatever. Again I went out to my stone.

A Yankee is seldom in so tight a place that he can't wiggle out, and I knew if I could only think hard enough I could solve the problem. Going back, I said to my friend, the storekeeper:

"If you knew that there was a sum of money deposited in your name in a certain bank in Cincinnati, would you give it to me?"

He answered, "Yes."

I telegraphed to my friend Harrison, who must have sensed that I would have trouble on the way and had told me to be sure to call on him for anything whatever.

"Place one hundred dollars to the credit of Sam Atkins in the First National Bank of Cincinnati."

He understood, for after a cashier's confirmation for the careful Mr. Atkins, I received my hundred, less five per cent, and was on my way again.

We were in the real West now. All along, beside

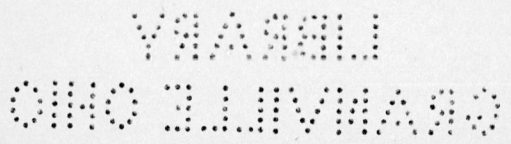

the tracks, were huts built of piled-up abandoned railway ties. Here men had tried to spend the night crawling in over a fire, many having been burned to death this way. It was surely an example of the survival of the fittest. Constantly, from the car window, could be seen the former emigrant wagon trail, and everywhere were the bleached bones of bison and oxen. Every time a hill rose high enough to count, there was a little white cross, marking the graves of a baby or perhaps a wife whose ashes were scattered, like those of the engine, God knows where. No calvary could have shown more evidences of pain and suffering than the trail of these first argonauts across the plains.

A fat man on the train took an interest in me, and it flattered me greatly. I have since met his type all over the world: he is what is called in gambling parlance, a "capper." I was dressed well and he probably thought I was wealthy, for he turned and asked me if I did not want to get off with him in Green River and go to a place where we could get beer and free lunch (then unknown to me) for one "bit." This idea pleased me, as the meals at the stations, which included bear meat and all sort of luxuries, were one dollar. The town was nothing but sagebrush and hills, with one little straight street down to a dive.

While we were eating and drinking, in came a man whose type I had been warned against in Cincinnati, where all the talk was of the West. He was a handsome, sharp, keen, inbred Yankee with a fur coat down to his heels, and kept swinging a bunch of mink skins while simulating drunkenness. I should have known that he was the three-card-monte man, as he fitted perfectly the description that had been given to me; but he was such an artist that, in my youthful ignorance, he convinced me that he was the *real* drunk that the three-card-monte man imitated. Swaggering around the room, he fished in his pocket for some money and, pulling out a roll of bills, threw it on the floor in disgust. Taking out a lot of gold, he indicated that it was the only money he cared to use.

"I've been in the land of Mormons," he cried, producing a pack of cards, "and I learned a new game which I'll show you. It's called 'Find the Mormon.'"

All the men, including a crowd of my acquaintances from the train, who had come in, crowded around him, myself in the front row. My friend, the capper, tried his hand and won several times, making a great haul. Then he urged me to bet and, upon my telling him I was broke, thrust a twenty-dollar bill into my hand. I bet it and won, paying back my debt, and then held out the other bill to the bartender to change so I could divide with my "pal." He reached his head down below the bar and I suddenly felt the atmosphere change. . . .

I turned to my friend. He was gently fingering a gun. With a cold, steely eye, the three-card-monte man stood, a pistol in his hand, with one end lying on the bar, casually pointing my way. In front of me the "barkeep" had risen with another. I looked behind for help, and all the men from the train had silently melted away. Leaving the twenty on the bar, I turned and walked slowly out of the place, not daring to increase my pace by one second until I reached the train.

I told my story to the conductor, and he said if I had carried off any winnings these men would have followed me to the ends of the earth and taken it from me. If I had been killed, they would have hitched my body to a horse and dragged it out into the sagebrush, leaving the coyotes to do the rest.

As an unpleasant sequel to this, I read in one of the first papers I picked up in San Francisco an account of two brothers from Vermont who got in with the same men. The first lost all of his money and borrowed all of his brother's, finally getting into a row with the gamblers, and was shot dead. The other brother escaped and somehow got to the train, going on to Salt Lake City, where he telegraphed home for more money. Watching his time, he went back to the saloon, shot the "barkeep" and capper dead, and left the three-card-monte man dying on the floor.

I carried a pistol on this trip, but up to this time I had had no chance to use it. However, since I had looked down the barrels of several myself, I was beginning to feel very brave. That romantic idea of "avenging one's honor or that of one's women" had quite got into my blood. The train broke down at Winnemucca, in a country covered with six feet of snow. A crowd of us had been having a good time amid much good-natured talking and chaffing, when I saw one of the trainmen, evidently drunk, sitting beside a woman passenger, with his arms about her, kissing her violently. Her husband was standing beside the seat, protesting, with no effect. Instantly I was at the head of a crowd that took the offender by the neck and threw him off the train. Without my counting the cost, I became the hero of the hour. But all was not finished. Our intoxicated friend came around under the window and raged threateningly until there was nothing for me to do but go out to meet him. Drawing my pistol, I strode on to the platform. The minute he saw me his hand went to his pocket and drew out his gun, but I had him covered.

It was just a question of who dared to shoot first. My blood ran cold; but just at that moment four hands came round the corner of the car, two had him by the back of the neck and two had taken his gun away. Then slowly but surely he was withdrawn from view. The conductor asked me not to report the occurrence, as the man was a fireman, a family man, and all right when sober. I was so glad to get away with my life that I would never have told a soul. Furthermore, I sold my pistol as soon as I reached San Francisco, and have never carried another.

The rarest sight I ever saw was the sudden change from six feet of snow to the southern slope of the Sierras. With a plunge from winter into summer, the whole character of the landscape changed. The air was balmy, the sky was a soft blue, and looking like orchards of apple trees of enormous size were the live oaks that covered the slopes of those mighty mountain sides. But best of all, beside the tracks, and almost denying the month of February, was growing tender young green grass! I picked some of it, put it in my buttonhole, and cried. I had fallen in love with California.

After that every shanty station saw me out of the car, smelling the atmosphere and feasting my eyes on the beauty of this big, good-natured, sweet, mild country. At one of these mountain stops, feeling hungry, I bought a large slab of custard pie. Beside the tracks was a cage on wheels in which lay a big female grizzly whose owner was taking her to San Francisco to be sold. The man was nothing loath to explain his prowess in capturing such a fearsome beast, and we all crowded about, myself, of course, in the front row. Looking at us while talking and gesticulating, his hand went fairly well within the bars, whereupon the lazy grizzly, seemingly dozing, closed her mouth over his fingers and backed slowly to the rear of the cage, pulling his arm in with her. With that he whirled, fed his arm in between the bars and, quickly looking around, grabbed my pie and slapped the bear in the face with it. Of course it splashed, and she immediately let go of him to lick her chops, but his hand came out with the mark of every tooth upon its back. In spite of its lack of humor, I truly believe that this is the original custard-pie story.

San Francisco was a very different city in those days from what it is to-day; the sea came almost up to Montgomery Street, and beyond Van Ness Avenue there was nothing but sand dunes shifting and changing every minute. This is practically all new now, as the great fire of 1906 swept it away. I remember the Bay and the ferryboat, the long pier at the Oakland Mole and passing the romantic and lonely Goat Island. The water seemed strangely quiet and strangely blue to me, whose only experience of the sea was the coast of Maine.

The Chinese and Mexican quarters of the city were a

marvel, for both of these peoples had managed to take bits of their own countries in their entirety and transplant them on this sandy soil. San Francisco is unique (as American cities go) in being able to keep within her bosom the civilizations of foreign peoples, in their original state, long enough for them to fertilize and bring forth the best of themselves. Visitors to her shore do not immediately change their manners and customs to agree with hers—perhaps for the very good reason that she hasn't any to agree with—but if it were no uncommon sight to see a Mexican sombrero, it was no less a common one to see a Chinese woman in native costume, feet bound, in high-stilted slippers, looking for all the world as if she had stepped down from an ancient vase, and propelled up Market Street by her big-footed "amah."

This thoroughfare seemed to fade away at the old city hall, which was then only in the process of construction. In fact, the only landmark which appears to have survived conflagrations and the march of progress is the Cliff House. Although it has burned down several times, each new building immediately takes on the air of the old, and whether, by the intention of its builders or the architectural limitations of the rock upon which it is built, it looks the same to-day as it did when I first saw it in '75. However one may deplore the mushroom existence of his familiar landmarks downtown, one has only to take a trip—now shorter many minutes by the change from horse to gasoline—out to the Pacific Ocean and, from a little table, sheltered by glass from the might of the winds, look out upon the same horizon, the same calm blue of the waters, and, best of all, the same Seal Rocks with their brown-coated inhabitants (grown woefully smaller in numbers now), sunning themselves and teaching their young that protection lies in remaining near at home.

The most characteristically Western survival of the 'days of forty-nine" were the San Francisco bars—not speaking of the smartest ones, for those I seldom invaded. There was nothing less than ten cents in the town; nickels they gave away and pennies were thrown down the gutter. Everything was sold in terms of "bits." Of course, there were two- and four-bit coins, but a one was the survival of the mixture of currency that had gotten into the land. Mexican, Canadian, French, etc., small silver coins were all bunched together as "bits," and eight were called a dollar, making one the value of twelve and one-half cents. A drink theoretically cost a "bit," but if you gave a quarter in payment, you received ten cents change. They were bound to take ten cents if you offered it, but too many deals of this kind in the same place elicited some such muttered remark as, "Tight Easterner," or, "Why don't you take some of the furniture along with you when you go?" The free lunch, which was *really* free, was served by gorgeous big men in clean white aprons, and for the price of one drink, you could have such a repast as boiled mutton and caper sauce, salmon and cream gravy with mashed potatoes, all sorts of biscuits, apple pie, fruit, and coffee. Should you dare offer a tip to this husky waiter (or, indeed, to anyone in all California at that time), you ran the risk of a strong right arm or, worse still, a tongue-lashing such as you had never heard in the effete East.

The price of a newspaper was also vague, but you were on the safe side if you offered Willie no less than a dime; for silver and gold were the only metals this child cared for. Coppers and nickels he threw into the gutter and made you a present of the paper, remarking that if you were so poor as that he would give you one. Willie was a character. We never knew where he came from or where he lived, but he had a face like one of Sir Joshua Reynolds's angels and must have been the model who sat to the Lord for the type of "Mother's Darling." He was under ten years old, slight and rather tall, with great blue eyes and curly yellow hair. His occupations were selling matches by day and newspapers by night, and when business was slack he amused himself by calling ribald verses—parodies on such popular songs as "Pop Goes the Weasel"—at the bankers who passed by without buying. He stammered badly, adding much to the effectiveness of some of the lines. His passion was gambling, and his first utterance on meeting an aquaintance was, "M-m-m-m-match you for a dime?"

One day one of the clerks, a Southerner, and myself put up a job on Willie and offered to show him "three-hand matching." Each choosing a different side of the coin, we won all of his cash in about ten minutes. Still in the game, he bet his matches, and, of course, we skinned him again. His lip began to tremble, but he pulled himself together and, saying, "B-b-b-busted, by God," stalked out of the place as pretty a gentleman as ever there was. We called him back to get his matches, and tried to explain. At first he was furious at our daring to think he was no sport, but finally he saw the joke and a light came into his eyes.

That was at noon; at six o'clock, passing the Chronicle building, I saw what appeared to be a pile of boys, all absolutely absorbed in something going on in their midst. In the center was Willie, beside him a pal, and between them one of those formless caps that boys affect, entirely full of dimes and quarters. He looked up and saw me; not a muscle moved in his face, but after a second, his left eye slowly closed as if in sleep.

In spite of its being wide open, San Francisco was then one of the cleanest towns I have ever known. The French spirit had invaded it, and here again the Western civilization had taken the best from these foreigners—in this case, their cooking. The Poodle Dog and Marchand's were already flourishing with their *Cabinets Particuliers* and for the first time in my life I saw wine drunk everywhere. The prostitutes were kept to themselves in one section of the city, and any woman who stayed out on the streets alone at night dared not stop and look in a shop window or loiter on a corner, as she would be taken by the arm by a large policeman and sent to Dupont Street.

This street led up the hill to Chinatown, and all along its sides were rows of one-story buildings, divided into small cubicles, each with one window and a swinging door that led directly in from the sidewalk. Everyone walked here, and it was the thoroughfare for one of the most fashionable churches, even though, sitting at the windows or leaning on the swing gates, were women of all nationalities, addressing the passers-by in the language of their country.

Everywhere were the earmarks of a populace plunged suddenly from hard work and poverty into riches greater than they could conceive of, and with no time to make the necessary adjustments. There were some attempts at making social distinctions, but it was difficult under the circumstances. Mrs. So-and-so, who lived on Nob Hill, was probably only one generation removed from the washtubs of Cripple Creek, while I, a poor assistant salesman in a department store, was a graduate of Harvard College. The father of one young woman upon whom I used to call had been so busy counting his recent millions that he had not had time to build himself one of those mansions with a drawing-room, but still stuck to a "parlor," and used to retire gracefully to the kitchen and allow his daughter to entertain me, uninterrupted, in the front room of the house. In fact, he never made his appearance, and I saw the mother only once, both evidently departing to the nether regions at the first ring of the doorbell. Such a situation would never have been allowed in New England unless the young couple were engaged, but out West the second generation held full sway.

One home, now devoted, I think, to an art institute, had, in the front hallway, a terra-cotta dado with Greek heads running around it; and, lest there should be no mistake, the name of each hero was painted below. But the artist was no Greek scholar. Many words were mispelled, and in several cases (worse still) the feminine article η was placed, instead of o, before a masculine name. What cared the lady of the house for a small thing like that, when she could take me up in an elevator (almost an unknown thing at that time) and show me, stowed away in her attic, fifteen bales of Oriental rugs? And I had tried to sell her *one!*

Quite in contrast with this residence was that of David Colton—pure white marble of Greek architecture, with a beautiful lawn sloping down to a hedge of enormous calla lilies. Some months after leaving San Francisco, I heard of Mr. Colton away up in the Shasta Mountains. I was working out my poll tax by mending roads, when an Irishman, working with me for the same reason, stopped and, leaning on his shovel, asked me if I knew any of "the bloods" in San Francisco. Dave Colton had started when he did and far outstripped him, but had never ceased to be his friend.

The Haggins' was another of these homes where one felt the evidences of good taste and refinement. I shall never forget one party I attended there. One of the family had been to our store in the afternoon and purchased some merchandise, placing special stress on the necessity of having it delivered that day, as it was needed for the reception in the evening—the same to which I had been invited. In the rush of closing the store, it was noticed that these things had been overlooked, and, as the Haggin house was on my way home, I agreed to deliver them myself. Accordingly, I proceeded to the back door and handed these sundry brooms and saucepans to the butler, who received them from me in shirt sleeves as man to man. Later in the evening, with a friend from Harvard whom the young ladies especially desired to meet, I alighted at the house from a carriage, this time at the front door. The butler, who was English, received me with a suspicious air, but let me get into the drawing-room, when all of a sudden, with the light of memory in his eye, he made rather a threatening movement toward me, but, thinking better of it, made his way up to Mr. Haggin and, drawing him aside, whispered excitedly in his ear. That gentleman burst out into loud guffaws of laughter and could not refrain from telling the joke. The butler had whispered the awful news that I was a tradesman!

No Britisher, even a servant, could possibly be expected to understand the Californian of that day. The bigness was not confined to the natural characteristics of the country, but seemed to have invaded the spirit of the people, making them pleasure-loving and easy-going, and, above all, gave them a magnificent, even if childlike, sense of humor. Then the richness of the land and the abundance of everything made them careless of property. Imagine a city where every humble clerk owned a horse and carriage; imagine, if you can, that same horse and carriage to be absolutely at the disposal of anyone—a friend or stranger—so that if you came out of a building onto the sidewalk, and your own vehicle had disappeared, you simply hopped into the nearest one and proceeded to your destination. Think of the president of the Stock Exchange being driven out of his seat by beanshooters operated by the members! Business was slack that day, and this was merely a form of amusement. Bring them any sort of a new toy, and they were ready to play with it immediately. We had an oversupply of ice cream freezers at the store, so I made up my mind to get rid of them. Every day at a certain hour I gave a demonstration out on the sidewalk, lecturing all the time I was freezing the cream, and handing out free samples of the stuff to the assembled crowd. These same members of the Stock Exchange thought it a great joke to join the antics and chaff me, while trying to force me to accept five-dollar gold pieces for the ice cream. Of course they bought out the entire stock of freezers; Californians are always eager to pay for their fun.

Every once in a while there were earthquakes. The small ones were ignored, but the large ones would send everyone tumbling out of the buildings onto the sidewalks. It was excitement, and we lived on it. During the Sunday sermon in one of the churches the building began to shake, and it is told that the clergyman rose and said:

"Remember that you are in the hands of God here in church as well as outside . . ."

At that a piece of plaster fell on the pulpit and he finished:

"But the vestry is good enough for me!"

It was through the store that I met Laura Fair. Hers was a tragic life. One of those women born to be a companion to men—she was not strong enough (or was it hard enough) to withstand the buffeting of man-made laws. Up in Virginia City, where she lived when young, it was said that "the front of her house always looked like a country funeral," so many one-man teams. It was here during the Civil War that she got into her first trouble. Wrapping herself in the Stars and Bars, she paraded the streets, daring anyone to stop her; and over her house, which was the resort of the leading Secessionists, she flew the Confederate flag, saying she would kill anyone who attempted to lower it. One day a Union man pulled it down and she shot him dead.

A. P. Crittenden, a lawyer from South Carolina, then championed Mrs. Fair's cause, and she was acquitted, due to his passionate and eloquent appeal at the trial. A close relationship between the two ensued and they moved to San Francisco, where she was known as the attorney's common-law wife. After some years, Crittenden decided to send East for his legal wife and family. Laura Fair told him directly that she would kill him if he did. Walking up to the family group as they stood on the Oakland ferryboat, she quickly drew a revolver from beneath her cloak and shot him, saying:

"You have ruined the reputation of myself and daughter."

The state of California has never executed a woman, and, while Mrs. Fair was sentenced to be hanged at her first trial, at her second one she was set free. During the 'seventies, she was living quietly, and I had only vaguely heard her mentioned, when one morning my boss came to the back of the store, saying:

"You must go out in front and wait on Laura Fair."

I went out to serve this person, who looked more like an elderly aunt than a murderess, and I marveled that any man would be afraid of so mild a creature. She seemed to have no charm whatever.

The bill for her purchases amounted to about eight dollars, and shortly after, just as a joke, I was sent to her house to collect it. The same thin, sallow, worn-looking woman greeted me at the door. She showed, contrary to my expectations, not the slightest touch of impropriety or dissipation, but—wonder of wonders—when this woman spoke, the sound was liquid music, and the words were followed by a smile so dazzling that one could not help imagining a withered bud suddenly opening into a beautiful flower. She called me Mr. Bill Collector and bade me sit down and have a glass of sherry; then she questioned me about my life.

I have been told she lived on, neglected by her daughter, and once attemping suicide, to a drab and commonplace old age; but I prefer to think of her as she was that day, calm and beautiful by some expression within, sitting in the quiet of her drawing-rooms, and showing the most enthusiastic interest in the absurd aspirations of a callow youth. Laura Fair was one of the few superwomen I have ever met.

My clerk's salary was augmented in small ways, and one of the most pleasant was taking the place of the literary and dramatic critic of the *Chronicle* while he went away for a two months' vacation. After the performances I used to sneak up to a saloon near the City Hall where Market Street tailed off into nothing, and write my criticisms of the plays over a glass of beer. I remember my chagrin when some of the members of Mrs. Oates's Opera Bouffe Company hunted out my lair and burst in upon me almost nightly. It was my good fortune to hold down my job at the time of the opening of the Baldwin Theater, and also my good fortune to have saved that structure from burning on the day before its opening.

Strange to say, not in my capacity of critic, but that of clerk in the store, I went back of the stage of the new theater to deliver some packages, when I saw a naked gas jet, which was jammed against the wall, with a flame ten feet long running up against unplaned boards. I yelled for the stage hands and ran for a bucket of water. In ten minutes it would have been a roaring holocaust and certain to have destroyed—not only the theater, but the hotel above.

The opening of this playhouse (named for Lucky Baldwin) was quite a social event, and everyone of importance was there. I was very anxious to show some attention to a certain young lady whom I admired greatly, so I decided to send her some flowers to wear on this night. My eyes lit on lilies of the valley growing in pots which were quite common and inexpensive in the East, and seemed unpretentious enough for the pocketbook of a poor department-store clerk. The florist assured me they would be twenty-five cents apiece; so, with my usual haste, I purchased a dozen pots, picking off the blooms myself in the shop (wondering at the sudden obsequiousness of the man who waited upon me) and ordering them delivered to the young lady's home. It was a beautiful present and a much-envied one, but a good lesson to me. The lily of the valley is about the only flower that does not grow prolifically in California. Instead of being twenty-five cents a pot, they were twenty-five cents a bloom, and my rashness cost exactly forty-five dollars. Determined to get my money's worth, I carried the despoiled plants out to my cousin; but even here I was doomed to disappointment, for she informed me that the lily of the valley was a biennial and the plants would not bloom again for two years.

Speaking of theaters, an amusing story is told of the earlier days in San Francisco when there was a semaphore on Telegraph Hill which signaled the approach of the weekly or monthly steamer. It was the habit of the citizens to drop whatever they were doing and run down to the wharf to meet the incoming vessel. One night there was a performance at a theater, and the heroine of the play was required to rush in crying:

"My God! What does this mean?"

This particular lady had gestures all her own and accompanied these words by waving her arms up and down like the handles of two pumps, and looking, at least to one member of the audience, like a human semaphore, for a voice from the gallery shouted:

"Steamer in sight!"

With that, every person in the theater grabbed his hat and coat and ran swiftly onto the street and down to the steamer dock, leaving a much-astonished actress on the stage.

My job as a critic had brought me in touch with the literary and stage folk, but I was eager to meet the painters. Alas! they were woefully few. Perhaps nature, in this part of the land, was too overwhelming; but I think it was because new countries seldom produce artists. However, besides Hill, there was almost no one but William Keith putting upon canvas the beauty of the California landscape. He was much more the traditional painter person than Frank Duveneck, and, although he really had money, he preferred to give the impression of the wild-eyed genius starving and striving to get along. I was still using my rattly old tin box, and it fascinated me to steal into his studio and watch this tousle-headed, pallid man put enormous quantities of paint upon large canvases in the most extravagant manner.

An artist who expected to live by his painting had a hard row to hoe. These rich miners cared not a whit for art, and any pictures they bought were purchased through Eastern or foreign dealers who took occasion to get rid of a great number of spurious "old masters" on the unsuspecting Californian. Most of the fortunes had been made quite unawares by illiterate and uncultivated men whose taste was vulgar to the extreme. These were the days of terrific financial excitement of the silver mines of Nevada, of the almost overnight millionaires such as Flood, Mackay, O'Brien, and Fair. The Comstock Lode, purchased at about two dollars a share from the poor prospector who discovered the vein, was selling, when I was out West, at something like $3500 for one-fourth of a share and paying a twenty-five per cent dividend quarterly. Is it any wonder they sometimes lost their heads?

Speculation ran riot, and the gambling instinct (which is almost a disease in California) had a chance to spread itself over an entire population who would almost sell their souls to bet upon what the deep, dark earth would yield on the morrow. In my small way I was affected; but I can remember being in only one real deal. My cousin ran into the store out of breath one day, saying:

"Have you any money? Don't ask me why, but give it to me."

I had diligently saved about sixteen dollars, and it amused me to try the gamble.

In a few days he returned and spilled two or three hundred dollars in gold on the counter. My winnings! As secretary to Adolph Sutro he had got a tip before the Stock Exchange heard of it. This sort of thing was happening every few days.

Adolph Sutro was one of the few educated men of the time. He was a black-bearded, serious, learned Jew, and more of an artist in his line than the others. He carried out many plans for beautifying San Francisco, built the Sutro Gardens and the large baths out by the ocean, and tried to encourage an interest in the fine arts by sending students abroad to study. I have sat many a time in his downtown office and heard him talk about his plans for the Sutro Tunnel. He had seen the suffering of the men in the mines on account of heat and bad air, and the troubles that occurred from the water that had to be constantly pumped out. So he worked out a theory for the construction of a tunnel into the Comstock and other mines, which would begin at a low level and run deep into the mountain, meeting the mines, draining them, and forming a passage through which the ore could be brought out. After encountering many difficulties in financing his project, he obtained his capital from the East and even from Europe, but the hardships had just begun. The first attempts were failures from an engineering point of view, but the final result was of inestimable benefit to the country. Mr. Sutro helped personally with the work, and could be seen with coat off at the head of a gang of laborers, helping with his bare hands to make his dream come true.

Hospitality stretched to its utmost limits in California during the 'seventies. Anything the state produced belonged to the meanest of God's creatures. I remember being invited to visit at a country place and, walking over the estate, hesitated to pick any of the fruit. I was laughed at.

"The fruit grows on the trees for any man to pick," said my host.

It was literally true: but the memory of being whipped, in Concord days, for climbing a wall and picking a pear, was too recent for me to understand this point of view.

One of the most lavish entertainers, and a man to whom the city of San Francisco owes a great debt, was William Ralston. He started numberless civic enterprises, one of which was a hotel which was to make her famous the world over; and he imbued that hotel with a spirit, a hospitality, and an atmosphere which have endured to the present time. Into every detail of this hostlery he put the most loving care. After the fire of 1906, which completely demolished the inside, the walls remained as stanch and firm as they ever were and completely earthquake proof—due to their enormous thickness.

The rooms were built around a central court, very much like a patio. Horses and carriages drove right in here, depositing guests almost at the office desk. The furniture for all the rooms was made of solid mahogany which Mr. Ralston brought all the way from South America in a big white fleet sent down for the purpose. Nothing more completely Western or completely comfortable could be imagined. If you

In Search of a Career

stopped at the Palace Hotel, you were certain to get the feeling that you were somebody's personal guest and that that somebody had taken a great deal of trouble for your ease and enjoyment.

In his own home at Belmont, Mr. Ralston was an extravagant host. The immense house was always crowded with guests, and from a specially constructed gallery he looked down (like an Emperor of Rome) upon these numbers of people, each one amusing himself according to his own personal desire. But emperors fall, and there are always people jealous of a dictator, no matter how just he may be. Ralston lived for others and consequently trusted others; therefore, the blow must have been harder to bear when it fell.

I saw him the day he was asked to resign from the presidency of the California Bank. It was right after he had left the board of directors. He did not act in any way unusual, but came out of the building, went straight to his carriage, and drove away. That was in the morning. The evening papers had the account of his suicide. He had gone out to North Beach to have his daily swim, and, contrary to his usual habit, left his watch and valuables in the life saver's hands, waded into the water, and was gone.

One could hardly pass over the dreamers of the West without telling of the greatest of them all—the Emperor Norton. His was a vision worth having, for he believed himself the deposed ruler of the vast kingdom of the United States. Foully ousted from his throne, he was only biding the time when he would come into what was rightfully his. I suppose "the few faithful subjects," who stuck to him were the citizens of San Francisco. At any rate, they furnished him with a living and the few luxuries he deemed necessary in his exile. They called him a "natural," but I often suspected him of being more clever than they knew.

The Emperor looked very much like General Grant, perhaps because of his bushy beard and long blue army coat. In his top hat he wore a feather and elaborate gold epaulets on his shoulders, while across his breast were rows and rows of medals. He was in no way shabby, and, in *spite* of his costume, gave the impression of mighty dignity. No one laughed at him, no one interfered with him, and he went his way, receiving everything he wanted without paying a cent. Charity? Not at all. He took it as his right. The street cars belonged to him; therefore, he rode for nothing.

He always looked neat, with his boots beautifully polished—again gratis—by any bootblack in the town. Many times he came into our store, asked to see some articles of merchandise, looked them over carefully, and selecting what he wanted, said ponderously:

"I am the Emperor Norton. I will settle for this when I come into my throne."

No one ever knew where he lived. He never asked to have anything sent home, and his purchases were never extravagant. His imagination was slow when it came to material things, or he may have been sly enough to know just how far to go. If he needed a little small change, he sold, at a discount, beautifully made out drafts on his future exchequer.

Many a time I have seen him walk into a restaurant with measured tread—he never hurried. The head waiter would rush up to greet him respectfully. The Emperor would ask:

"Is my food ready?"

"Right away, Emperor."

He would be seated at the best table and given the best the house afforded. Having finished, he would walk out majestically without paying, of course. The Emperor Norton *never* got out of his part.

This could never have happened in the East. In Concord, Massachusetts, people would have lifted their eyebrows and given him food and raiment as if he were a tramp, but indulged him in his whimsies —never! In New York, those smart society women who send their daughters out upon Fifth Avenue to beg money for various charities would most certainly have had the Emperor Norton put in an institution for the insane.

Chapter IV: On Being a Tenderfoot
North of California

> Twenty miles from Water,
> Thirty miles from Mail,
> Forty miles from Hell,
> Girl Wanted—Inquire within.

RUDELY printed and stuck at a rakish angle upon a tree, hundreds of miles from civilization, or indeed from any visible touch of human habitation, this sign greeted the astonished eyes of the passengers who traveled on the stage line from Redding to Shasta in the north of California in '75. Leading from it, off into the woods, was a tiny newly trodden path—an invitation that any adventurous young woman could hardly fail to take—had any come that way. But there was the joke—few did.

These Westerners made jests of everything, their loneliness and misery in particular, and the characteristic is not dead yet. For just thirty years later, in the city of San Francisco, people forced to rush from their homes by a great conflagration, leaving all their worldly possessions behind them, put up outside their improvised tents and shacks such ridiculous signs as these:

> Old clothes for sale.
> Beer, five cents.
> Fortunes told.
> Dew Drop Inn.
> Rooms To Let.

And while the fire still raged within the walls of that hostelry of which they were all so proud, there appeared over the poorest and most tumble-down shelter of all the words:

PALACE HOTEL.

California still may be young, but, better yet, California is still brave and unspoiled.

The distance to Redding by railway seemed to take hours and hours. There were no fences, no divisions of property, no irregular stone-wall separations, as in the East, and no parti-colored plaids of green and brown denoting "this is mine and that is yours," that I was to see in Europe later on. It was my first view of large acreage—miles and miles of it—and in the distance (real distance in California, which you soon find out if you start to walk it) great hills of red and purple, while right beside the tracks, unprotected from the weather, were endless stretches of sacks rammed full of wheat.

Most of the towns took the name of the first settler, and Redding was called for the father of Joe Redding, who has distinguished himself in many ways—one being to write the libretto for Victor Herbert's opera, "Natoma." One unsuspecting village named "Dorris Bridge," after its founder, had this changed to "Alturas" by a representative whom the voters had sent to the state legislature. When the populace heard that they were forced hereafter (by law) to be called by a classic name, they took their guns and prepared to meet that assemblyman as soon as he got off the stage. Needless to say, he never returned home.

From Redding on was a stage line, winding in among the immense hills, with turns in the road so sharp that the leaders of the six-horse team would have to climb the bank in order that the coach might go around the corner. On one occasion an animal which I took for a big collie dog, but which was in reality a coyote, ran behind us for quite a ways.

By this time I took any kind of a job—took it, and learned how to do it afterward; so at Bayley's, my first stop, I did many things, from picking blackberries to running a mowing machine—only knocking two teeth out of the scythe before I got the hang of it. Old man Bayley, being a democratic soul, played cards with his help at night, thereby taking away from them regularly what he paid them during the day. Life was profitable to no one but Bayley, so I decided to move on. Let me say that on my return trip I stopped again at Bayley's. I was greeted joyously. But I had learned a new game up in the country. I taught Mr. Bayley seven-up, and before I left that place I had won back all the money he had taken away from me when I worked for him, and fifty dollars "velvet"—incidentally paying my trip back to San Francisco.

Having no funds, I walked to my next stop, which was the United States Salmon Hatchery on the McCloud River. Livingston Stone, who had been sent out by Baird of the Smithsonian Institution to run the place, was a retired parson, but very wisely shed his religious ideas before going west. I'll never forget when he let me into the secret of the drink he gave the workmen every hot summer afternoon. A huge washtub full of cold water into which was put a quart of raspberry shrub and a quart of pure alcohol. The men did not realize what they were drinking, as it looked like pink circus lemonade. Mr. Stone knew the government would not O. K. large bills for rum, but pure alcohol might be used for anything.

To anyone who has not seen a fish hatchery it is a fascinating place. The big fish came up into the McCloud River to spawn, and from here most of the rivers of the world were supplied with their eggs. Exhausted from the trip up, for they never touch food from the time they leave their homes, an expert can simply reach down and catch them with his hand. The eggs of the female are pressed out into pans where the milt of the males is squirted over them, fertilizing them in water—the unimpregnated ones being sorted out. They are then ready for packing in cracked ice and swamp moss, some traveling as far as New Zealand. Nature hatches out twenty-five per cent of her salmon eggs, but it was considered a failure if we did not produce ninety-eight per cent in living fish. If we could only do the same with the human race, we could make perfect children and just the number the Government needed.

The Indians were of the tribe of Wintoon, called "Digger." They were dirty and lazy, and, although some of them had been educated in the public schools, they very soon lapsed into their original state. Even then it was against the law to sell them whisky, but I have seen a young Indian boy take a quart, sit down in the sand and knock off the head against a rock, clap the hole to his mouth, and drink the whole thing without stopping. Needless to say, he fell over as if stunned with a blow, and would have rolled into the river if he had not been rescued.

The Indian women were certainly not attractive. In the winter they wore thickness upon thickness of old sacks and rags wound around themselves, principally their legs, and these never came off until they rotted or the summer heat drove them to take knives and cut the dirt-caked and incrusted stuff away. Along toward spring they were objects to keep away from, but in summer they were more bearable, as they bathed in the river almost daily. I remember venturing into their particular swimming pool one day and being taken by the arms and legs and almost drowned, they thinking it a joke. I believe the Indians were the originators of the Turkish bath in America. They had a religious ceremony very much like it which was about as good a way of getting rid of the unfit as I know of.

On the hottest summer day (and the temperature, like everything Californian, was generous—114 degrees in the shade being not at all unusual) they would strip themselves of all but their war paint and feathers, build a fire in a cave, and dance around it. These convolutions began slowly and rhythmically, gradually getting faster and faster, until, at the height of the ecstasy, with wild war whoops they would dash into the water of the McCloud River, whose average temperature was forty degrees.

One day, during work, a crowbar was needed. George Campbell, a Yankee whom I had heard was married to an Indian woman, came to me and asked if I would walk up to his home in the woods, a matter of nine miles, and fetch one down, telling me I could take my time and have breakfast with his family. I should have remembered one or two of George's characteristics and been wary. He used to come in to meals, look his hands all over, and say: "Well, what won't rub off won't eat off." Also, I remember one day noticing him scratch his thigh. I asked, "Got a flea?" He answered: "Flea? Think I'm a Digger Injun? No, it's a louse."

However, I disregarded these small pleasantries and went for the crowbar. There on one side of the tepee was a dead fire, and in it sat the Indian grandmother, ninety years old, entirely naked, and spilling the ashes over her ugly, brown shriveled legs. Some distance away was the wife, rather good-looking, cooking salmon at another fire. When it was done she rubbed it up into meal which made a sort of pemmican when dry. In the large bowl, into which she put this when ground, sat a naked and very dirty baby, quietly amusing himself in the midst of the family dinner! I took my crowbar and departed breakfastless.

Henry Casey, a young architect from Richardson's office in New York, was the cause of my going to the north of California. We met in San Francisco, where he was building some houses, and as the doctor had ordered him to lead an outdoor life, we planned to make a camp in the wilds. I went up in the spring and he joined me in August. Casey was suffering from tuberculosis, and the rough life and high altitude were supposed to be his only salvation. We were two foolish tenderfoot boys, and our amateur attempts were dramatic and almost disastrous—for Casey.

The camp—no tent or cabin, but only a brush shelter—was pitched in a curve of the falls of the McCloud River, which flowed through a gorge, making the volume of water deeper than it was wide. We planned to live by hunting and fishing, with the addition of one or two staple foods, and helped by the large bloodhound I had purchased in one of the towns. All went well for awhile until it began to rain; Casey came down with a violent attack of pleurisy, and our hunting dog proved to be the type that would run back three weeks into the past unless we pointed his nose in the right direction. Poor Casey! What he must have suffered, lying on that damp, improvised pallet with that terrible pain in his side! The rain did not stop for days. It streamed through the shelter, keeping everything eternally wet and all but put out the fire. I did the best I could. First I painted him with iodine, then, taking the gunny sacks in which we had brought food, I hung them (damp from the rain) on stakes about the flames, and clapped them steaming hot to the side of my pal until I absolutely scalded a square piece of flesh off his body. The doctor told me afterwards that it was the only thing that saved him.

For days the rainfall kept up, and it seemed as if the heavens were soon to fall. We were exhausted. Except for one partridge and a rabbit I had managed to kill, our food had been bacon, coffee, and bread of my manufacture. The wood was wet, and it was one man's job to keep the fire going. Life to me was becoming a serious matter. If it had not been for abounding youth, I think I should have thrown up the sponge. . . . Then without any warning, the rain stopped.

I shall never forget the morning it cleared. I had been up for two nights and had snatched only an hour of sleep before dawn. Waking before six o'clock, I went down into the river cañon, unable to get the customary mental reaction from Nature's vagaries. I was pretty tired and the sunlight did not cheer me. Sitting down on a rock in the river gorge, I gazed into the water. Then something turned my attention and, looking up quickly, I saw the picture. Snowcapped Shasta, which had shrunk like a corpse in the graying weather, suddenly towered like a giant, to meet the rosy dawn, and, proud in its setting of the river of low oxidized silver, it rose (as do certain flowers), seeming to unfold on their stems to say "good-morning" to the sun.

Those lines of Tennyson came back:

> And on the glimmering limit far withdrawn
> God made himself an awful rose of dawn.

We do not get these sensations often in our lives, and when we do we do not always recognize what they mean. A Bach prelude in its rhythm, accord, and beauty of sound; a dancer who at moments seems to reach that perfect co-ordination of movement and balance; and certain color combinations—always put a stop to light thinking, and there is—a pause. If we touch the realm of high beauty, we enter the realm of high thinking, and no matter if the effect is produced by the hind legs of a dancer or the thumb of a sculptor, if we get there, we are at the edge of the goal and something whispers:

"Be careful; tread slowly; you are on sacred ground."

I had felt and *realized* my first artistic harmony, and it was in the realm of color.

The sun was high in the heavens before I began to think of Casey's breakfast. Walking out on a huge log that lay across the river and in some past time had been leveled off, making a bridge wide enough for horses to pass over, I gazed into the water. It was clear as a crystal and far down—too far for a line to reach—I could see the lazy fish moving languourously in their glassy pools. All of a sudden, upon the improvised bridge, which was decayed and sagged into the water in spots, appeared a female otter, her coat as sleek as a wet seal's, her long tail dragging after her, and in her mouth she held the most beautiful silver two-pound trout you ever saw. What a perfect breakfast dish!

It all happened in an instant. I was out upon the log with a loud cry of, "Wow!" The little animal snapped into the water and, before I could think, the fish, gills between my fingers, was flapping in my hand.

Casey was asleep when I carried the steaming dish and put it under his nose, crying:

"Wake up, old man! The sun is shining. Here is a king's breakfast for you, and to-night you are going to sleep between dry blankets!"

That day, resting much along the way, I carried Henry Casey on my back five miles to the nearest cabin, belonging to a man named Scott. The next day he was driven to the stage, went to San Francisco, took the boat for Panama, and arrived in New York to spend just three weeks with his family before he died of tuberculosis—not pleurisy.

Sissons was four or five miles from the base of Mount Shasta in Strawberry Valley, and here it was that I went, after the departure of Casey. I wanted human companionship and I needed a job. As usual, the place was named for the first settler; and in this case

Sisson was the hotel proprietor and owner of practically all the worth-while land about. He was a small man and very pugnacious, but he had been in the woods for twenty-five years, and that he had managed to keep his equilibrium for so long was pretty good testimony as to his strong character. Most everyone went to pieces before that time.

This was the country of which Bret Harte wrote. Overlooking the valley, where nestled the homes of twelve families, stood that strange sentinel—Mount Shasta—snowcapped, but inside, a seething mass of fire and lava causing bubbling springs to burst forth in many places, and one at the top so hot that an egg dropped in it would be perfectly boiled. Out of her sides (no paltry spring forming its source) rushed the McCloud River, full born, as Minerva leaped out of the brain of Jove.

Here we were fifty miles from the Oregon border, and no way to get there but by sea.

One day while looking down the side of Shasta through the vast cathedral of trees, I saw, about a hundred yards off, what looked like a rabbit. It proved to be a man on horseback, a half a mile away. A red-headed woodpecker, which is about the size of a robin in the East, is as large as a pigeon in the north of California. All nature is in scale, so that one does not realize the immense size of the trees and mountains. We mowed a field of timothy, and it was so tall that I constantly lost sight of the head of the man who went before me. The stems were as large around as my thumb.

The northwest slope of Shasta looked like a great

big beautiful lawn, and I had planned to go up and make a sketch from there some day. What I had thought to be soft grass proved, on close inspection, to be brush, fifteen or twenty feet tall and so interlaced that a deer could walk on it in summer. One loses one's sense of proportion completely. Even the snowfall, not to be outdone by the other elements of nature, was prodigious in its generosity. One winter I made a notch upon a tree, and the next spring, when the snow had melted away, it was so far above my head that I could not touch it—a matter of eighteen feet or more.

The health of the community at Strawberry Valley was greatly benefited by the numberless springs that gushed out of the sides of the slope, bringing cold water of the first purity. Some of these formed streams which ran under the houses, and if a busy housewife had neglected to prepare anything for dinner, all she needed to do was to open a trap in the floor, put in a colander with some meal scattered on the surface, and pull up one or two flapping trout ready to clap into the frying pan.

The hotel was the stopping place for teamsters, and very rough. The main room held a bar, a table for poker, and a fireplace lined always in winter with these men who drove horses or mules all day and played cards and told stories all night. As I remember Sisson's family, it consisted of his wife; Ivy, about five years old; Joe, of two years—and "Lizzie." Lizzie was a short name for "lizard," and she was taken for granted, the same as one of the members of the family, by the hotel boarders. They would speak about her much as if she were a maiden aunt, and she did not seem to be a particular pet or noticed much. One night a number of these men were sitting in a circle around the great open fire after supper, when a man, new to these parts, came in and joined them. They were chewing tobacco and swapping yarns, when all of a sudden Lizzie ran out from her hole onto the stones of the hearth and played around fearlessly, as she did every evening. The new man grunted and, taking careful aim, spat a squirt of tobacco juice on the little animal. Instantly the others were upon him. The air was blue with oaths, and he was punched and clouted ten feet. Ashamed and very much abashed, he picked himself up without offering any resistance, and the group reassembled as if nothing had happened. These men did not cease to be poets just because they carried guns and had never gone to school.

Justice was administered quietly, and each man was his own judge. The theft of a horse was punishable by death, as a horse meant a man's whole existence. I remember a man who lost his brace of mules out of his wagon as he was sleeping under it. He borrowed a team from Sisson, but returned them the very next day. He had met the thief on the Ridge and had calmly shot him.

My duties were varied at Sissons. I was general help on the farm; I waited on the table at meal time; tended the bar—under which I bunked; and was village postmaster. In the last capacity it was necessary for me to get up at four-thirty in the morning, meet the coach, and change the mails. I shall never forget this. Six feet of snow, the moonlight, and away down the road, a half mile or more, from amid the great trees came the weird cry of the stage driver calling for me to get up. Then with rattle of harness, loud screeching of brakes, the unwieldy vehicle came to a stop, still swaying and swinging on the leathern supports, like a ship at sea. And the effect upon the occupants was very much like that of a sailing vessel. The men rode outside, but if there were women and children they were within, and the memory of the smell of musty seats, close air, sweat, and stale vomit that issued forth upon the opening of the door has remained with me ever since. It was my business to have whisky ready for these poor, suffering souls, and it was certain that some of them could not have finished their journey without it.

There was always some new job presenting itself for me to do. Quite unexpectedly, on the day and night of the 24th of December, twenty-five hundred merino sheep began to lamb. It was dry, cold, with a heavy snow. The mothers, showing the quality of inbreeding, did not want their lambs, would not nurse them unless we tied them together. The Cotswold, of far less value, is a perfect mother, but the high-priced Spanish merino would, on a drive, walk behind a bush, lamb, and go on without it. There is everything non-aristocratic in being a perfect mother.

Another one of my occupations—and, indeed, one in which all of the help about the house joined—was keeping track of Sisson's glass eye. He had a beautiful fifty-dollar eye which he wore to market and down to San Francisco, but this one we rarely saw. His cheap ten-dollar one was constantly slanting in the wrong direction, and then Mrs. Sisson would say, "Sisson, northwest." Back it would go at its proper angle, and all would be well again. But the great excitement was when it was lost entirely. Everything stopped until it was found, which was generally in the wooden gutter that led away from the washbasin under the pump. Coming down in the morning, with it in his mouth, he would place it temporarily on the shelf while washing, and it would roll down the gutter, where it remained—gazing fixedly with mute and silent reproach at the diligent searcher. Sisson, being small and of a combative temperament, was the butt of many a joke. Old Andy Gregg passed one day just after a new and beautiful sign had been put up, announcing that the place was:

SISSONS.

"Hello, Andy! Bet you never seen a name with so many s's in it," said the hotelkeeper.

"Oh yes, I have!" said Andy. "'Ass!'"

Any intellectual job—of which there were few—was given to me. I was called "Boston," and was supposed to have a great amount of book learning, so it was my extreme pleasure to be the clerk of the polls at a Presidential election in Strawberry Valley. There were seven voters, and six voted early. They were Republicans. After casting their ballots, they stationed themselves at different positions, one hundred feet from the polls, and, cocking their Winchesters, sat there all day. The one Democrat rotated about that voting place until the sun had fairly set, but it was no use; he was not allowed to vote. I was forced to turn in a unanimous majority for Rutherford B. Hayes.

One Sunday there was nothing to do. I was loafing

around the gateway in my working clothes when the stage arrived. I noticed that the driver looked cross. The passenger—"a dam' Britisher"—who sat on the seat beside him, had evidently "got his goat," for, contrary to his usual habit, he unstrapped the trunk from the back and dropped it into the dust of the road. The Englishman, looking hopelessly around, spied me, and said in the manner he obviously kept for service:

"My good fellow, give me a hand with this luggage?"

I was perfectly willing, so I hoisted it on my shoulder and carried it upstairs, where he fished in his pocket and handed me a quarter. To give a tip in California in those days was an insult, but I was an Easterner and it only amused me to take it and thank him in a respectful manner. After staying long enough to try all his British contraptions for hunting and fishing (with no result), he gave up in despair when the salmon refused to rise to a fly, but could be caught in myriads with the old-fashioned bait—their own eggs—and left, seeming to feel a personal injury.

Some time later I went to San Francisco to be at one of the celebrations of the Harvard Club, when who should sit next me at dinner but our Englishman. I had an important part in the evening's doings and he asked my name, saying he was Sir Rose Price. Then giving me a searching glance, he said:

"I've met you before some place? In town?" To an Englishman, "town" is London.

I said, "No, I met you in Siskiyou County, in the north of the state."

"Oh, but you are mistaken. I met no gentlemen there."

"Nonsense!" I replied. "I carried your trunk upstairs in the hotel and you gave me a quarter."

He stared, got blood red, and turned his back on me for the remainder of the evening.

Great news in town—the "schoolmarm" wasn't coming back! I resolved to apply for the job, which paid seventy-five dollars a month. The board met in Yreka, which was thirty-seven miles north of Sissons, and I went in to see Mr. Jenkins, who was president, treasurer, and seemed to be the whole boss. Seated in his office, which was in back of his grocery store and had a door leading into the bar, he put his feet upon the table and heard my request.

"I want to teach the school at Strawberry Valley."

I told him my name and that I had been educated at Harvard.

"Oh, I don't know; you might lie about that," he replied. "Have you ever been in jail?"

"No," I said.

"Well, how do I know that?"

Searching around for some credentials to prove my honesty to this most suspicious man, I pulled out a letter from John Forbes, who was very influential and owned railways in the West. He looked it over and said:

"Yes, I remember hearing something about him, but how do I know you didn't write it yourself?"

I was nonplused. It was harder than I thought, but I had a last suggestion which I put very timidly indeed.

"I have a letter from Mr. Emerson."

He was adamant. "Which one?"

My voice almost disappeared in my throat, but I managed to stammer, "Ralph Waldo."

"What!" he yelled, flinging his feet to the floor. "Let me see it!"

I handed it to him, and he turned to the end first, reading not a line of my recommendation from the Concord sage. But taking one look at the signature, he ran to the door of the saloon, shouting: "Say! Boys! Come here and meet the new 'schoolmarm' of Strawberry Valley! The drinks are on him!"

That was my examination.

And who can say that art is not more universal than riches, when an illiterate saloonkeeper recognizes the signature of a writer, but does not know the name of a wealthy railway president?

The schoolhouse was a half mile from Sissons, and some of the pupils came a distance of five or six miles. The building was situated in a heavy growth of pine and fir trees, and through this mass of great columns could be seen the fourteen thousand feet of Shasta. Four sugar pines growing in a square had been chosen as a basis and cut down so that the stumps made a foundation. On this the schoolhouse was built of the newly cut trees, leaving a space below which at once became the favorite hiding place of truants.

The pupils, of which there were thirteen, were of all ages, ranging from Ivy Sisson, five years old, to Dick White, a Hat Creek Indian of twenty-one. There were six Sullivans—girls in their teens, and Sammy, about eight. The first day's examination proved that I had a class of varied accomplishments. Dick White could draw, paint, and play the violin well enough to be the musician at all the dances, but had no capacity for book learning and would not obey orders. In the midst of the examination he calmly walked out of the room and went home. The rest of the pupils were at various stages of "readin', writin', 'rithmetic," until it came to Ivy. She piped up:

"I know letters, read words, and can spell. I know my Primer to O. O—x (looking at the picture); that spells 'cow.'"

"No, no, Ivy," I said. "Look again and tell me what o—x spells."

She pursed her lips, searched in the book, and then, with the most cherubic expression on her face, looked up at me and said:

"Damned if I know."

These children of nature had never seen a bible, never went to church (in fact, there was not a place of worship within forty miles), and yet they came to school dressed in the latest fashions—gowns made of material and patterns that had come from New York. Sitting on the rough pine seats of this rustic, primitive school, these girls seemed like little princesses of some fairy tale—that is, until they spoke. I made up my mind that it was my duty to teach them—no creed—but a knowledge of the Bible.

The announcement was made by me that those who chose to give up the Wednesday half holiday would be told stories and shown drawings of people who lived thousands and thousands of years ago. The first week they all stayed out of curiosity, and after that nothing on earth could have kept them away from such things as:

"A long time ago a king of one tribe got into a fight with another tribe. On one king's side was a boy named

David." Then the story of the challenge and pictures of each one. Continuing:

"What do you suppose they had in the way of guns? David had a pouch tied around his waist, and a sling."

"What's a sling?"

Not one of those thirteen children had ever seen a sling; so, of course, the rest of the afternoon had to be devoted to making one out of an old shoe. The next morning they all had slings, and before I arrived one of the boys had become expert enough to kill a woodpecker.

"God" had been nothing but an oath to them before; "Christ" was a little more familiar; but I resolved to stick to the Old Testament. The girls were interested in Judith, and understood her, too, but I was obliged to suppress the profanity that was hurled at Delilah when I told the story of Samson.

That these tales produced a definite result was proved in the case of little Sammy Sullivan. After recess, on a certain Thursday, everyone came in but Sammy. When I asked where he was they all giggled, so I went outside to find him, carefully locking the door behind me in order to keep my scholars from departing in a body. I had not gone far when a something made me realize that Sammy was not out there. There was no brush, and fifty feet away I saw a slight motion among the trees. Stalking him from the back, I heard weird sounds, and there, stuck up against a yellow-pine tree, was a small boy's cap, and standing off from it, with a sling, was the boy himself, taking careful aim at this imaginary adversary. Sammy was fighting over the battle of David and Goliath and fighting it like a male, but the flood of oaths that came rippling from his rosy lips would have shamed Satan himself.

Learning is acquired in various ways—at times, better outside the schoolhouse than within. I tiptoed away, never letting him know that I had seen him, for I felt that Sammy was getting his education.

A new school was to be opened with a grand celebration lasting from 7 P.M. until 7 A.M. Everyone for twenty miles around would be there, the men with rum and pistols in their pockets, and the women in their gowns of latest New York style. The stage driver's wife invited me, her husband having to be on duty and so could not take her. She seemed very old to me—over thirty, at least—and I was inclined to be flattered at the invitation—until I discovered the reason for it. Her baby of eight months had been brought to the party, and I was supposed to take care of it. At the height of the merriment this frivolous woman, instead of devoting herself to me, as I had expected, thrust her crying child into my arms and went off to dance with all the beaus of the place. I was a "tenderfoot" and "schoolmarm," and now had become "nurse." I did not like it. I sat in the dressing room, a sorry figure, for every time I put my charge down he began to let out unearthly yells. Something had to be done, I cared not what. Gathering together a heap of women's shawls and putting them in the bottom of a box, I laid the child upon them and, looking about for something to give him to play with, I saw a flask of whisky on a table. It might kill him, but I was past caring. I poured a little down his throat and rushed out of that room.

A few hours later, daring at last to peep into my improvised nursery, I saw my charge sleeping as peacefully as an angel.

The business of being a teacher embraced more than drilling the children in their A-B-C's. I was supposed to be the arbiter of morals, family counselor, and was in at the births and deaths. In one or another of these capacities I was kept very busy by the Sullivan family. These children—there were six in the school—were the offspring of perhaps the poorest stock America has produced, the parents being part of the flotsam and jetsam which the swirling eddies of the mining times caught up in their mad rush and left high and dry with the lowering of the tide.

"Doc" Sullivan, so called because his uncle was an apothecary in Yreka, had a brother in the state asylum for the insane at Stockton, and he himself had spent some time in that institution. His wife, who was the washerwoman of the town, was addicted to drink.

The day before Christmas Mrs. Sullivan had stopped at the shop of Mrs. Barlow, where I boarded, and asked for whisky. She was refused—in fact, she was never able to get liquor unless some traveling salesman "hit" the town and took her on a spree. Seeing a case of Jamaica ginger on the shelf, she asked what it was, was given a bottle to taste, drank it all at one gulp, and immediately bought the dozen.

In the middle of the night I was awakened by a frightened voice calling outside my window. Snow had fallen and about five feet of it was lying on the ground in that calm, big-sided way it has in California.

"Mr. Simmons! Oh, Boston! Oh, Schoolmarm! Oh, come!" was repeated over and over, and dancing first on one foot and then the other, in her nervousness, was Sally Sullivan, a girl of sixteen.

"Ma's actin' so queer," she cried. "I can't wake her up!"

Sure enough. We rushed to the house, and there was Mrs. Sullivan lying on the floor, stone dead. By her side were the twelve empty Jamaica-ginger bottles, with another smaller bottle, smelling of camphor or some such drug, which in her stupor, she had reached for and drunk.

"Doc" behaved himself at the funeral, swearing only at the end of the ceremony. That was Christmas Eve. On New-Year's night there was a full moon and the same snow. The whole town was again sleeping peacefully, when it was awakened by a loud and barbarous noise. There was "Doc" Sullivan standing in his wagon—he was the head of a road menders' gang—beating his horses with an ax. He had stopped at every milepost along the highway and clipped off the number, saying that he wanted no lies on his road. He had gone suddenly raving mad!

There was a man named Charley Williams living near by, and he and I followed up to the Sullivan house. Charley was old, but he was fearless. I once saw him walk right up to a man who was pointing a loaded pistol at him and take it out of his hand. He always said:

"There ain't no danger in a gun."

When we arrived at "Doc's" we saw a strange sight. There he was, kneeling on the floor, praying, with Sammy in his arms, and every time he uttered "O

Lord!" he jumped, with the strength of a giant, six inches in the air, coming down upon his knees again until they were nothing but a mass of huckleberry jelly. While Charley went for help I promised to keep watch over this maniac, and it took all of my mental powers to control him. He seemed to realize, in his subconscious mind, that his children had a terrible heritage, so he decided to destroy them. First he started to lug all of the things out of the house, smashing them, as he did so, with the ax. His intention, he confided to me, was to burn it and then start out after his children. All the time he kept muttering about "those chains at Stockton—you bet I'll keep the kids away from those chains at Stockton." On the promise that I would marry Sally and take him East he gave up his ax, and by the time Charley had come back he was quite willing to go down to Sissons.

Charley had got the one physician of the countryside to go on ahead and say we were coming, and, although the men had all promised to help, there was not one in sight when we "hit" the town.

From here "Doc's" nephew, a puny kid; old Charley Williams, who was brave but physically weak, and myself, started to drive him on to Yreka, the physician going ahead once more to make the arrangements and warn the police. The thought of that trip is one long nightmare. His mind worked so fast it was almost impossible to keep up with him. I was his especial friend and pal, and, getting it into his head that I had a cold, nothing would do but that I must have some mountain balm. This we procured after much trouble, and my whole journey was enlivened by eating whole bunches of this herb and washing it down with gallons of water. His chief amusement was to jump up in the air, kick the horses, and land with both feet and with such force that he finally knocked the bottom out of the wagon.

All of a sudden, without the slightest sign, he was over the dashboard and rushing across the fields toward a farmhouse we were passing. When I got up to him, there was "Doc," kneeling beside the pump, drinking water, while beside him stood Mrs. Hall, the farmer's wife, stroking his head, petting him, and talking to him in a low, controlled voice. Strange is this power of women to realize a situation. I got him away, but we learned afterward that when her husband came back home, an hour later, Mrs. Hall was lying at the pump in a dead faint.

We arrived in Yreka at six. The police showed up at nine. We tried to keep "Doc" in a barn, but his spirits were rising every moment, and I decided to tire him out; besides, I had a grudge against the police and citizens for being such cowards and deserting us. I had to play the game with "Doc," and ours was certainly a tour of destruction. Every place we went into was wrecked—bottles broken and bars smashed. It looked as if a cyclone had hit Yreka. Finally, he said he was hungry, so we found a restaurant. As soon as we went into a place it was ours, as everyone faded away. There was no waiter in sight, so the proprietor waited on us himself, bringing in a huge steak and—I had hard work to keep my balance—an enormous butcher knife to carve it with! But "Doc" did not want to cut his meat. He merely grabbed it up in his hands and wolfed it.

Just then I saw faces pressed to the window (his back was toward the door), and for one moment my mind left his. This was my only danger; but there was a sudden feeling of reaction at the thought of relief and I let go.

"Say, Boston," he said, "you're goin' back on me!" and taking my nose in one hand, he picked up the butcher knife with the other and pressed it against my Adam's apple. Instantly, my mind was back and controlling his again.

"Don't be a fool," I said—it *sounded* calm—"and kill the only friend you have left." He subsided.

"Oh, all right."

I made an excuse to go out in the back, and a sicker youth than I could not have lived to tell the tale.

But I had to finish my job. Although I am very much afraid of any physical hurt, I am not a coward mentally, and you can control any drunken or crazy man if you stay just "one think" ahead. He was looking at the faces and I knew it had got to end. I said:

"'Doc,' they're after us. I think it's me as well as you. We'll go through 'em like a dose of salts. You go ahead, walk slowly, and when I say, 'Now!'—then, 'Doc'—rush!"

We started for the door, I saying all the time:

"Slow—slow."

And then when he was ten feet away from the crowd I cried:

"Now, 'Doc'!" and put my foot in front of him to trip him up.

By the time they got to him, there on the floor, he was unconscious and frothing at the mouth. The next morning I was so bruised from his affectionate handling that I could hardly walk, and there was a cut on my Adam's apple; but I went around to the jail to see "Doc." He was back in the terrific chains that he had so dreaded in Stockton. As soon as he saw me he lunged forward, yelling and screaming.

"Yes, they got me"—ripping out a thousand oaths—"but they didn't get you. I'd like to eat your black heart out."

They took him to the state asylum, and I don't know what happened to him later; but I shall never go back to Sissons unless I am sure "Doc" Sullivan is dead.

Walter Scott's cabin was twenty-two miles from Sissons in Huckleberry Valley, and here I went during vacation time to help him tan hides and smoke venison. Scott was over six feet tall, with bright red hair, a straight Greek profile, and absolutely illiterate. But a more joyous creature never lived. With him was a man named Peter Klink—a silent German who had been a miner in the days of '49.

One day I was out hunting for the camp, and on one of the benches that ran down from Shasta, with brooks between, I started a doe. I let "rip" and must have "creased" her, as she went down like a shot. Dropping my gun, I went for her, knowing that if I could close with her before she got up, I could knife her. In my mad rush I suddenly took a header. This was unusual in that country, as the ground was free from stones or small brush. Rumpling up the pine needles, I found a pick head; the handle had rotted out, showing that there had been mining there once. Near by—a very uncommon sight—was a large stone.

That night, after the guns were cleaned, the dogs fed, and a brisket of venison hung near the fire, ready for each one of us to cut off a slice with his hunting knife before we went to bed, I told my experience.

"That's Benny Russell's stone," said Peter, and by the light in his eyes I knew, if I kept very quiet, there might be a story.

Taking his pipe out of his mouth and giving me a searching glance, he said:

"You didn't heist that stone over, did ye?"

"Turn it over, Peter?" I replied. "How could I? Think I'm a young Hercules? Besides, what would be underneath?"

"Yes," he said, ignoring my question, "it's nigh onto twenty year since Benny Russell died."

Never taking his eyes from the fire, but pausing to take long-drawn pulls at his pipe, he told the following tale:

"Minin' camps are queer places, and sometimes the folks that comes ther' are the kind—wal, you wonder why they come, that's all. It was 'long 'bout the year '55, a crowd of us fellers was livin' in a central camp and goin' out prospectin', each one for hisself, when 'long one day in spring comes a young feller, rosy cheeks an' soft hands, and asts if he can jine us.

"I'll never fergit the way he looked when he rolled in on us—more like a play actor than ennythin' else— all got up in new minin' clothes, high boots and all, and luggin' with him the darnest lot o' pickaxes, ropes, and contrapshions that ever you see. We was all fer laughin' at him, at fust, but he was so young an' so soft like, that it would o' bin jest like makin' fun o' a gal, an' we didn' hev the heart. So we jest give him the nickname 'Bub' and tuk him in.

"He was 'bout twenty-two year, but he didn' look sixteen. That boy could work, tho'—and l'arn?—l'arned quicker 'n lightin'. 'Twarn't mor'n two days till he had off his store togs and borryed a pair o' overalls. An' he was so happy-like an' joyous, singin' 'round all day like a canary in a cage.

"Seems like luck was ag'in' him from the first, tho'. Nothin' he teched turned out right. Thet boy would give up a claim he'd bin workin' fur months, with never a sign o' color, when 'long would come some feller the very nex' day and strike it rich with one turn o' the shovel. Yes, Bub was allus jest one shovel o' dirt away from vict'ry.

"He didn' 'pear to mind, tho'—not as long as Joe Bascom rode up ev'ry month or so with the mails and brung him one o' them big fat envelopes writ on baby-blue paper. Bub used to walk down the road, sometimes five mile, t' meet Joe—he was that anxious to git that letter. We all knew 'twas a gal, and used to josh him 'bout it, but I didn' guess how serious 'twas till he come to me one day an' said:

"'Peter, I've got to strike it soon, and I've got to strike it rich.'

"'Wal,' I answered, 'this is one deal where yer cain't stack the cards. If you got luck, you'll hit it, and if you 'ain't, you won't.'

"'But I must hit it, you see.' He was more serious 'en I'd ever seen him. 'Fact of the matter is, Peter, I'm in love, and she won't marry me till I can show her twenty thousand dollars.'

"'Whew!' I says. Then to cheer him up: 'Bub, don' be scared; if she loves you she'll take you without a cent.'

"'Maybe, Peter, maybe, but that's the sum she named, and I'm a-goin' to git it.'

"He was allus that way after a talk—seemed to raise his sperits.

"Long 'bout spring things changed. He come in a whoopin' one even' 'bout sunset, and nearly turned the camp upside down. He'd struck it at last. Not much, but gold—real gold—and in this game you never kin tell what's layin' jest 'round th' corner.

"A few months later he come to me agin.

"'Peter,' he says, 'my pile's gittin' big. It ain't gonna be so very long till I have twenty thousand, and I want you to promise me this. When I leave I ain't gonna say good-by to no one, but I'm goin' to slip you somethin' for a celebration, and I want you and the boys to have the rousingist farewell party this camp has ever seen—after I'm gone.'

"Not long from that a trader come into camp—the kind that carries 'round all sorts o' dam'-fool trinkets and changes 'em fer 'most ennythin'—nuggets, dust, er even skins and hides. 'Mong his pack was a passel tied up in newspaper. We all grabbed fur it at onct, then decided we'd play cards fur it—not fur what was inside, understan,' but ev'ry feller wanted to git the first chanct at that thar newspaper.

"Bub won it. We lost heart in playin' against him when we seen how anxious he was.

"He tuk it and begun readin' us the diff'runt items of int'rust, laugin' and commentin' in between—when all of a sudden his eye lit on somethin'. I never seen enny human bein' change so in the same len'th of time. He jest stared—seemed to be readin' it over and over ag'in.

"After what 'peared to be a half hour, but I guess was 'bout five minutes, he looked up—an' when we saw his face he had changed from a boy to a old man.

"We was standin' quiet, not darin' to ask what happened. Most of us thought his folks was dead. But then he threw that paper down on the ground and laughed—the kind o' laugh as I could believe the devil would give ye if ye was goin' down to hell. Then we knew 'twarnt no act o' God had upset him, but some dam' trick that could only be thought out by a human bein'.

"That was the last we saw o' him. He went off into the woods. Joe picked up the paper and said he couldn't find ennythin' on thet page to disturb a body—mostly women's fashions and one piece 'bout a gal elopin' with a feller. I didn' say nothin', but I guessed it. That gal had sent him up to the mines to git a fortune and then gone and chucked him.

"We was all nervous at supper 'cause Bub didn' come in, and 'long 'bout ten we set out to look fur him. The woods is dark at night, an' we couldn't find a trace till Joe, searchin' up at Bub's claim, come on that thar bowlder you seen to-day, and, curious to say, he stumbled over somethin' same as you done, but 'twarn't no pickax head—'twar a human bootleg. Puttin' his lantern down low, he seen Bub's foot a-stickin' out from under that rock, and the whole plumb thing had let down and flattened the life out o' him.

"'Twas a long time afore I went up to examine the place, and when I did thar was nothin' to see but I figgered it out fur myself, and this is how it must 'a' bin.

"Bub had most likely bin diggin' under the rock and gitting out the pay dirt, and when he'd git so fur in he'd put in a plug to shore up the thing and keep it from fallin'. That day when he read that paper and he felt the whole world crumblin' 'round his head, he jest made it literal by goin' up to his claim, crawlin' under the stone, and kickin' out the plugs."

There was a pause.

Peter rose; cutting a piece of the roasting brisket, he started for his bunk, but stopped before climbing in.

"That's why I ast you if you turned over the stone—but I hoped you didn't."

Scott had been fifteen years in the woods and wanted to settle down, saying he would like to see some little Scotts running around. So when the summer camp broke up he looked about for a location. He found a log house that had been built by a man named Carrick, who was hated in the community, principally because he held mortgages on nearly all the farms for twenty miles around. Carrick did not have a right to this particular homestead, as he did not live on it, so Scott went in and jumped the property.

Knowing Carrick would try to use the land, Scott was ready for him, and when he tried to put his sheep in, Scott, who was waiting in a hole in the ground, rose with his gun in his hands, saying:

"*Don't touch them bars!*"

Like all crooks, Carrick was a coward at heart, and, instead of settling in the usual way of this part of the country—as man to man—he took Scott into court. With no money in back of him, Scott won his case, his extreme honesty and simplicity impressing the judge. For instance, I remember there was a question as to whether he was an American citizen or no, and he answered:

"Wal, Jedge, the first thing I remember is livin' in a town about a half a mile over the border into Canada, but my mother allus said I was born in a little red house that we could see across the line, an' I took her word for it."

And so did the court.

I had left Scott and Peter Klink and had gone back to Sissons, when one morning a man we called "the Texan" came racing down the town's one street on horseback, yelling:

"Scott's shot! Scott's shot!"

Scott had been beloved of all, and everyone was aroused. It was quite awhile before we could get the story out of the Texan, but it finally came to this. He had come across a wagon standing all alone on the road, filled with the groceries Scott had bought in Yreka. It was turned around, with the horses facing downhill, the whole weight of the wagon bearing upon them. They were nosing toward home and evidently had been there all night, as they were covered with snow. Looking about, the Texan had seen a trail into the bushes and, going in a half mile or more, he found Scott's body. There was a rope around the neck and he had been dragged into the woods.

The memory came to me of one night when I was camping with Scott. The conversation had turned on death.

"How would you like to die?" I asked him.

"Shot in the back and never know who done it," was his quick answer.

Scott had had his wish.

Death meant nothing to these men. It was all in the day's happenings, but to me, at this very moment of writing, visualization of Scott's body, as it lay on the rough pine bed in a back room in Sisson's Hotel, is as clear as it was in 1877. The rope had been taken from his neck and had left an impress, above which rose his purple head, looking like an eggplant, with the shock of red hair, the pale blue eyes wide open, and the rows of perfect teeth showing, his mouth drawn into a snarl. His body was green-white, the blood having all gone to the head, and under the left arm, where the bullet had gone in, was a little blue spot. But under the right arm, where the bullet had come out, was a ghastly hole through which protruded torn pieces of flesh. I did not know that men died that way.

A few minutes after the body was brought in a woodsman was found who had passed the wagon—it must have been while the murderer was disposing of the body in the bushes—for he said that a Ballard rifle was leaning against the wheels. He had thought the driver of the wagon was off in the woods and would be back presently, so was in no way surprised at the sight.

The minute the woodsman mentioned the gun I was convinced as to who had committed the murder. I had seen Carrick's Indian with a Ballard rifle. It had a broken extractor, and he had to use a withe to poke out the empty shell. Sure enough, beside the road we found a withe covered with powder. An Indian tracker told us, from his examination of the trees, that the murderer had worn a red tippet and was riding a sorrel horse with a white star. The evidence was conclusive enough for us to start out for Carrick's ranch.

We were a posse of four—the Texan, who had been in the Civil War and was a real leader; Joe Johnston, a friend of Scott's; one of Joe's hired men; and myself. We were prepared for a fight, for, as Carrick hated Scott and was probably implicated in the affair, we figured he would protect the Indian.

The way lay over fertile, grassy country, and on the road we passed bands of sheep and cattle. One herder rode several miles w.th us and, on hearing our errand, said:

"If you help me git these cattle together I'll tell you something I know."

It seems that the night before he had been at Carrick's house. It was getting quite late when he heard a mysterious whistle under the window. Making an excuse, he went outside and looked about. There in the corral was a horse—sorrel in color with a white star on its forehead—evidently just returned from a hard run, as it was covered with lather. At that moment he heard a sound, and coming out of the kitchen door was Carrick's son, carrying something in his hand. He disappeared into the barn. Creeping up to a crack in the building where a light shone out, he peeped through and saw the boy giving food to an Indian.

Our evidence was piling up.

Along toward sunset we rode up to Carrick's place. The sheep ranch extended for many acres to the north, while the house, barn, and corral were on the banks of a low willow creek. Carrick was sitting on a bench out in front. Going directly up to him, the Texan said:

"Scott's bin killed—shot."

"The hell you say!"

"We think your Injin Jim done it."

He pretended great anger.

"Well, if he did, ketch him and string him up for it. He'll be back in a little while."

We waited.

It was not long until several horsemen appeared and rode up to the gate. Joe Johnston's hired man, who was a fool and easily excited, marched up to Injin Jim and said:

"We're here to arrest you."

I have seen a prestidigitator work the most astonishing disappearances of material things, but I never saw a human being take himself off into space as quickly as this one did. Jim gave one flick and was flying into the woods. I was off and under my horse in an instant, but my pistol missed fire. He had disappeared into the willow creek, which was overgrown with grass, with here and there patches of water covering treacherous quicksand. Our only hope was to close round him and ride him out.

I was in a bad way. My horse had poll evil, and my pistol would not shoot without the use of an oaken plug. I had seen Jim kill rabbits on the run many a time, and, adding this to my grief at my friend Scott's death, I was working up a great case of true tenderfoot fright. I was so scared that I would not have recognized Jim if I had seen him, but I kept on. Finally, the Texan saw that I was rattled and stopped and drew me behind the others. To think of anyone noticing my condition drew the tears of mortification to my eyes.

"Go up the hill," he said, handing me a Winchester, "and watch and see that Jim does not leave the valley."

This was a diversion, and I was certainly glad to get away from the others. I must have stayed up there several hours, and all the time the hunt was going on there was an accompaniment of wails from women and children of the Indian camp near by. They would moan and cry to an even rhythm, and then all of a sudden there would be a pause. The silence was extraordinary.

At last the Texan called me to come down from my vantage point. Jim had sent a deputation of squaws to say that he would give himself up if we would promise not to lynch him. An Indian is afraid of hanging only because he believes—as the Greeks did—in the Animus. The breath is the soul, and he will never get to the happy hunting grounds if he is killed by cutting it off.

We accepted his surrender and began the journey to Johnston's. Jim's legs were tied under his horse, and I can see the procession now, the Western sun hitting them as they rode on ahead of me. The smell of sweat, saddle leather, and alkali comes back to me as pungent as if it were yesterday. The two Carricks seemed to be loath to leave us, and the old man kept crying repeatedly:

"There is a good hill. Hang him now. What is the use of waiting? Hang him to onct."

He tried to be jocular, but he overdid it. He was talking too much.

I, being the scribe, was delegated to take down Jim's confession. His hands were tied and lying listless on the table while I rolled him cigarette after cigarette. In a corner of the room sat his sister, who was a girl of the town, lolling back on a cot and looking over the whole scene with a contemptuous curl to her lips. Jim told his story with the utmost composure. It was no more to him than killing a deer. He was a chief of his tribe and had been educated, but the seventy-five dollars and a horse which Carrick had given him to commit the murder were more than he could withstand.

He told how he had sneaked up behind Scott, shot him, and, taking his own boots off, ran away. Gaining courage after a while, he crept back. "He wasn't bawlin' no more," so he took the trace from the harness and dragged the body into the woods. All this time the boys were outside, making ready for the hanging—it was impossible to keep him from them—so I was truly relieved when I heard the loud beat of horse hoofs and a deputy sheriff arrived on the scene, saying:

"Christ! I'm too soon!"

A party of us went out to Carrick's that night. There was a white blanket of snow gleaming in the moonlight. We formed a cordon around the house while the sheriff went up to the front door. There was a wild scream when Mrs. Carrick opened it. She had sensed our errand.

In a little hotel away up in the redwoods, many miles

On Being a Tenderfoot

off, the father and son were taken next morning before dawn. They had stopped, in their flight, to have breakfast when the sheriff came up to them.

I did not see the trial, as I had left California before it came off, but the papers stated that Carrick and the Indian were hanged and the son was sentenced to twenty years. Over the grave of Scott, however, who had been my bunkmate and friend, I placed a headstone, the naïvete of which I am afraid I was unaware at the time. In 1915 I was told by a woman I met in California that in her early childhood up at Sissons, she used to sit for half a day at a stretch and wonder what it could mean, this piece of redwood, carved with the words:

WALTER SCOTT [date, etc.]
MURDERED!!! R. I. P.!!!

Certain types thrive on rough life, and others deteriorate. They might be likened to iron and steel. The true frontiersman is like the common iron as it is dug from the ground. His feelings and sensibilities have never been refined; therefore, contact with the elemental things of life has no debasing effect upon him. The educated person is more like steel—something produced by being subjected to a great heat and which must be tempered to the climate. Hard steel breaks at a low temperature; so does human intelligence break under rough handling. Place a gentleman back in the primitive life and he is pretty sure to become a squaw man or a crook; only a person of refinement has the will and cleverness to be criminal.

I was getting scared. The murder of Scott had given me a jolt and I decided I had had enough of California.

I had been playing poker every night until I owed the Chinese cook so much money that I had to sleep with him for two months and let him collect my pay. I thought this was about as low as I cared to go; so, picking up my traps one day, I started for San Francisco—and home.

A third-class ticket was sixty-five dollars—we called it the "emigrant train." Peddlers sold pieces of canvas and straw mattresses at the station, and these we stretched across the seats in such a way as to make a fairly comfortable bed. The rule was that if sixty people got together they could go through as a "car" and be a law unto themselves. So we "fired out" the married men, the women, and the children, and made up our own crowd. We had neglected to get the full number, however, so the authorities put in twelve Chinamen, and I remember sleeping with my feet against the bald head of one all during the trip.

It had taken me seven days to get out West, but the trip back was thirteen. We were never certain where our car was to be from day to day. A freight train would come along and we would be hitched to it, jogging along slowly, only to be dropped at some God-forsaken flag station, with no way of knowing how long we were to wait. Then, of a sudden, would come on the express, whisk us up and whirl us along for several hundred miles.

At every stop a line of boys and girls passed through the car with cans of fresh milk, pies, cakes, etc., and, augmented by a basket I had brought from San Francisco, my food cost me only ten dollars for the whole trip. A passenger was rude to one of these children, knocking him over and spilling all of his milk. We promptly put him out of our car, back with the women and children.

We were a motley crowd—all nationalities. There was the usual "bad man from Texas." He talked loud, swaggered, and bluffed, and kept the car in a general uproar. His food for the trip—as far as we could see—consisted of several feet of bologna sausage which he had hung from the rack above his seat. When he deemed it time to eat, he would take out his vicious-looking knife and "hit it a lick." However long or short the slice, he would eat it, saying:

"The Texan only eats what he can get by the might of his right arm."

Every once in a while his "might" would get beyond all control and he would knock a hunk of the sausage in among the crowd of poor chattering Chinamen, frightening them almost out of their senses. Then, to make matters worse, he would dive for it with his dangerous-looking knife. I used to argue with him about this action until the bald-headed Chinaman in the seat in front of me *knew* I had saved his life. Every morning a pot of tea, made hot by the stove at the end of the car, was on the floor beside my bunk.

It was the Texan who told the other men not to play poker with me, as my hands were "too soft" and I must be a card sharp. When I accosted him with it he only said, "Well, how *did* you get those hands?" and was much amused when I answered, "Painting pictures."

We never left the train that we did not encounter some strange adventure. At one station, in a shed for horses, we saw the body of a negro with sixteen bullet holes in it, a sight that would have been carefully guarded from the eyes of first-class passengers. At Ogden City we bribed the trainman to tell us that we would have several hours to spare. There was a camp of seventy-five tramps on the border of the lake, and their antics had been terrorizing the citizens. These men of the road accepted us as bosom companions, told us stories, and finally fed us a wonderful dinner of chicken and all sorts of delicacies, cordially inviting us to join them permanently.

Instead of being a bore, the trip was one of the most delightful I ever made and, except for one small aftermath, marked the closing of a definite chapter in my life. I had been back only a short time when I was walking along Howard Street in Boston, my thoughts everywhere but out West. Noticing a crowd in front of a house, I drew up to see the excitement. It was nothing unusual for those days—a gang of toughs were wrecking a Chinese laundry. Standing at the door, uttering most horrible sounds and brandishing an ax in his hand, was an old Chinaman. Just then he saw me, stopped yelling, dropped his ax, and, to the astonishment of all, fell on my neck. All Chinamen looked alike to me, but there could be no doubt about it—it was my friend of the emigrant train. Of course I appealed to the police and the toughs were dispersed; but I had an awful time explaining to this frightened Oriental that I was not his savior.

Chapter V: Adventures in Æstheticism
Paris and Student Days

MY first trip to Europe cost me forty dollars and my faith in human nature. The former was the price of an emigrant ticket on the boat and my food from London to Paris; the latter was caused by my lending a fellow passenger—a Frenchman—my best overcoat and never seeing it again. As he taught me a great deal of French, however, I may have been repaid.

There was never an idle moment in the steerage. Every noon we were all hustled up onto the deck—even to a man with a broken back—and our bunks washed out with chloride of lime. This was before the days of wholesale fumigation, and the company was taking no chances. At mealtime were brought in huge baskets of bread and large cans of coffee; we produced our own dishes and were fed much in the fashion of a barbecue, with hunks of meat. After two days I was invited by the purser to sit at his table, and so dined in splendor with the cooks, steward, and "barkeep" on virtually the same fare as the first cabin.

One night we arranged a mock marriage between a giggling Irish girl and rather a crazy fellow with a gray beard. I was the high priest. The barkeeper had given us some whisky and the noise of the merrymaking must have reached the upper deck, for just at its height the leading lady and some members of a well-known opera company that was crossing came down with the captain to see our show. I knew that this would mean the dampening of all our fun, so I stopped them, saying that we had not been invited to their entertainments, and demanded that the privacy of the emigrants should not be broken. The captain seemed amused, but agreed, and they went away, much to the annoyance of the opera star.

I remember being very much impressed with the shore of Ireland which showed once through the fog, looking so like a large emerald that I immediately saw where the island got its name. This dark, dark green, soaked in rain, was very extraordinary.

A brief stop at Liverpool, where a pretty barmaid drew me a tankard of stout that was the nearest thing to God's nectar I ever tasted; then on to London; directly to Paris; the Hotel de Londres and—Julian's!

Off the Passage de Panorama, which is just off the Boulevard, is the Galerie Montmartre. Here, up one flight of stairs, over a public *cabinet d'aisance*, in the dingiest place imaginable, was the Académie Julian. The room was dirty and dark, despite the skylight above; at one end a platform, and near it a soiled bit of drapery behind which the women models stripped. On a hot July day, what with paints, dirty Frenchmen, stuffy air, nude models, and the place below, this room stank worse than anything I can think of. Not much calculation for comfort, but possibly an enormous inspiration for genius.

Julian had his office below, but was not there with any regularity, generally coming in to loaf or to see new girls. He was a Hercules and quite a romantic figure, about whom there were many stories. They say he was the Masked Man who used to wrestle on the stage and at county fairs. This hulking fellow had been rather a good painter and had become a most successful business man. Born an Italian peasant, he had spent the early years of his life as a goatherd. To me he always looked exactly like a great big orangutan. The three hundred francs a year he received from each one of us seemed a small sum; but the models were paid only a few cents a day, the rental of the studio must have been negligible, and such men as Lefebvre, Boulanger, Bougereau, Tony Fleury, and after him Tony Robert Fleury, gave their instruction gratuitously. So it was not such a bad business deal after all.

One of the older students was the *massier*, or boss. He chose the model for the week or had one voted upon from the crowd of poor devils who lined the stairway every Monday morning in hopes of a job. This day we grabbed our places; first come, first served. If anyone came into the room, other than Julian or an *ancien* (old student), there were hurled at him paint tubes, stools, cigar butts, oaths, and comments upon his appearance and clothing. This was a tradition of the school and had to be lived up to.

Some of the pupils were old men with gray hair who had been there fifteen or twenty years, still working away, I suppose, like some men who stay in prison after their terms are up, having got used to the place. One day a tall Englishman—I think he called himself Vernon—turned up. He was about fifty-five years old, hollow cheeked, with sad eyes looking out from under great brows. He came every day and worked hard, but his painting was not very good. He always made a pretty model's legs look like twisted rope. One morning he called me over to criticize his drawing, and I asked him why he was doing this. He told me he was an art lover, owned a great many pictures, and thought he would get a far greater appreciation of them by doing the actual work. He stayed about two months and some time after we learned that he was Lord Dufferin, who had just come from the post of Governor-General of Canada and was on his way to St. Petersburg. Imagine the shame of a certain pupil from England who had constantly boasted in a truly British manner (and, indeed, in "Mr. Vernon's" very presence) of his close friendship with Lord Dufferin!

But all the students were not old. Most of them were quite young, and some very unsophisticated. I remember a blond fellow, green, and straight from the country, who had received a hundred francs a month from the citizens of his home town to complete his art education. One day he came running into the studio, breathless, stammering out a most amazing story. He had been staring in a jeweler's window when a beautiful woman, "an angel," approached him, saying:

"Who art thou?"

"Your servant."

She took him by the arm to her barouche, and he drove with her to a magnificent house on the Champs Élysées. There servants took charge of him and arrayed him in fine clothing. The details of the next three days were very vague, but he lived in a dream. One of the things he did was to drive with her into the country at 4 A.M. to drink milk fresh from the cows.

It was another story of Diana and Endymion, but all he could say was:

"She was a goddess."

We were inclined to disbelieve his tale until one evening we took him to the Variétés, whose back door opened into the same *galerie* as Julian's. There, on the stage, he discovered his "goddess." She was Judic, a famous actress of the day, well known for her curious amours!

Most of us students were poor. I had fifty dollars a month allowance, but I roomed with a fellow who had only twenty for everything—and he made it do. We lived in the rue de Douai in Montmartre. The room, six flights up, with a trapdoor for a window, was furnished with two iron cots and very little else. I remember we used champagne bottles for water ewers. For all this we paid thirty francs a month. No heat, of course, and in winter the cold was unspeakable. One night I got an idea, and, taking my blanket, started across the icy red-tiled floor to get into my roommate's bunk. In the middle of the room I ran into something. It was he coming to sleep with me! We laughed and went out and bought a roast chicken and a bottle of wine. It did not take much to start a party in those days.

We could not afford the theater, but would go now and then to sit on the boulevards over our beer. The wicked thing was to go to the Café Américain and drink with the girls. Here one night I saw an amusing thing. A little fellow with varnished boots, loud clothes, and a gay tie, showing every outward vulgarity that some Americans can show, was sitting on the balcony with two large, fat women.

Suddenly, a row started below—bad words and then loud oaths in English—and a blow. The French do not do this; they slap the face, but do not use the fist.

"*Un coup de poing Anglais!*"

We looked down. Five or six Frenchmen were upon two Americans; and then one yelled:

"Any Americans here?"

The little fellow got up. He was terribly drunk, but, stepping on his chair, he climbed upon the railing of the balcony, balanced himself a moment unsteadily, and then leaped wildly into the crowd, shouting:

"I don't amount to much, but here goes!"

When the calm was restored it was seen that his action had had the desired affect, for several arms were broken and one or two Frenchmen were completely knocked out; but for an exhibition of true heroism and Americanism, it was gorgeous.

A great event was the Bal Bullier—the students' ball; everyone went, and it was "artist" all through. Things always went well unless some one broke one of the unwritten laws. For instance, all the women who amounted to anything wore masks, and to take them off was an invitation to everyone. One evening at one of these affairs I suddenly heard:

"Any Americans here?"

In the middle of the floor, surrounded by dozens of Frenchmen and fighting with his fists, was an upstanding male in a cowboy hat—a fashion then unknown in Paris. Some one had broken the rule and taken his girl away from him. In a flash I recognized him as Charley White, a man I had known in the north of California.

I looked about me and yelled to each corner of the room:

"À moi, Julian! À moi, Julian!"

Instantly dozens of men sprang from all sides with cries of:

"À toi, Simmons! À toi, Simmons!"

In a second they were upon their brother Frenchmen, had downed them, and had hustled Charley White out of the room. No matter where one is in France, he can always call his class to his side; architects stick to architects, actors to actors, painters to painters, and so on. I could never convince my friend, however, that I did not employ private police.

These nights of revelry were few and far between; our evenings were spent in the studio, and I always see them in "black and white." Black were the shadows in the recesses not reached by the big gas flame, black were the heads of the Europeans, strange beings to me at that time, some of them with beards; while the body of the model, the straining faces of the students, and the paper on the easels before us were a gleaming, glaring white. We did drawing alone at night.

Up to this time there had been one and only one real influence upon my artistic life, and that was Doctor Rimmer. While at the Boston Art Museum I used to go over to the Institute of Technology to his classes in art anatomy. Dr. William Rimmer, who is only to-day being given any recognition, probably occupies in the artistic world somewhat the same position that Samuel Butler does in the literary world. Rimmer's work is being dragged out of obscurity to-day by men like Gutzon Borglum, as Butler's was by Bernard Shaw.

He was a large man with a foreign accent, a crank, but an enthusiast and very excitable. His absorption in his work was that of a crazy genius, but his knowledge of the structure of the human figure, combined with his delicate sense of beauty and vigor of execution, was of inestimable value. In his life he was absolutely impersonal and cared for no man. Doctor Rimmer did me more good than any other man except one—Boulanger.

I had been told by Crowinshield, in Boston, that I had something that would be of great value in the future, but was very dangerous then—*chic*. With the conceit of youth, I thought it meant something, so I began to paint as soon as I joined Julian's. My first work was the head of an Italian; it was very bad. Boulanger stopped in back of me and said:

"If you go on this way, you might as well go home and make shoes."

A thing like that had seldom happened to me; I couldn't help showing off, and it hit hard. I realized that the criticism was right, but I thought that he should have told me how to cure myself. So I left the room and waited on the stairs for a half hour before he came out. Seeing me, he tried to push by, but I stopped him, saying:

"I admit everything you said. I do not know anything, but I came here to learn. (By this time the tears were streaming down my cheeks.) You shall *not* leave here until you tell me what to do."

He thought for a moment. "Well, have you seen the outline drawings by Gérôme?"

I thought them the finest things I knew of, and said so.

"Go back and make one, and mind you, young man, see that you take a week over it. Good morning."

These drawings were larger than the academy paper, so I got a three-foot stretcher and put wrapping paper on it. They wouldn't let me in the front row at school because it was too large and obstructed everyone else's view; I had, therefore, to go in the back of the room and stand up to see the model. In two days I had finished it, and I started it over again, rubbing out so much that I wore holes in the paper. After one every week for three weeks, they came easier.

Boulanger was away on a vacation, and when he came back he passed me by as though I did not exist. July, August, September went by and still he ignored me. I was too scared and miserable to speak to him. Finally, one day he walked in back of my easel and halted as if shot! Turning to the whole school, he said:

"None of you could do a drawing like this, and I doubt if any one of you could copy it." Then turning to me, "Let's see you make an academy."

I switched from being a loafer and *chiquer* from that moment, and realized that only by eight hours' daily work and hard digging could I become a painter. The next week there was a prize offered of a hundred francs for the best drawing—and I won it.

My first showing was at the Salon of '81. We students used to congregate at the Palais de l'Industrie and watch the four or five thousand pictures arrive for selection. From these only about two thousand were chosen. We were a great crowd, lining the grand stairway or sitting on the balustrade, and it was everybody's business to be funny. First would come vans and wagons from which would issue twenty and sometimes forty pictures; then messengers; poor artists with their one creation; and last the commissionaires who carried the canvases on the easel-like thing they had on their shoulders. Of course, the barnyard pictures brought forth loud cackles and crows—this being my special accomplishment. Every now and then some girl would arrive with a portait of "Mother" (too poor to have it sent). Everyone would weep copiously. Up the stairway, with great ceremony, would come a portrait of some high official; we would all assume a manner of awe, but as it turned the corner—loud shouts of *"Merde!"* I remember mine (I was so ashamed of it) in a big frame so large that it had to be borne by two men. It was a portrait of a Scotchman in kilts.

"*À biens l'horreur!* It is of our friend Simmons. Shame! Shame!" (for the bare knees).

Up it went, and a big red-headed man from Julian's rose and said:

"Silence for a while and tears."

At last a wave of quiet—serious this time—and whispers all up and down the line.

"Sh! It is the master!" A Jules Lefebvre had arrived.

Pictures accepted and hung, varnishing day was the next excitement. Everyone of importance and all fashion turned out. New York society cannot conceive of what a place the fine arts have in France. Women of note at the gates with their *quêteuses*, soliciting money for charity; inside, great masses of people go through the galleries together, with some such person as Sarah Bernhardt at the head and the lesser following. I remember seeing Madame De Gautrot, the noted beauty of the day, and could not help stalking her as one does a deer. Representing a type that never has appealed to me (black as spades and white as milk), she thrilled me by the very movement of her body. She walked as Vergil speaks of goddesses—sliding—and seemed to take no steps. Her head and neck undulated like that of a young doe, and something about her gave you the impression of infinite proportion, infinite grace, and infinite balance. Every artist wanted to make her in marble or paint, and, although she has been done innumerable times, no one has succeeded.

At one Salon, in the early 'eighties, two Frenchmen, with flowing ties and low collars, stepped in front of me to look at a landscape by Boutet de Monvel. One said:

"There is a girl in England named Kate Greenaway who is doing some very clever work. She doesn't know anything about drawing or color, but her idea is certainly original. Some day some man will take it and get a great name by it."

I never forgot this, for the speaker was De Monvel himself, and he certainly did scoop the idea.

One who always attracted a crowd was Rosa Bonheur—she who was made famous and wealthy by American dollars. She looked like a small, undersized man, wore gray trousers, Prince Albert coat and top hat to these affairs. Her face was gray white and wizened, and she gesticulated, speaking in a high, squeaky voice. I have never seen anyone who gave a more perfect impression of a eunuch.

The Salon was not all fun; there were many tragedies. One day I called on my friend Renouf, a first-medalist, who was painting a decoration in the Palais de l'Industrie. The Salon had been closed a month, but there were hundreds of rejected canvases standing outside that had never been called for. Some were not even framed. He hauled out several pathetic attempts; then, coming upon one, said:

"Did you ever hear of a painter named G——? He has just been locked up; crazy."

The picture was about six by ten feet, had no frame, but it was signed in large letters. It was a scene of a long corridor, with two barred windows on the side and a man crouched against the wall, with the most maniacal expression on his face. I never have forgotten the horror; he must have painted it when he was going crazy. I often think of poor De Maupassant, whose extreme intelligence warned him of approaching insanity and who, having a gun, desired to take his life. Of course, the gracious Christians surrounding him preferred his earthly sufferings to his heavenly happiness, and so prevented him from doing it.

Ten years after a man of prominence in the artistic world dies the French give a showing of his work. This places him historically as an artist. Some of his pictures are purchased by the government and, after this exhibition, if the authorities deem him great enough, pictures by him are moved to the Louvre. I remember the ten-year show of Courbet. He had been an anarchist, also one of the leaders in the Commune, and his work was considered frightfully "modern." He was the brutal sort of painter that our present-day young men try to emulate, but, though he died many years ago, Courbet was a far abler painter than any man now alive in America.

Of course, this realism of execution brought forth much criticism from the members of the so-called old-school artists, and among the leaders in denouncing Courbet (while alive) was that classic authority, Tony Fleury. He considered this type of art worthless and all wrong and, if I mistake not, expressed his opinion of the modern man in the newspapers.

On the opening day of the Courbet show (there was a smart crowd, as there always is at these affairs) I noticed the attention was suddenly turned in one direction and people seemed to be following some one. Sure enough, with his hands behind his back under coat tails was that notorious enemy of the dead painter, the venerable Tony Fleury, pottering around the room and examining each picture with great care. Then a striking thing happened—so theatrical and so French.

Whirling and facing the audience, he spoke:

"Gentlemen and ladies, for many years I have said that this man was a bad painter. I was mistaken. He was a genius!"

Whistler was a well-known figure at all Salons, but I first met him in London, where I visited him with a letter of introduction from my aunt Fanny, who had trotted him on her knee when he was a baby. He was charming, said there was something he had to do, and, if I could wait for him, the day was mine. He handed me a portfolio of drawings to look at while he was gone, saying:

"Some things I picked up in Italy."

When he came back I told him, with the arrogance of youth, that I hadn't cared at all for some of the etchings and wondered why he had bought them. He was very curious to know which ones I meant, but never told me, what I found out later, that they were all his own! The well-known Venetian etchings!

We lunched at the Hogarth Club and back to his studio to look at his work—me to drink in fountains of knowledge and he to be much amused at my untrained conversation. The studio was large, dignified, and very bare. I remember multitudes of little galley pots in which to mix colors. His painting table had a glass top, and I made a mental decision to have one like it. Whistler always had his own canvas made for him and was extremely careful about all his materials.

His accent was very English and he was full of mannerisms, constantly fooling with his eyeglass or the lace at his throat. He asked about Paris, and I told him of the first show of the Impressionists, held on the Boulevard des Capucines; of Monet, Sisley, etc. The pictures had looked crazy to the people of the day. Whistler said:

"Oh, I know those fellows; they are a bunch of Johnnies who have seen my earlier work."

Considering that his earlier work looks pre-Raphaelite or stuffy German, this was a curious remark.

A large manservant in full livery brought out the pictures to show us. He wore white gloves and was careful not to touch the surface of the canvas. I remember the portrait of Sarasate; it was very large and the servant acted as an easel, holding it on his toes, with his two hands at the sides. Our conversation became quite interesting at the moment, and his master left him standing in that position for more than half an hour while we talked of other things. I thought this very inconsiderate, as we had never treated servants that way. It was this same portrait of Sarasate that I later saw finished in the Salon. Whistler had kicked up a great row, because it had occupied only the central position of the left-hand room instead of the right, which was more popular. He spoke to me about it, and I told him that he should not care, as the poor fiddler looked as if he were trying to commit suicide in the Metropolitan subway. He tried to get angry and wanted to know why. The figure was all black, with the signature (a gold butterfly) looking like the headlight of an engine, about to dash it into oblivion.

Whistler could always find plenty of adorers to sit at his feet and let him use them as a doormat. The Claimant in Lemon Yellow told me that he was hurrying home with him one evening in the rain, when the master spied something that pleased his æsthetic taste. It was a little lighted grocer's window. He stopped like a pointer dog, ordered the Claimant to go home, a mile or more, and get his box. Then he started painting like mad in the dark, and for more than an hour the Claimant held his umbrella over him and handed him his materials. Truly, the man had an hypnotic power.

Whistler was all heart and all pocketbook to any

poor unknown and, for all his arrogance, the servants loved him; but he could never resist a chance to rap Authority. He sent his "second-class thanks" for a second-class medal awarded him at the Salon. Considering the fact that this is the highest honor a foreigner gets, it seems, for once, that the little man lost his sense of humor. He couldn't resist getting in his knock at the English, either. I remember a phrase in a letter written by him to a friend of mine.

"Yes, Sid, here I am again in Paris and gentle Peace seems at last to be inclined to take up her permanent abode in my little pavilion; but I shall drop back across the Channel, now and again, just to see that too great a sense of security may not come upon the people." They reveled in it; he was master then, and the British love to be patronized by some one who has arrived.

I once rented a studio that Whistler had used, and the decorator, who had a shop below, told me that he had changed the color of the wall to agree with every new picture he painted. On one side of the room was a large space filled with palette scrapings. When I think of Abbott Thayer, I know I must have missed a good business deal by not cutting them off to sell to his admirers in the U. S. A. Mr. Thayer was giving an outdoor lesson to a number of girls and, wishing to sit down, and also having on a new pair of trousers, he went over to a near-by barn and got a shingle. When he left he heard a sound like a football rush. The girls were fighting for the shingle!

There is a letter of Whistler's, written in the 'sixties, to Fantin Latour, which I am going to quote, trusting there may be some young artist, in however remote a land, who, reading it for the first time, will say:

"I will profit; I will learn my trade."

DEAR FANTIN—I have far too many things to tell you for me to write them all this morning, for I am in an impossible press of work. It is the pain of giving birth. You know what that is. I have several pictures in my head and they issue with difficulty. For I must tell you that I am grown exacting and "difficile"—very different from what I was when I threw everything pell-mell on canvas, knowing that instinct and fine color would carry me through. Ah, my dear Fantin, what an education I have given myself! Or, rather, what a fearful want of education I am conscious of! With the fine gifts I naturally possess, what a painter I should now be, if, vain and satisfied with these powers, I hadn't disregarded everything else! You see I came at an unfortunate moment. Courbet and his influence were odious. The regret, the rage, even the hatred I feel for all that now, would perhaps astonish you, but here is the explanation. It isn't poor Courbet that I loathe, nor even his works; I recognize, as I always did, their qualities. Nor do I lament the influence of his painting on mine. There isn't any one will be found in my canvases. That can't be otherwise, for I am too individual and have always been rich in qualities which he hadn't and which were enough for me. But this is why all that was so bad for me.

That damned realism made such a direct appeal to my vanity as a painter, and, flouting all traditions, I shouted, with the assurance of ignorance, "Vive la Nature!" "Nature," my boy—that cry was a piece of bad luck for me. My friend, our little society was as refractory as you like. Oh, why wasn't I a pupil of Ingres?—How safely he would have led us!

Drawing! by Jove! Color—color is vice. Certainly it can be and has the right to be one of the finest virtues. Grasped with a strong hand, controlled by her master drawing, color is a splendid bride, with a husband worthy of her—her lover, but her master, too, the most magnificent mistress in the world, and the result is to be seen in all the lovely things produced from their union. But coupled with indecision, with a weak, timid, vicious drawing, easily satisfied, color becomes a jade making game of her mate, and abusing him just as she pleases, taking the thing lightly so long as she has a good time, treating her unfortunate companion like a duffer who bores her—which is just what he does. And look at the result! a chaos of intoxication, of trickery, regret, unfinished things. Well, enough of this. It explains the immense amount of work that I am now doing. I have been teaching myself thus for a year or more and I am sure that I shall make up the wasted time. But—what labor and pain!

One advantage in not having money in Europe is that it forces one to live with the natives and not mingle with transplanted America, vulgar with luxury, that exists in every large capital. We had a good chance to learn the French nature, bear with its eccentricities, and appreciate its wonderful charm. They never miss a chance to make a witty remark. I remember a girl about twenty-five, but looking sixteen, with bobbed hair (unusual in those days), conspicuously short skirts, and woolen stockings, looking distinctly the poor gentlewoman, walking down the boulevard one day entirely alone. Under her arm was a violin case, looking exactly like a coffin. Each café has its character, and as she passed the Café de Madrid, with its gathering of literary people, a perfectly dressed Frenchman, lavender tie and all, at one of the outer tables rose, raised his hat and said:

"*Ah, Mademoiselle! Tu vas enterrer la petite?*" ("You go to bury the little one?")

There was dead silence until she was out of sight, when every man in the café rose and lifted his hat to the speaker. We, in America, are not in consonance with wit and beauty as they are.

If you make good in Paris, it is all right. The students once carried a nude model all over the city, and the citizens respectfully bowed to Beauty. Again, conversely, an actress who appeared in a play in the nude was madly applauded—until she made the fatal and inartistic mistake of taking a curtain call. She was hissed off the stage. I remember Rochegrosse, a fellow painter, picking up a red-velvet-and-gold hat of the Louis Onze period, one day in the studio. It made him look exactly like a mediæval page. Without thinking, he wore it out—the whole length of the boulevard. No one thought to laugh, but all stopped and said "Admirable." You must not be ridiculous in France, but you are not necessarily ridiculous just because you differ from the crowd, as you are in America.

My only meeting with the *haut noblesse* of France did not leave me with a very good impression of that society which it is practically impossible to penetrate. I had been asked by a friend of mine, in Colorado, to play gallant to the beautiful singer, Marie Van Zant, to whom he was betrothed. My first act of friendship was to try to protect her from a marquis who had been forcing his attentions. The marquis had bet forty thousand francs that he would make her his mistress, and wrote, asking her to be a party to his game and share the money. Receiving no answer to this proposal, he sent a bouquet to Miss Van Zant's dressing room in which was a note stating that if she did not accept his offer he would publicly insult her as she left the theater. Then she appealed to me.

I had a carriage waiting at the stage door that evening, into which I quickly bundled both singer and her mother and, in order to avoid any further scandal, sent them off alone. But I was mistaken. The marquis must have been before me and bribed the coachman to go to a different address. Before they knew it they had stopped before a brilliantly lighted restaurant and the young man was running down the steps to meet them. Marie succeeded in avoiding him by threatening the coachman with arrest if he did not take them home.

But some woman got hold of the story, and there was a scandalous article in one of the papers in America. Twelve days after it appeared my friend was in Paris and, coming to my rooms, asked me to meet him at a certain hour as he was going to shoot a Frenchman. He asked me to be one of his seconds and I carried his challenge to the marquis. The nobleman was a mere boy and pleaded that he was too nearsighted to use pistols, and, as my friend did not know the use of swords, the duel came to nothing. I did not know enough to ask for a Jury of Honor or he would have been forced to go on the field. One very characteristically French thing came out of the affair, however, when the marquis tried to pooh-pooh my overtures for a fight on the basis that no "actress" could be insulted in his country and that it was only because we were Americans that he would consider the matter at all.

We sometimes went to the Closerie des Lilas, at the corner of the Boulevard St.-Martin. This was quite in the country, in the days of Henri Quatre—a sort of road house where the young bloods went to drink. The women of the court discovered this and used to go out there, disguised as milkmaids, and flirt outrageously with the tipsy members of the nobility. Alas! the lilacs are gone now and sportive milkmaids no longer frequent the place; but the Cafe des Lilas still has its stories, and in my day there was at least one interesting habitué. He was a major whom everybody knew and spoke to familiarly. He was gray bearded and must have had his title from the Franco-Prussian War. He and his cronies had the same table, played piquet, and sat for hours over their coffee. His was a *mazagran*. The first time I saw him I noticed he had a funny trick which he repeated every night. For a *mazagran* the waiter leaves three lumps of sugar; he always used two, left the other in his saucer, and became exceedingly annoyed if, by any chance, it got wet. In his right-hand waistcoat pocket was his watch, with a great fob that went across. With the utmost deliberation, he would reach into the left-hand pocket, take out a piece of brown paper, beautifully cut into a square, and fold into it the extra lump of sugar, carefully putting the package back in his pocket again. For many nights I watched this proceeding and made up my mind that, being a thrifty Frenchman, he used it for his morning coffee. But not so. Some time after, I read in the Figaro that Major P—— who lived in Montparnasse (there was no mistaking the name and place), had died suddenly, leaving no estate and no personal effects; but behind the door of his small bedroom had been found—a cubic yard of sugar!

Verlaine sometimes came to this café—Paul Verlaine; I often paid for his beer. A plain, hairy, dirty figure, seeming physically very feeble; you would not think to look at him twice except to marvel at his ugliness and disorderly appearance, unless you saw his eyes. If he looked at you, you knew you were in the presence of your better. He was worshiped by all, and they fought to pay his check, hovering about him like crows around dead carrion, waiting to snatch at anything that dropped from his lips. I was not a good student of character in those days and in no way realized his importance, but I could not help feeling his charm. One night I had a dispute with a Frenchman as to what was the meaning of courage. One of us argued that it was an admirable quality, and the other that it was vanity and stupidity—therefore, idiotic. At the height of the discussion Verlaine came in and was appealed to to decide the question. He first demanded beer and then listened carefully to one and then the other. Looking at me, he said:

"I decide for the young American."

"Well, why?" asked the Frenchman.

"Because you are right and he is right; you are wrong and he is wrong. But *he* believes what he says."

To him, *truth* was of no importance—the question was *belief*—and this seems to me to be the secret of his whole philosophy.

There is a corner in Paris where Arthur Cosslet Smith says, if you sit there long enough, you will meet everyone of importance of your day—the corner of the Café de la Paix. Here one day I was sitting, having an *apéritif* before lunch; at a table in the corner was gathered a group of *jeunesses dorées* and a little farther back I noticed Barbey d'Aurevilly. The young men began to discuss literature with that cocksureness that is the quality of youth the world over. Victor Hugo was still alive, and it was the fashion to "knock" him, which they proceeded to do, outrageously. Finally, one said, so the whole café could hear:

"Oh, your Victor Hugo, he is stupid."

At that I *felt* a figure rise behind me and come forward; then I saw this wonderful vision. About seventy, handsome, tall, dressed with the most exquisite care, lace at his sleeves and neck; D'Aurevilly was a count and noted duelist and distinctly of the old school. Looking as if he had stepped straight out of a book of Dumas', he walked up to the young men. Instantly, their conversation was hushed. He did not present himself, but said:

"My young friends, I also care for literature; and that is my excuse for speaking to you. I heard your talk of Victor Hugo and I came to tell you that I agree with you in your estimate of him. Alas! he *is* stupid—stupid as the Himalayas!" ("*Il est bête——bête comme les Himalays!*")

We are fond of saying that things are not the same as they were when we were young, but I fear we are wrong. The change is in ourselves. When I went back to Paris in 18—— I visited some of the old familiar haunts. One was the little café, where I used to breakfast every morning when a student. Everything looked the same—the dingy walls, dirty floor, but spotless tables—as the French tables always are; the waiters calling out the orders for their well-known patrons as soon as they showed their faces in the doorway; the poor, half-starved grisettes eating their sou's worth of bread—I could hardly believe I had been away for so many years.

But why did the food taste so strange? The *croissons* were soggy, and the coffee, with its abominable taste of chicory—bah! Was it possible I could once have lived on this fare and actually liked it? I could not even call back one old thrill.

After such a disappointment, I was almost afraid to visit Julian's, but with rather a sinking heart I turned into the Passage de Panorama, around the corner to the galerie, up the still dirty stairway, and opened the door. Instantly I was greeted with French oaths and comments, and I found myself running a barricade of paint tubes and what seemed to me all the furniture in the room, hurled at my head. I stopped and swore in every language I knew, crying:

"If anyone here is as old an *ancien* as I, I'll kneel to him, but if not, get down on your knees, the whole crowd of you!"

"Who are you?" they asked.

I pointed to the wall where hung a drawing—the very one which had won me the hundred francs in the contest. Instantly everyone in the room was on his knees.

The tears streamed down my cheeks; I was not disappointed. My old Paris had come back to me!

Chapter VI: The Middle Ages
Brittany; Spain

AMERICA is a country without tradition, and the large cities of Europe are too cosmopolitan to impress one with the fact of fixed manners and morals. But not so in the provinces. From '81 to '86, I lived in Concarneau, on the Breton coast, and made a trip of several months into Elche, Spain. I felt as if I had suddenly plunged back into the Middle Ages. The superstitions, manners, customs, and dress, as well as ideas, of both those places, were unchanged from centuries ago.

Around the part of Concarneau where the poor live is a wall built by Vauban; inside is a fortress with the sea making a moat. The bridge, which could originally be drawn up, is now stationary, but the doorway for a passage is still there. On the other side is the ferry to Pont Aven. Inside the inclosure the streets are narrow and paved, with little houses on either side. Outside is the smart part of the town. The beauties of the sea, and, as usual, the low cost of living, brought the artist to Concarneau.

My studio was a wheat loft, and any peasant was a model for a few cents. We painted them in their native dress, which was picturesque enough, and, besides, no virtuous Breton woman would allow you to see her hair, so that it was obvious that the coif stayed on. These headdresses gave them a distinctly mediæval air, and each town has a certain style, more fixed than the laws of the Medes and Persians, so that you can tell immediately where a woman comes from. Underneath this white coif, which is always beautifully laundered and starched, is a tight cap which holds the hair, and this, I think, is seldom removed. The remainder of the costume (which makes them look like Noah's Ark women) is a heavy woolen skirt and a double-breasted blouse. This is held together by a huge shawl pin of brass, and under no circumstances can they be persuaded to use buttons. Of course there are stockings and sabots.

Blanch Willis Howard wrote her book called *Guenn* in my studio and it afterward became one of the popular novels of the day. I think she greatly exaggerated the romantic quality of the artist who fell in love with his model, however, as all the Breton peasants I ever saw washed below the chin only twice in their lives—once when they were born and once when married.

The peasants dance all day long. Every day seems a fête day, and the celebrations are always held in the market place. The dance starts with a procession, with a man at the head playing a *biniou*, an instrument (the same in every Celtic country) very much like a bagpipe. They serpentine, as do the college boys of today, and whirl madly, couple by couple, with nothing but a clatter of sabots. The virtue lies not in the grace or time, but in keeping it up the longest.

The Bretons seine their fish (sardines) in a long net with large corks at the top and weights at the bottom. Myriads of forty-ton boats start out before sunrise, making a picturesque sight with their few feet of deck and large fore and aft sails, originally dyed brilliant colors, but always faded to lovely tones of rose, gray, and tan. The sails drop at the fishing grounds, they let out their nets, and the men begin to row, while one, the boss, stands in the stern to throw the bait. This imported egg of cod is called *"rogue,"* and as he throws it from side to side the play of his body in action is more beautifully Greek than anything in all Europe. Whenever I saw this I wondered if Christ might not have performed his Miracle of the Fishes in somewhat the same way. The catch is enormous. I have seen a net sink, breaking a manila rope the size of my thumb. When the boat comes in it looks as if it were entirely full of shiny fifty-cent pieces in a flutter, and every scoop of the bucket is one of pure silver. When cooked in that flapping condition, in beef drippings, and served with a boiled potato, they come nearer to being perfect human food than anything I know of.

Georges Pouchet, the ichthyologist, used to come to the Vivier in Concarneau to study the fish forms. He was a friend of Pasteur, and they were studying mammals as a basis for the investigation of the human body. I lunched with him in his bachelor lodgings during the Salon every year. He had an original way of entertaining. The invitations were always written and very formal. I was always received by the same man-servant; lunched with him alone and upon the same menu. We had but one dish. The servant brought in a bowl fully two feet across, full of écrevisses; then bread, wine, and a basin with a towel and fresh water. He said it was necessary to wash while eating these shellfish. Of course we finished off with coffee and a smoke.

Pouchet was an intimate friend of Alfred de Musset and told me much about him. The poet had many fads inherited from the days of swords, pistols, snuff, and powdered hair. For instance, he would under no circumstances accept copper money; in fact, he would not touch the metal in any form. Toward the end of Musset's life he frequented a certain café in Paris—used it as a club. He would go there to write his letters, read his paper, etc., and with him would be a quiet man in plain clothing whom you would not notice. At a certain time in the evening he would make a gesture to the waiter, who would serve him with two carafons—one of brandy and one of absinthe. He would pour them together in one glass and, looking at them, take out of his buttonhole his button of General of the Legion of Honor, and put it in his waistcoat. He would then down the mixture at once; the quiet man would approach and take him to his carriage. No one but a Frenchman could have done this; he would not get drunk as a member of the Legion!

Sitting one time with Pouchet and a well-known authoress, discussing sex, he said:

"You make a mistake, mademoiselle, there are four sexes. Male—Mr. Simmons; female—your charming self; neuter"—pointing to a stuffy judge way down the room; "and potentially male or female. This sex can be recognized by the human hair. It is long in the men and short in the women. Let us call it the professorial sex." Women's rights, divorce laws, etc., were then unknown in France, so this was quite an advanced idea.

The last time I saw Pouchet was in New York. He

was about sixty-three years old. We were lunching at the Players and I asked:

"What brings you to America?"

"To study the question of tonsils."

"Are American tonsils different from European?" I asked.

"Oh no! We are interested in the tonsils of other mammals—of the whale."

Just before he went back to France I asked him what conclusion his investigation had brought forth.

"A matter of great importance," he answered. "The fact that the tonsil is of no importance."

I have since heard this disputed, but I thought it very interesting that these learned men should work so long and so hard for such a result.

The British artists passed by Concarneau and went on to Pont Aven, where there were ready-made landscapes for the water-colorists. Truth to tell, they were frightened by the bigness of the coast and left it to the French and Americans, who formed a very happy crowd, all living at the Hotel des Voyageurs. There was Thaddeus Jones, who has since painted a portrait of the Pope; Alexander Harrison, the famous marine painter; Frank Chadwick; Howard Russell Butler; M. Brion; Emile Renouf; Paul Dubois, the sculptor; and Bastien Le Page. Bastien was the first in importance in the Concarneau older set, being almost the father of the Realistic movement. He was a quiet, well-bred person, swift at repartee, and could write as corking a letter to the press as Whistler.

One day I caught him painting a sketch of the little stone church on the shore at the edge of the town, something we had all tried. He was drawing and painting, with meticulous care, every slate on the roof, each with its little lichen. I brought the subject up, after dinner, when we were sitting on the sidewalk having our coffee.

"M. Bastien," I said (no one ever called him Le Page) "we have all been taught by Le Febvre, Boulanger, Cabanel, and Durand to *ebaucher* our subject broadly and put in only the details that are absolutely necessary. I saw you to-day painting every slate on that roof for its own sake. How about it?"

He laughed.

"I have tried all these different methods, but none of them got me what I saw; so now I do everything as truthfully as I am able, then take my picture to Paris, where, in my studio, away from nature, I can consider it broadly and remove all the unnecessary detail."

"Yes," said Harrison, "but when we younger men see your picture in the Salon we don't think you have done what you say you do."

He threw his hands in the air.

"*Helas! Helas! Sacré Nom de Dieu! Vous avez raison.* I am so much in love with it when I see it in my studio that I cannot bear to touch it."

Bastien was born in Domremy, which was probably the reason he made such an admirable painting of Jeanne d'Arc, now in the Metropolitan Museum. He told us the details of the work. There was no one model, except for the body, and he used several to carry out his ideal of the head. You feel that she is a working girl and not a pretty peasant by Bougereau. Albert Wolff wrote a stinging criticism of it, commenting on the charm of the figure and the excellence of the drawing and painting, but saying that the visions in the air were idiotic. Bastien replied that the visions were not supposed to be those of a learned man like Wolff or, indeed, his own, but those born in the brain of Jeanne d'Arc, an uneducated girl of sixteen, whose only knowledge of kings and queens was of the figures of the saints she had worshiped in church.

He handled this canvas in quite an original way, and not a very successful one. It was painted in two pieces, so that it could be easily carried to the orchard where he worked. When finished, he and the village cobbler sewed them together by hand, with the best linen thread and cobbler's wax. They then stretched it and hammered the joining, which was filled with white and siccatif and scraped down. When it was firm and dry, he went over it so there should be no question of the surface, and repainted it, and, as he said, "I wager anything that that crack does not show in a thousand years." Alas, it is plainly evident in the Metropolitan to-day, and the repainting must have changed, as the color and tone where the crack is are all wrong.

Bastien was one of the most lovable men I ever met, bright, smiling, with a certain undercurrent of sadness—the mark of tuberculosis was upon him then. I remember one day attempting to tell him the meaning of an American negro song he had learned from one of the boys, but he refused to listen, not wishing to be disillusioned.

"No, no, Simmons, I do not wish to have it explained. I know what it says. It is a pathetic song of a lover mourning for one he has lost."

And he rendered it in a voice that would have brought tears to the eyes of the average audience.

> "Ze lobstere in ze lobstere pot
> Ze bluefish in ze panne;
> Zey suffere, oh, zey suffere not;
> What I suffere for my Marie Anne."

Poor Bastien! He was gone the next year.

It is almost impossible to speak of Bastien without mentioning that young woman, made famous by the remark of Gladstone that she had written the best book of the year, the woman who meant so much in his life—Marie Bashkirtsev. Fresh from the hands of her maid, she was a fascinating blond "vamp," but in about twenty minutes the charms began to go. Her hair became unruly, buttons refused to do their duty, and slipper strings burst. She had beautiful feet and was inclined to wear her shoes too small. I once sent her a message saying that I would give her a sketch for one of her slippers. She replied:

"I know the value of a new pair of slippers, but I do not know the value of one of your pictures."

On the apartment mantelpiece of Bojidar Karageorgivitch was a semicircle of shoes, a slipper in the center, and two bell jars covering riding boots at either end—all belonging to his cousin Marie. Borjidar was a charming person; the son of a king, his mother a Russian princess and second in line for the Serbian throne. His brother Nicolas was a weakling, and Peter, the king, was no good. Slight, pointed beard, and aquiline nose, he looked more the fashionable Frenchman than anything else. Like Pierre Loti, he was smitten with the divine Sarah, who visited him at Concarneau and left her painting materials behind. Borjidar always seemed to be surrounded with a halo of romance. One day we were sitting out on the pavement and some one mentioned thumb-nails. It is said that the larger the white moons, the greater the aristocrat. This royal prince had no moon at all, thus indicating no ancestry; but if the sign is true, it is not strange, since his grandfather had been an ignorant butcher who had jumped the throne. Through his mother he had a delightful touch. Years later I met Bojidar in Paris, and what do you suppose he was doing? Such a brave, fine thing! He was selling jewelry, which he designed himself, to the English snob and really making good at it. Many people like to buy from the son of a king.

There came to Concarneau a young girl, wide eyed, eager, temperamental, thirsting for a knowledge of life, but knowing about as much of it as the bird just out of the egg. She was alone and studying Art. She asked of the women folk the meaning of marriage, and wanted to be chaperoned until she had made up her mind whether to take the big step or not. Not so long after her enlightenment, she announced her wedding, and with none other than the now well-known writer—Havelock Ellis. Ellis seems to me an example of a man who took up one subject, stuck to it, and absorbed it thoroughly—a procedure almost always destined for success when accompanied by brains. Some years after, I visited the Ellises in England. There had been no children from the union, but the one-time timid and childish wife had developed into a charming woman, and, strange to say, a full-fledged raiser of blooded stock. She it was who tended the wants of the baby bulls and colts, was in at the births and deaths of the animals; while Havelock sat by the warmth of his very delightful fire-place, smoking his pipe and probably mulling over the psychological effect of all this on the feminine mind. Anyway, I had a delightful time and, upon his refusal to help her, I held the head of a baby calf while she slipped a dose of oil down its throat, oblivious to the fact that I was ruining a beautiful new pair of white flannel trousers.

Halfway between Concarneau and Pont Aven (that place of predigested food for artists and ready-made motifs) at the summit of a rise in the road, is the Rocking Stone. It is twenty feet in diameter, almost spherical in shape, and so poised by the glacial period upon another buried stone, that, if pressed at a certain angle, it rocks. The legend is that the stone gained this quality at the hands of the comtesse of the château, whose husband went to the Crusades and left her, a bride, to his dearest friend to take care of. This he proceeded to do by trying to make her his mistress; he was rebuffed and became her enemy. Upon her husband's return from the wars, this so-called friend rushed ahead to meet him and told him his wife had betrayed him. The count drew his sword, walked ahead to meet her, and accused her of the infidelity. She placed her hand on the stone and said:

"God is my witness that it is a lie and, if I am chaste, will move this stone."

Thereupon, she touched it ever so lightly, and it rocked!

It was a habit of the peasants and fishermen to take their sweethearts to this place to see if they could move the bowlder. On such superstitions does the virtue of a woman hang.

* * * * * * * *

The Middle Ages

It was very dramatic, the way I first saw Spain. A cold and beastly night, changing into a hot day; third-class carriage and no coffee; the first sight out of the car window in the morning a dusty plain. It could have been an alkali desert in the West. In no sense like the Italians or French, the Spanish are haughty, silent, laconic, dignified, morose, and lonely, like their plains with every now and then a brilliant patch of green. Here and there would be a castle and, clustered around its feet, tiny houses. Human beings lived there! Farther on, bands of sheep or goats, and a herder whom one could imagine a Moorish horseman with a tall spear. There was a Don Quixote at every turn. At last, the plain stretched and widened until there was a hill line like the horizon of the ocean. Suddenly, the two horns of a snail stuck up, getting larger and larger, until the animal seemed to be creeping toward us out of the distance. A cloudless sky, vast stretches, with no sign of human habitation anywhere—and the horns of the snail suddenly changed into the towers of a building—the Cathedral at Bourgos!

At Madrid I saw Titian for the first time; the ones in the Louvre are of no importance. On one side of a narrow gallery in the Prado will be a Titian, and on the other side a Velasquez. The former looks five hundred years old, and the latter very modern, the difference being due, apparently, to the surface of the canvas; also the movement in my day was toward Velasquez— the free brush work and the blond note. There is one marvelous canvas of his here; no one ever did anything like it. He had painted Phillip, the king, dozens of times, and did the dwarfs and ladies of the court.

Evidently the queen was tired of these, and said to him one day:

"I want a picture for myself. Do just as I say. Paint my daughter in her new gown, the fool, dog, and parrot, and the king and myself looking at you while you do it."

A large order, but see what he has done! He stands in the center with his canvas; at one side the infanta, a squat dwarf, and the dog, while the king and queen are seen at the back in a doorway, with the background of a garden. Of great value to us is his palette, which he is holding in his hand, plainly showing what colors he used—red, yellow, black, and white.

Upon arriving at Elche (from the Roman Illici) under whose walls Hamilcar Barca, the uncle of Hannibal, died fighting, I realized I had quietly stepped back four or five hundred years in the history of the world.

One could almost forgive the superstitious and general ignorance of the Mediæval Age when one realizes the beautiful things that have been bequeathed to us. Nothing could be more fascinatingly romantic or more un-Yankee than the Sereno—the man appointed by the city to go about at night announcing the time and the weather. His name, meaning "serene," comes from the fact that the weather is nearly always clear. In fact, during all the time that I was in Spain there was only one day when I saw a cloud in the sky, and I am afraid I should have missed that if my attention had not been called to it by a proud native.

On these clear blue evenings you would go to bed amid a profound silence and just be dozing off into a half dream, when away down the street would come to your ear two or three weird little notes, faint and far away, seeming to be part of a song or the cry of a bird. Perhaps you would go back to sleep, and again it would seem only five minutes, but in reality it would be a half hour—would come the sound, this time nearer and much more distinct. Each repetition would be louder, until you would hear the "toc, toc, toc," of his stick, stopping now and then as he banged on the door of some heavy sleeper who had paid the Sereno to wake him. Perhaps he wanted to make a train—or was it "reasons of love"?

Then right under your window would come the song, "Eleven o'clock—Serene," beginning loud and finally disappearing into the night.

Las do - ze y Me - di - a Se - ra - no.

The Spanish nature is a mixture of politeness and cruelty. There is something to excite the blood every day. I have seen them gather together all the stray dogs and give them poison, then heap them up at the corners of the street. Those that are not dead escape and run away howling, and the great sport is to jerk them up on a rope, hurling them high in the air. Everyone thinks this a splendid game and the children yell with glee. But as to the manners—those of an illiterate farmer are better than the average clubman's of New York. If a Spaniard offers you anything three times, you must accept it, and then offer him something three times so that he may accept. I remember a farmhand hailing an old-fashioned coach which ran from Elche to

Alicante. Boarding it slowly, he raised his hat to everyone, saying:

"Good morning, ladies and gentlemen. Will you permit me?" Rolling a cigarette, he was suddenly struck with a thought, and, turning, offered the tobacco to the coach in general. In a café, if you sit down beside anyone—peasant, priest, or dude—he offers you a drink. The third time you are obliged to accept. The same formula is gone through with in every situation in life (like the Arabian who must always walk with a guest to the limit of his property), but I rather think democracy is doing away with it.

There is no art among the provincial people of Spain. In fact, I do not know any place where there is such an utter indifference to it. Once the hotel keeper came into my bedroom and saw a water color I had done hanging on the wall. It was a careful rendition of the passageway in front of my room. There were the tiles on the floor, the plaster walls with the door halfway down, and, at the end, beneath a window, stood a large jar (exactly like the one in which I imagine the Forty Thieves were concealed) full of pampas grass. I should have thought a child would have recognized it. But mine host said, politely:

"One of your artistic results from our river?"

"No," emphatically.

"Oh, then it is the cathedral?"

I gave it up. Had I been a sensitive man, I think I would have stopped painting then and there.

The Church is the doctor, lawyer, teacher, amanuensis, and theater. The festivals are more beautiful than I have seen anywhere. From May to October there is never a cloud in the sky, and during this time is held the Fiesta de la Vieja Negra. The ceremony takes place in the public square, and at midnight of that July night the roofs of the town are crowded with people while the sky looks like an inverted bowl of black over their heads. The legend is that the little Virgin, only three feet high and carved out of dark wood, landed in a boat on the shores of the Mediterranean. In her hand was a scroll which directed that she be drawn inland by two white oxen and that where they lay down must be built a temple. This is the Cathedral of Elche, the roof of which is of blue tiles and glitters like an amethyst or turquoise. The procession of the fiesta begins at twelve o'clock and proceeds in stately fashion to the square. Everything connected with the Virgin herself is black—black-robed priests, black casket and draperies—with all else a blaze of light and color. I was much affected and ready to fall on my knees and become a Roman Catholic. The mayor, in evening clothes, awaits her, carrying in his hand a black velvet flag about ten by twelve feet, with no insignia. When the procession stops he walks solemnly forward, all alone, across the square. When directly in front of the Virgin he raises the flag in his hands and, amid dead silence, waves it slowly in her face, back and forth. The third time the staff snaps and down falls the flag at her feet. There is a wild yell of: "Fiesta! Fiesta!" Everyone believes a miracle has happened.

The story is that when the Vieja was first installed, a Moorish chieftain jeered at her and waved his flag in her face, wherefore she caused it to break in his hand, and he fell down converted. Now year after year the miracle is repeated. I was told that the flagpole is cut to the center on one diameter and gauged, when turned, to break at the right moment.

The fiesta of Elche takes place within the cathedral. I was fortunate enough to be able to witness the ceremony from a small window just below the dome and hundreds of feet above the people. The first part is the cleansing of the temple of the Jews. A large crowd in rags and gabardines, with beards, evidently false, attempt to come in, but are fallen upon by the audience, flagellated, and flung out of the church. All having quieted again, a most dramatic thing happens. Suddenly, seemingly, the whole dome (a part twenty-five feet in diameter) begins to move and slowly come down. From my seat I could now and then see the operation of the windlass, but to the people below it must have looked like the petals of a water lily detaching themselves and opening into a golden flower. The stamens held two men angels with golden wings and wearing costumes hundreds of years old, so beautiful that I did not notice the colors. I have never seen any fabric so wonderful except the old Breton communion lace and the costumes of the Javanese dancers. The pistil had, for a stigma, a cherub—as far as they could see below—in empty air. He was a beautiful ten-year-old boy held only from behind by a gilded shaft of steel with two little places for his feet. As he descended and came about opposite me, he fainted away, but the two men's arms flashed out to hold him, so that it was not noticed below. Then the angels scatter the pollen—little bits of gold leaf—all over the church, and as this is supposed to be very holy and of great curative value, everyone

The Middle Ages 157

strives to pick up a piece. The boy angel, supposedly come down from heaven, delivers to the Virgin the palm branch which is symbolic of a productive year. Just at this moment a tiny sparrow (not on the program) circled our heads like a soul in flight. The angels begin to rise, are carried to the dome, the petals of the huge flower close, and the whole ceremony seems to have been but a figment of the imagination.

One's point of view of the human race out of doors becomes exactly reversed upon going from Brittany to Spain. In the former country one sees the head, with the coif, as a white spot against a background of green; and in the latter the head is black against the landscape. The ideas of modesty are also exactly reversed; for a Breton peasant to show her hair means that she is not virtuous, while the Spanish constantly go about with the head uncovered. The Spanish have no sense of privacy; they stare on every occasion and do not hesitate to go into anyone's home without knocking—there are no locks on the doors, so one cannot prevent this. They never pull down the shades from any desire of seclusion, and rather think it taking away their privileges if anyone else does. A beautifully dressed woman and daughter will pass you with downcast eyes, but if you turn quickly you will probably see them standing perfectly still, facing you and gaping. The children go about naked, and used to climb upon the grill of our veranda to stare at us and beg to taste our food.

A few days after my son was born I noticed something peculiar in the actions of the midwife and the women about. They kept wailing:

"Poor little heathen. He will not live. He will not

live. Seven-months child. Condemned to the fires of hell."

To tell you the truth, I did not care much at that time whether or not he did live, but for the sake of the nerves of the household, my own included, I was forced to ask them to explain.

"Why, he is a heretic!" they said.

"What do you mean?" I asked.

"He is not baptized."

"Do you want to baptize him?" I asked, rather jokingly.

"Will you let us? Oh, Medica, Medica, run, run! We will baptize the little heretic!"

I was in for it, so went to my friend Don Paco, who was a very wealthy and influential man, and asked what I had to do.

"Oh, *you* have nothing to do," he replied. "You do not count. Only the godfather matters, and that will be I."

His duty, besides officiating at the ceremony, was to promise to do his utmost to keep the child in the Catholic faith.

Well, I got into the church by fighting, to see one of the worst-looking babies you ever saw held up, entirely naked, by the medica, while four or five big priests crossed the different parts of his body with holy oil—changing a Concord Unitarian into a Roman Catholic! Truly, the reclamation of a heretic. After the baptism they did acknowledge my existence, for I rode in the carriage with Don Paco and the medica, who held the baby. The godfather had to get us out of the church by striking women right and left—a woman does not count for thirty cents in Spain. We rode in a four-seated carriage with two horses, and a brass band going before us. The crowd was so dense (more than twenty-five hundred people on that small street alone) that we could proceed only at the slowest walk, and at that we broke the arm of a small boy who was pushed under the horses' hoofs.

Back at the hotel, the landlord was so overcome at the advertisement that he almost lost his head, giving us a wonderful feast—downstairs for the band and upstairs for the dudes, priests and contessas, the last having been invited by Don Paco and come from far away for the occasion. I learned afterward that one of the reasons for all this excitement over my child was that Don Paco had told that both parents lived in California (their El Dorado), and somehow they had gotten the idea that I owned most of the state. One little touch that reconciled me for all the trouble the baby's christening had caused me—the doctor, one of the first in Spain, who had brought him into the world presented me with a bill charging ten cents a visit and five cents whenever we called upon him.

My exit from Spain was not so romantic as my entrance; in fact, it was in the nature of a flight. Walking into Alicante one day, I was grabbed by the American consul, who said:

"Get your family and bring them here as quickly as you can; I cannot explain, as I must not speak English any more."

Cholera had broken out, in spite of every precaution to keep it from coming over the border from France, where there was an epidemic. If we did not get out immediately, it would mean three months in Elche, surrounded by troops, and the possibility of contracting the dread disease. I shall never forget the misery of that journey. As usual, I had very little money. It took us sixty hours to make the trip, and we landed at Concarneau at 3 A.M. in a blinding snowstorm.

I think I spoke of the politeness of the Spanish farmer. Not so the dude. We had started third class, but had been driven out by the number of people to the second and finally the first class. Upon changing to the last, I saw the train was about to start and was all crowded except one compartment, marked "Reserved," which I opened and entered. There were four well-dressed Spaniards lying down with their feet upon the seats, occupying the amount of space legally allowed for eight people. They looked up, saw the woman and baby, rolled over, and did not move. I explained politely and asked for a seat. Not a move. I then pushed one of them over and stood on him while I made room for my family, folded my arms, and waited for these people who kill, assassinate, and duel to come forward. There were many oaths and much talk about "wishing I had my sword," etc., but not a shut fist.

Just before we got to Irun, which is the last town before you cross the border into France, I got into conversation with a very well-bred Spaniard. He pointed to a little house at San Sebastian, way below on the seashore, and told me it was his and that he had just arrived home from South America and had seen his family for the first time in three years. He then spoke of his impatience at having been kept such a long time in quarantine in France.

The Middle Ages

"But you are going away again?" I asked.

"Oh, I left an important parcel in Irun and am going back to get it," he answered. Then, pointing to a bit of red worsted tied to his umbrella, he continued, "This was put on by my wife, who knows how forgetful I am, so that I may be sure and not pass the border."

While we were talking, he suddenly looked out of the car window with a wild exclamation:

"My God, we have passed Irun!"

In spite of the red worsted reminder, he had gone over the border again into France and would have to spend another three weeks in quarantine!

Chapter VII: From Breton to Briton
St. Ives, Cornwall; London

GOING from Concarneau to St. Ives was like moving up from the thirteenth to the seventeenth century. No more thatched roofs, no more floors of beaten earth, no more manure piles in front of the houses. The roofs are of slate, topping little stone houses, with quite proper floors; the front yards are clean, and the Cornish farmer is most likely a Wesleyan, but he may belong to one of the other thirteen denominations that flourish in this town of five thousand inhabitants. It is true that there is a circle of stones which archæologists say was placed before the time of the Picts; there are some customs handed down from centuries before; but most of the "ancient laws" are no earlier than Henry VIII, and the old traditions are so changed that the original makers would not recognize them, for the Englishman *will* think for himself, even though he thinks badly.

The waves that come to St. Ives Bay are straight from America, and there is nothing to equal the beauty of the cliffs and sand except the coast of Maine. The climate is five degrees less than that of Naples and never goes over eighty degrees in summer or much below freezing in winter, so that vegetables and flowers flourish. In January are growing violets, dahlias, and fuchsias for the markets of London. South of St. Ives are five miles of flowers blowing in the breezes. The real beauty of the country is the constant storm, shower and sunlight. If it is not raining, it is shining, and there is a rainbow almost any day—a little Legion of Honor wandering around by itself.

Of the different religious denominations, there were the Christian Brethren, Temperance Wesleyans, Plain Wesleyans, Lady Huntington's Chapel, Church of England, and the Catholic. The butcher, grocer, and carpenter were all preachers on Sunday. Perhaps the most interesting of the sects, however, were the Primitive Christians. They do not believe the altar or the pulpit is any more holy than other parts of the church, so you will see them kneeling with their faces to the back, to the sides, or any way whatever, while the minister is hard at work preaching at one end.

Right in back of my studio, which was a storehouse for pilchard nets and consequently on the sea, was the old graveyard. Here the stanch Cornishmen were buried four or five layers deep, and occasionally the tide would wash a hole in the wall, scattering the bones, and rolling skulls up and down the beach. The new graveyard was much more modern, with a careful division between the Church of England and the Dissenters, the different entrances separated, as I think my dear mother thought heaven was—one gate for the Unitarians and one for the remainder of the world. I remember a carpenter who accidently cut off his thumb. He was not nearly so worried about the pain as that he might go through all eternity thumbless; so he anxiously saved the piece and, waiting until there was a funeral, dropped it into the grave, being very careful, however, that it was on the Dissenter side of the cemetery (he being a Wesleyan preacher on Sunday). The picture of any part of his body wandering around in a Church of England heaven was something he could not bear to contemplate.

The Cornish have some peculiar uses of the English language, some of the expressions going back to the Elizabethan period. They never use an objective, but say "to I" or "for we"; then there is "on" for "in" and "coolth" and "dryth." "Minching" means stealing or playing hooky and comes from the same source as "Miching mallecho" of Shakespeare.

Nearly the entire life of these people is spent in the fishing industry, as it is in Concarneau; only here the pilchard takes the place of the sardine. All along the shore are built little whitewashed cabins, glistening in the distance like seagulls. Here, during the fishing season, men sit all day long, watching for that unmistakable faint purple ruff on the water that indicates the run of fish. At the first sign they stand upon the cliff and wave the branch of a tree. Everyone quits work; children rush up and down the shore, waving green branches and shouting the fishing call at the top of their voices. If you look out upon the water you can see a place where the "hair of the animal" has been rubbed the wrong way. There is great rivalry as to which company gets the best schools of fish, and they row madly to beat one another, sometimes having very serious fights. The costume is very different from that of the Bretons, the men wearing tarpaulins and high boots; but the catch is just as large, sometimes taking three days to empty the large circular nets that have been drawn up like a purse.

When I went to St. Ives it was unknown as an art

colony, the place where they gathered being Penzance, about ten miles away. Whistler had been there two years before, but Robinson was the sole representative of the clan upon my arrival. When I left, five years later, there was an Art Club of one hundred members. The term "Cornish school" came into being from a remark of Stanhope Forbes to Whistler's enemy, Harry Quilter, the critic, who asked:

"Why do all you men of the Cornish school paint alike?"

(They were all painters who had studied in France and learned their trade.)

"We use the same model," answered Forbes.

"Ah, that's it! Who is she?"

"Nature."

Seeing this colony form in St. Ives made me study out how such things happen. The artist finds a place that is beautiful, undiscovered, and suits his pocketbook. He goes there for two years. The third year other artists follow him; the fourth year come the retired British admirals and "vamps"; the fifth year the artist leaves; the sixth come the wealthy people who spend a lot of money on it, making it as ugly and dear as possible, but soon tire and go away. Then the artist comes back again and begins all over, picking the bones of what the Money Bags had killed.

The home of Leslie Stephen, in St. Ives, was the gathering place for all sorts of interesting persons. He married Thackeray's daughter, knew many notables, and was the biographer of most of them. He entertained such men as E. W. Gosse, the critic and brother-in-law of Alma Tadema, the famous painter of finished Greek subjects. It always seemed to me so extraordinary to see one of his Greek slaves with manicured toenails, leaning up against a marble column upon which you could see the polish, with a truly Bostonian expression on her face!

Curious to say, I met Lowell here, and, although he immediately called me "Edward" and spoke of my mother as "Mary," I did not remember him at Concord, and was ignorant enough not to know much about his work. One day Stephen remarked that music, like eating, should be done in the bathroom. It always sounded to him like an infernal din. He was the ultra-literary type, who wished to be rid of all things physical; he even envied Harriet Martineau, who had no sense of taste. Lowell said:

"Edward, this foolish friend of mine really has some excellent Scotch whisky. Come away with me. If you listen to him you will surely be contaminated."

Mental corruption for a young man was much worse in his opinion than teaching him to drink Scotch whisky.

I remember walking with Lowell and my uncle when the conversation drifted to walking sticks. My uncle said he had cut his on the grave of Wordsworth. I sniffed and said it was not half so good a stick as mine and that if it had been cut on the grave of Shakespeare it would have no added value for me. Lowell turned and said:

"My boy, you are like most of the great men of the world—lacking in one quality, that of deference—and *all* the fools." Considering that I had heard of this poet in his youth, marching through the streets of

Cambridge with the young woman to whom he was betrothed, draped in white, with wreaths upon their heads, and the people in the procession cheering, as a tribute to virginity, I could not help but think: Is it better, I wonder, for a young man to be lacking in deference or a sense of humor?

Leslie Stephen was an editor, and used to get his friends to look over some of the manuscripts submitted to him before he gave his final opinion. One day his friend, Robert Louis Stevenson, ran in, on his way to Scotland, to say good-by, and he asked him to take some poems by an unknown writer along with him and give his criticism of them. R. L. S. wrote a most enthusiastic letter, saying he was so interested that he had hunted up the author, in the hospital, and taken along his best beloved book, *The Viscount de Bragelonne*.

"If he did not like that, I did not want to know him," he said, "but he knows it better than I do. Publish his work at once."

This was the first the world ever heard of the Hospital Sketches of Henley, who showed his gratitude after Stevenson's death by coming out with a statement publicly criticizing him for his debts.

Anders Zorn and his wife, who was the daughter of a wealthy merchant of Stockholm, came over from Spain to St. Ives. He was known principally as a watercolorist before this, but had painted portraits of some of the royal families of Europe, and was patronized by the king of Sweden. Zorn had a disposition of sweetness and light, and, although he had inherited a great charm and delicacy from the paternal side of his family, he cared nothing for society and manners, and thought like a simple peasant; therefore, like a child.

He was large, fattish, built on a small skeleton—a man who would break easily—and had the head of all the colorists—that is, a square forehead, delicate but square jaw, slight aquiline nose, and enormous pale-blue watery eyes. His drooping yellow mustache was long but not thick, and his hands were of the softest, most personal and interesting character. He was a man wth a great hypnotic quality who did not talk much, but dominated without speaking. When he got into a tea fight, he would stand around a short time, listening, then saying, "Yes, I agree," saunter over to the window to the light and, taking a ring off his finger, begin to carve. He had many of these in all states of completion, and one I recall as especially clever was of two little girls with feet twisted and hands holding the jewel.

Zorn loved beautiful women and the human body from an artistic standpoint. His wife understood him as no other being could, and his unrestrained, childlike disposition and natural manners were never misinterpreted by her. In fact, she took care of him as of a most valued property, and added much to the success of his career as an artist. She and his mother seemed to be the two great influences in his life. Every year he sent a lovely sealskin wrap to his mother back in Sweden, and the dear old woman had chests in her garret full of these coats which she evidently delighted to take out and show to her less fortunate friends.

I never knew Zorn to get angry; he was as smooth as cream, but always gave his absolute opinion when asked for it, and always expected others to do the same.

Quite a contrast to a well-known American artist who wanted to turn me out of his house because I did not praise everything he showed me. I asked:

"What did you ask me here for, to give you compliments?"

"Yes," he answered.

The first thing Zorn painted in oils he did out of the window of his little stone house on the embankment overlooking the bay and island. I helped him set his palette, and he jokingly called himself my pupil (I had told him what materials to buy), being as peevish as a child when I dared to criticize the fact he had put the moon in the due north.

"But don't you think it looks well?" he said. This canvas was bought by the French government and now hangs in the Luxembourg.

Zorn was one of those artists who are always showing much originality in the use of their materials and combining this with a sense of humor, which often produces fine results. I went into his back yard one day, and he had a six-foot water color leaning against the house, and was throwing pails of water on it—"bringing it together." He had a great success at the Grosvenor Gallery with a picture of boats, sails, masts, and the seashore sand, with a fat fish-wife walking toward one. (In those days he thought the only beautiful women were fat ones.) He laid this on a box hedge in the garden when a thunderstorm came up. We all rushed out and it seemed to me ruined.

"Now I can make a fine picture," he said. He painted out the smudges from the sails and fixed the dirty sky, but in the foreground, in the sands, were large spots of raindrops. These he turned into footprints, and their naturalness has been commented upon more than once.

One of the most exquisite things he ever made, and one of the greatest works of art, considering its size and sentiment, was a little carving of poplar wood about four by six inches in size. A feather bed, in the center of which, as if she had been dropped there, was a tiny naked figure, sitting up, playing with her wedding ring—the most eerie, fairy creature, with not a touch of the salacious.

Zorn never really got over the sin of water color. He was an all around artist, but hung next to Sargent's his portraits had all the life taken out of them. He did not seem to go beneath the skin except in his etchings, which are perfect, but had a wonderful dexterity and absolute truthfulness combined with an artistic eye that refused to see anything ugly. He once did a portrait of a woman seated on a plush sofa, which looked like the traditional boarding-house affair—thumbed wood, worn, and not pleasant in color. The picture gives you an idea of a beautiful piece of furniture. I said:

"You did not harm the sofa any, did you?"

"Mine is a copy," he replied. He would not deny the truth, but being a gentleman, did not call names.

It would not be fair to leave St. Ives without mentioning Mr. Knill. It is true, he lived many years before my time, but he left a permanent money legacy and a personality so redolent with humor that he will never be forgotten. He was not serious, even in death, and built his tomb long before his demise—a large crypt and granite sarcophagus with his coat of arms—upon the top of a hill as a landmark for his smuggling fleet to get into harbor. Having completed this, he made his will. He directed that every five years there should be given ten pounds to the oldest widower, ten to the oldest widow, ten to the town fiddler, and ten each to ten young virgins, provided they all joined hands and danced around his tomb (led by the fiddler) to the tune of "Old Hundred."

This celebration had developed into a pathetic thing. They selected the poor who needed the money and the dinner, which originally was to cost two pounds a plate, but had been reduced to two shillings, even the Cornish not being above a little unpardonable economy. The whole thing was very English, and just like the lichen which comes on a tree when it is old.

One of the greatest jokes Mr. Knill played upon the populace was to go to London and die in a hospital, so that his body was dissected by the medical students. I was telling this to a crowd of Londoners, saying that it was such a joke that he should have painted as his motto on his tomb:

NIL DESPERANDUM.

"Yes," they said, "but you see his name was spelled with a 'K.'"

London is a male, a great, gloomy being, sitting up on his island, rough, unshaven, besmeared with cinders and smut, and glowering across at the courtesan Paris as she graciously smiles back at him with every wile. For Paris is a woman.

In London nobody wants to see you. There is a "get out" sign on the side of every wall, and broken glass on the top. Even the weather frowns on you, making you feel that you are not wanted. But in Paris, the very first man you meet, from the cab driver to the waiter in the café, is very glad to see you and gives you the impression that you are his personal guest. On the north side of the Channel, the Atlantic Ocean roars like an infuriated bull, while on the south side it hurls itself against the coast like an angry woman. In fact, all the male characteristics are those of London—dignity, strength, coarseness, and brute force—but in Paris there is never a trace of these. There is only charm.

Paris never shocks you. There is much low life and there is crime, but it is treated in an artistic way. Every so often they have a wholesale raid to get rid of the undesirables. At a stated time, on a summer evening, suddenly will come marching down all the streets which lead to the tenderloin district hundreds of police, walking four abreast and making a dragnet which sweeps everything before it. Everyone who cannot tell his business, any solitary woman, is caught in its meshes and brought up before the authorities. I was sitting in the Café Américain one night, with a drink before me, when a woman in an evening gown rushed frantically up to my table, saying:

"You are my brother."

Nothing loath, I took the cue, but asked, "What is it you want to do?"

"Oh, don't you know what is happening?" she said. "It is the *cordon*."

She took my arm and I escorted her to the door, she all the time protesting her eternal gratitude. If she had been seized alone by the police, that last shame would have been hers. She would have been "put on the card" and become automatically a registered prostitute.

Nothing like this happens in London. There, in the first dusk of evening, little girls hardly twelve years old walk past the Criterion Bar and the Haymarket, dressed in long skirts, smirking and smiling and proclaiming their profession to any male they happen to meet. These children are unmolested, and no one seems to object to it in the least, although their manner and language are disgusting as well as pitiable. Then again there are the old women, drunken, disorderly creatures, always ready to engage a chance loiterer in conversation and taking the opportunity to whisper vulgar remarks in his ear; their flabby bodies and flying wisps of coarse gray hair and the ages of vice in their countenances almost denying their human origin. But to all of this London is blissfully unconscious—it is merely the gross side of a male—and, as such, is ignored.

My first visit to London was when I was still a student in Paris. I was given one hundred dollars by a patron, evidently with the best intentions, to go across the Channel and paint a portrait of the last of the old-fashioned tallyho-coach drivers. I was a stranger in a strange city; I had never felt the frosted shoulder before. Every other place I had been, even in the north of California, I had been able to make myself at home almost instantly, but here in the country of my ancestors, where every man was as near to me in blood as the people of Concord, Massachusetts, I was as much an alien as if I had been of Oriental origin. I managed to locate the coachman and found him an interesting character, but I could not make any arrangements about painting him; it was impossible to do it in his house. I could not find a studio, and before I had hardly turned around I found my pile reduced to about thirty-five shillings. I decided it was about time to go back to my friends.

Choosing the longest and the cheapest trip across the Channel, I found I could just about get to St. Malo, third class, if I did not have a stateroom. I had a right to occupy one of the berths in the downstairs cabin, but, upon finding it filled with about eighty seasick butter merchants, drinking and yelling, I decided to escape the vile odors and bluff it out on deck, with my ulster to keep me warm. I have never been sick on the water before or since, but the whole situation and my worried state of mind drove me to it, and I shall never forget the pathetic picture I must have made curled up in the scuppers, trampled on by the crew, my greatcoat covering myself and a cabin boy who was making his first trip and was also in a very bad condition. There was a blinding snowstorm, and we lay to the leeward of the Isle of Guernsey, making the crossing last eight hours. Upon landing, the cabin boy recovered first and carried my grip, while I went across the gangplank on all fours and just managed to reach a hotel and telegraph my friend Frank Chadwick, who was down in Concarneau, to bail me out.

After such memories, I was rather loath to go back to the great capital of my ancestors, and have never made long visits to London. But the English are gentlemen, and, as gentlemen, have a delicate sense of humor. *Punch* will be stupid for six months at a time, and all of a sudden will come out with some witty picture or saying that will ring around the world and be remembered for years.

London is the center of the English-speaking race, and its opinion goes for all of us; but it seemed like a foreign land to me every time I entered, and I was glad to see that I was not alone in my feeling. I never read the travels of Robert Louis Stevenson that I do not realize that when he went to England he instantly felt himself among strangers. Be that as it may, they do not treat us as they do colonials, toward whom, if they do not ignore them, the shoulder is always hunched. They, at least, do us the honor to scrap with us, which shows they consider us worthy of much consideration. In all these arguments, it is best to get in the first blow and then you are all right.

Only once do I remember feeling perfectly at home in London, and that was the first time I visited Westminster Abbey. I must have been in a prophetic mood or else the atmosphere of so many dead warriors influenced my mind, for the friend who was with me wrote to me in 1917—more than thirty years later, saying:

> We went to see the historical sights of London, and you were particularly moved in Westminster Abbey. As we stood in the corridor outside, you made a solemn prediction to this effect: "Twenty or thirty years from now, when Germany conquers France, as she surely will unless England has the sense to step in in time—she will then try to conquer England. This she can do, unless America comes to the rescue. When Americans face the destruction of Westminster Abbey, they *will* come to the rescue. Then at last the war of 1775 will come to an end."

On one occasion, while entering the city by the railway (I was feeling fine from a reinforcement of several real old Scotch whiskies), I took out a coin, a penny, and said:

"This is a wonderful country. I no sooner get here than for a couple of our copper cents (with a picture of an Indian, badly done, upon the face) I receive this large, weighty, and dignified coin of pure bronze upon which is a bas-relief of Her Gracious Majesty, Queen Victoria."

From the other side of the compartment leaned forward a retired British major—a man you could see had evidently conquered with difficulty his childish habit of dropping his aitches. In a gentle, deprecating voice, he answered:

"My dear young sir, permit me to hope that during your stay with us here you will refrain from any desire to make a mock of our holier institutions. Do not, I pray you, carp at Our Gracious Majesty."

He did not get down on his belly on the floor—only mentally—but I had the awful feeling that he was longing to do so. Queen Victoria (and that was long before the admirable book by Lytton Strachey) could never produce such an effect upon a sane Yankee.

Speaking of aitches, I once told Leslie Stephen that every Englishman was careless with them, even himself. He roared and insisted that only the lower classes dropped them or added them. I then asked him to say, "White witch which I met on the Isle of Wight." Of course he stumbled. This softening of the aitch to a point where it seems to disappear is a habit peculiar to the inbred Britisher—just as the "r" is to the Bostonian and the "d" to the Spaniard.

I once discussed this with an educated and learned Englishman from the commoner class. He was only a graduate of the College of London, but knew his Latin and Greek better than any American and had been spending his time teaching the children of the vulgar rich of Pittsburgh. He insisted that the habit of dropping the aitches was prevalent in those parts of England where the Romans had permanently settled— all along inside the Wall. He cited a poem of Catullus which mocked at the fashionable dudes of Rome for the foolish habit they had taken up of dropping and adding their aitches. If this were the fashion in the mother country, it would certainly have penetrated to the Roman settlers of England.

My later attempts at an artistic invasion of London were no more successful than my first poor effort to paint a cockney coachman. In the year 1888 I sent two pictures to the Royal Academy which were duly accepted and hung. Imagine my joy when a large and formidable communication found its way to my studio in Paris, asking the price of one of my canvases and signed by the Chantry Bequest. This was a well-known fund created to buy pictures for the government to place in its permanent galleries, and everyone knew that, once the price had been asked, it amounted to the same thing as a sale. In fact, according to the British precedent—which is generally iron-bound, a request *was* a sale. I replied, as they expected me to do (this was also according to rule), that my price was four hundred pounds. The picture, which I called "The Carpenter's Son," was a simple pose of one of my children in my studio. A blond boy with a light shining over his head sat dreaming, instead of sweeping out the shop, while his mother, in the back, told his father what a worthless son he had begotten. The shavings had accidentally fallen in the form of a cross, and the light seemed to be a halo. The *Scotsman* came out with a scathing denunciation of the work (not at the idea, mind you) but because, as they said, I had been sacrilegious enough to paint Christ in the costume of a French peasant boy! Of course, the Chantry Bequest did not buy—for the first time—after asking the price.

It was very amusing to hear that when the picture was afterward exhibited in America, a woman of the old New England type was seen standing before it and weeping, saying between sobs:

"Oh, what a terrible thing! They have crucified our Saviour again!"

This was more than a Concord Unitarian could understand.

The next year I took courage and sent another canvas to the Academy—this time an inoffensive thing of an old man kissing his wife good-by—which I called "Darby and Joan." Through some mistake, it was marked "sold" in the book which is left on a table to give the record of sales. Some of my friends seeing this, and having it confirmed by the person in charge, telegraphed me congratulations, I being away down in Cornwall. It was customary to notify the artist as soon as a sale was consummated and, as I heard nothing, I wrote to the secretary (whom we always called "Pants Exclusively," on account of his tradesman instincts) and asked him to confirm it. He answered that one of

"THE CARPENTER'S SON"

Hitherto unpublished photograph of the painting by Edward Simmons, now hanging on the walls of the home of Miss Amelia Jones, New Bedford, Massachusetts

Copyright by Edward Simmons; from a Copley Print, copyright by Curtis & Cameron, Publishers, Boston

the officials had marked the book by mistake and that the picture was not sold. I wrote and asked him to take it off the book and to advertise it as "still for sale." No answer. All through that exhibition my picture was hung and marked "sold," thereby preventing anyone else from buying it, and this in spite of the fact that I wrote to protest about it three times. Then I did a terrible thing! I issued a writ against the Royal Academy! British honor was sullied, British institutions had been assailed. Never before had anyone dared to invoke the law against that august and distinguished body—the Royal Academy!

My final letter ran something like this:

DEAR SIR—In my country, when dealing with gentlemen, I get an answer. In dealing with you, I do not. I appeal to the law.

I received a most pathetic letter from "Pants Exclusively" and a large, formidable parchment apology from the trustees of the Academy.

In the meantime the London papers burst out with indignant articles against the person who had dared to sue the Academy, calling him all sorts of names and saying it was a bit of "cheap American advertising." Immediately a flock of reporters came down to Cornwall, all ready to start a beautiful fight. I produced my parchment apology, resulting in the gentle fading away of newspaper representatives and a lovely article about me in the next morning's papers.

This carelessness of the Academy had been going on for years. I had known of several similar cases where the artist supposed his work had been sold and was afterwards told it was a mistake. One year a friend of mine, with true artistic optimism, gave a large dinner party to celebrate his good luck, and, of course, expected to settle for it with the check he was to receive. He was months paying for that dinner. At that he may have been lucky. He at least got his picture back. There were many lost and never returned, and any protest from the painter only met with indifferent silence.

The English are sentimental, though—especially where they do not understand—and, yes, I shall have to admit it, so are we of New England. Sitting in the drawing-room of a prominent British woman, I was astonished to hear her say, upon the announcement that a pianist was about to play a well-known selection of Mendelssohn: "Songs Without any Words! What a pity!" In painting they prefer canvases that have some literary significance; a story with a heart appeal frequently attracts more attention than a far greater work that is more abstract.

The year after Sargent had exhibited his "El Jaleo" in the Salon, his close friend, Ralph Curtis, was bothered to death by all the busybodies who wanted to know what the next picture would be. One day Curtis answered:

"I'll tell you. Sargent is painting, for the Salon, a circle of naked women sitting on red velvet cushions, called 'Daughters of Sin.'"

"But he can't send it to the Academy afterward," they cried.

"Oh yes, he can!" replied Curtis. "He'll just change the title to 'Waiting for the Omnibus,' and they will never think to look at the painting."

There was always a great deal of talk about Sargent's titles. At Paris in '89, I was dining at Stanley Reinhart's with a number of men when some one spoke of the portrait painter's Academy picture of that year. It was a beautiful thing of girls hanging Japanese lanterns in a garden of flowers at twilight. They said he had called it, "Carnation, lily, lily, rose." I said at once, "Damnation, silly, silly, pose." They thought it quite a joke, and some one wrote to Abbey about it, who answered that Luke Fildes had made that remark three weeks ago. His thought must have been almost simultaneous with mine, he in England and I in France. This shows how people may be falsely accused of plagiarism.

Of my own pictures, there was one of an old man with two children gazing out to sea, which I had named "Low Tide." My mother called upon the English tailor who bought it, as she had never happened to see it. He was very polite and treated her with great reverence, and then proceeded to explain her son's work to her.

"You see, the old man has just returned from sea and the little girl has laid her hand on his arm, telling him that his daughter and her mother—has passed away during his absence. It is called, 'Mother's Dead.'"

And this in spite of the metal plate on the frame which announced the title in large letters! Another time, a Yankee girl—dripping with sentiment about my poetry of mind and deep thinking—told me of the sad picture she had seen of mine of the poor mother who, having lost her first child, was mending its little shoe in expectation of a second. I was puzzled until she mentioned the title, "No. 2." In my earlier days, I started numbering my pictures—as a musician's "opus"—until one of the members of my family insisted that I give it up. I had gotten as far as 1 and 2, then stopped. It was a picture of a girl in a blue calico jacket with a darker blue skirt, mending a child's little blue varnished boot. Just a peasant I had seen; she was about ten or twelve, but I had evidently made her look older. What an astonishing explanation for my simple harmony of blues!

Frank Millet used to say, "Put a Bible on the table or a letter bordered in black on the floor if you want to sell your picture at the Royal Academy," and I think this is borne out by an incident that happened to a friend of mine in Cornwall. He was a bully fellow from a titled family which objected to his artistic tendencies. He came to me one fall, asking me what he should paint to send to the Academy, saying that it was very important that he should have a picture exhibited and sold, as his family had given him one last chance. I asked him to show me the canvas he had sent the year before. He fetched out a thing, remarking indifferently that it had been refused.

"Give me five minutes and some paint," I said, "and I'll bet you I can fix it so that it goes in and is sold."

"What will you bet?" he asked.

"Two guineas."

"Done."

It was a fairly good landscape of two tall poplars reflected in a pool in the late afternoon. I put a dab of rose on the tops of the trees and on their reflections, making the effect of a sunset light. Then I got a gold panel for the frame, painting on it in most artistic Old English lettering, these touching words:

"The last sad kiss of dear departing day."

It went to the Academy; it was sold for two hundred pounds; I got my ten. Of course, everybody *knew* where the verses came from—either Thompson's "Seasons" or Wordsworth, etc.—and I was perfectly willing to let the dead poets have the credit for such sentimentality.

Chapter VIII: Summer Adventurings
I. *Carrière St.-Denis*

I HAVE often wished I could have the faith of some Christians in the power of the Holy Book and, when I wanted to decide anything of importance, just open it to any page, put my finger on a spot, and proceed according to the instructions thereupon given. I have the gambler's instinct, but perhaps only for little things, and while I have never gone to the Bible for material guidance, I have many times employed the childish quotation, "My mother says that I shall do this"—pointing a finger at each word—and following the lead. This does not always prove a happy method of selecting one's future, but I think it is as near as one can come to it. There is only one case where I am certain it cannot fail, and that is for a very good reason—there is a prize package at the end of *every* string. If you stand in the center of Paris and start in any direction toward its environs, you will end at a place more charming than you can imagine. I have tried this experiment many times and have never been disappointed.

Carrière St.-Denis was discovered quite accidentally by two of my painter friends, and it was only after a long time that they let me in on the secret. Having traveled out of the city on the railway as far as Nanterre, you take your courage in your hands and get off at this place, which seems to have nothing more interesting than endless fields of vegetables. Despair not; cross the tracks and walk steadily on until you come to a canal. Here is a wooded island whose banks look like nothing so much as the old fishing place on the Concord River at home. All is quiet, with no signs of human habitation until you come to a post across from which a boat is tied. Here you must stop, put your hands to your mouth to form a trumpet, and cry: *"Passeur!"*—*"Passeur!"* After about the second call will come the answer, *"Attendez!"* and down the path from his little hut, which is entirely concealed by the trees, comes an old man bearing upon his shoulder a pair of oars. Without speaking a word, he comes over, you get into the boat, and he rows you across the canal, where, very gravely, he leaves the skiff and, again carrying the oars, he walks with you across the island. Here you are at the Seine, but a part of the river that you have not known before. Another boat is waiting, again the old man rows you over, but this time you land upon a gravelly beach flanked by a cliff so steep that you despair of ever climbing it.

At first glance this *falaise* reminds you of the familiar Palisades, only made of Caen stone, but, on closer examination, you are astonished to find that there are doors and windows cut out of the solid rock! The blacksmith shop is a former quarry, as are many of the homes of the humbler and poorer, their people having taken up their habitations in the same manner as the hermit crab—in the shell of a former owner. On the other side is the village, looking like an old-fashioned jewel in a rough setting, while farther along, on the outskirts of the town, are the fields of cabbages and beets. You must be very careful in wandering over these stretches of growing vegetation, for at any moment you may come to a hole like a rabbit burrow almost concealed by the grass. If you have the Alice in Wonderland instinct (and you will certainly have acquired it by this time), you will plunge down this rough tunnel to see what mysteries the underground holds.

Men have dug out this rock, from which Paris has been made, leaving a labyrinth of paths and chambers. Every once in a while there are flashes of light very much like the glimpses of the sky that one gets from the train when going out from New York at the Grand Central Station. Over the edge of these openings hang blackberry vines, and the singing of birds can be heard. You are reminded of that story told by Wells, of the race of people that lived under the earth and came out at night to feed upon those who lived on top. There is one long tunnel which leads to an amphitheater larger than the Hippodrome. It is dark as the night, and you feel as if this must be the cathedral of these underground men.

All at once, out of the dampness comes a new odor, something of the earth, but not of the deep earth. It is as if the plowshare had just turned over a bit of sun-warmed humus, and as your eyes become accustomed to the darkness you see that this vault, so much like a stage setting of Gordon Craig's, has small apertures in its sides where beds of mushrooms are pushing their way out of the ground. It is in places like this that the supply for Paris is grown.

Turning to the left, you will find a continuous passage, and if you have the courage to traverse its three miles of length you will come out to the light at the site of another red-roofed village—this one called Montessan—and strange to relate, there again is the Seine, which has coiled itself around like a snake and met you at the other side. Across the river at this point is a large and formidable building which seems by its modernity to deny the facts of all you have seen, for this is the Pavilion Henri Quatre, and Paris is but twenty miles away.

My hotel at Carrière St.-Denis was above a shop where pig meat in different forms was sold. M. Perdrielle, *charcutier*, was a genial host, and his wife's cooking did ample justice to his artistry as a butcher. We often went out there for a few days, and once I spent a month with these people who lived the life of the France of a hundred years ago. I was always called "M. Edouard le Dessineur," which is not French, but peasant argot, and they did not see anything at all generous in including cigarettes, billiards, and drinks in the two hundred and fifty francs a month they charged for board.

Berthe, the daughter of the household, was married while I was in Carrière St.-Denis, and I had the extreme pleasure of assisting at a true rural marriage. Her husband-to-be was a wine merchant and, wishing to do him great honor, she begged me to wear my evening clothes. A merchant *de vin* is on about the same social level with that of the owner of a corner saloon in America; but I was perfectly willing to show off for Berthe's sake.

The banquet began in the evening and was enlivened by many old customs. At a certain time a small boy came in with a giggle and ran away with the bride's garter, which was twenty yards long, and was immediately pulled this way and that by all the men, who fought for the pieces. One ceremony, which must have been a survival of the Rabelaisian period, was carried out by the bridesmaids, who came in singing an old French song (one of those delightful things whose meaning could be taken either of two ways) and holding aloft a *pot de chambre* filled with *dragees*, or sugar almonds, which they distributed to the company. The procession of young men followed with a pair of candy horns for the groom.

At the end of many toasts they all were sufficiently tipsy to begin their long pilgrimage, for it is the custom for the bridal pair to spend the first week of their married life visiting all their friends, taking all the bridesmaids and groomsmen with them. At each home they eat and drink, and on the seventh day an exhausted pair of lovers return home, dirty and forlorn, with their clothes—and their nerves—in tatters.

Every change of season has its corresponding duties to nature, and each one is made the occasion of a festival by the simple folk in all lands. Let the foreigner who wanders into peasant France in the autumn beware of letting himself loose among the grape gatherers. The *"vendange,"* as it is called, is the ceremony of picking these little fruits out of which the native wine is made, and it is during this season that the peasants let themselves go, like children. They dance and they sing and they play practical jokes, the most common being to catch the unwary bystander and rub him with the juice of the *tenturier*, the Spanish grape.

There are a certain number of these in every vineyard. They are called the "dyer" grape, and are used to give color to the *petit vin*, and assuredly give a lasting color to the poor victim. After the harvest they all come home in a tumbrel, the noise and laughter in no way indicating the former gruesome use for that vehicle.

When you have managed to tear yourself away from this interesting and strange suburb of Paris, and crossed the Seine, should you look back upon the scene of your former pleasures, you will see nothing of the villages with the red-tiled roofs, nothing of the cabbages and beets, indeed, nothing to indicate any human habitation. As far as you know, there is only a solid cliff of Caen stone—the same of which the Louvre is built—pale cream in tone and gray when the air touches it. I once dug my finger-nail into a soft piece of the rock and found it was made of an infinite number of seashells, a veritable paste of dead animals.

II. Barbizon

On the fringe of the woods of the forest of Fontainebleau is Barbizon. We used to go out here whenever we could, where, at the Hotel Siron there were always dozens of artists gathered together, hoping to pick up one of Millet's paper collars.

Most of the old Barbizon group were dead by the time I got there, but among those left were Frank O'Mara, Naegley, and Hawkins—all Englishmen—and Jameson, brother of the doctor of South African fame; my friends, Ruger Donoho and Charles H. Davis; Butler, who married a daughter of Monet;

and Jaques, the well-known French painter of sheep. Jaques was the last of the original French colony.

Babcock, an American painter, had lived there for twenty years. He was one of those beings who had been soured by time and had come to know that the world was all wrong. He almost always went out of his back door, and if ever he emerged from the front it was in the dead of night. He had sat at the feet of Millet and had a portfolio of twenty or thirty drawings that the great artist had thrown away. He told me with joy that Millet would crumple up his self-condemned work and throw it into a box behind the stove. Every once in a while Babcock would fish out one and open it up, Millet yelling at him all the time. Nothing daunted, he would retreat like a dog with a bone. Even the garbage can is not sacred to some people.

In Boston, Millet has been overrated (W. M. Hunt did it). Once he sold a picture for two thousand francs, the highest price he had received up to that time. He was most human and, like all artists, optimistic, so he immediately hired a professor to come out from Paris and tutor his children, and hired saddle horses for them to ride upon in the park. Of course, this period of affluence did not last, and when he died, at about fifty-nine years of age, he was supposed to be a poor man, cursed by fate; yet he had received an order from the Pope and decorations from his own government. This is not a case of neglected genius.

I was still under thirty when I met Mrs. Millet. She immediately asked:

"You paint? Then might I, as an older woman, give a bit of advice? Remember you run the risk of making any woman you marry unhappy." (I can hear her voice now, as we sat at the table d'hôte.) "A woman who marries an artist must realize beforehand that he will never care for her alone. She must look forward always to playing second fiddle to something else. If he is a true artist, it is his painting, if not—but she will always be second fiddle just the same. If she has the capacity to adapt herself to that position, she will be happy. I, myself, have been a happy woman."

Robert Louis Stevenson had just left Barbizon a short time before my first visit. I was avid to hear about him and tried in vain to get them to give me some details of his character and personality. But all the boys said, indifferently:

"Oh yes, he writes, but his cousin is much the cleverer author." And they had read the *Lodging for the Night!* Not a very good recommendation for the literary acumen of painters.

We led a lazy life out there, with rarely a tinge of excitement. We were all in the same financial class and, I imagine, in about the same state of blissful innocence and ignorance of the world. I remember a very pretty girl of the Paris gay life, who was advised to go to Barbizon for a rest and to freshen up a bit. We were thrilled at her appearance and entertained her as if she were a *grande dame*. She was evidently in no way pleased, but very much puzzled, when she went back to Paris and told a friend:

"*Crois tu, ma chere, pas un de ces cochons la m'ont offert le sous!*"

We made most of our own good times. One favorite

game at Sirons was to go out, each one of us, and lean a sketch against a tree, retire to a hiding place, and watch. Of a lovely afternoon, myriads of carriages would come out from Fontainebleau, the occupants leisurely lying back and gazing from side to side. Some of them would spy the painting there on the ground. If they looked at it, it counted one point; if they examined it carefully, it was two; but if they carried it off with them it was a sign that the painter was one hundred per cent perfect and he had to pay for a bottle of wine for the crowd. I once had one of my sketches taken away and it cost me two bottles of fizz, but I was a very happy man. Some one had liked my work and had stolen it! And what was one sketch? It was so easy to make another.

A man, perhaps not so well known as the Barbizon painters, but certainly much more interesting than the majority of them, was Professor Lainey. He looked an old man when I knew him, white haired and a chatterbox. For years he had taught drawing in the schools of Fontainebleau.

In his youth Professor Lainey had hoped to become an actor and had joined a class to study for the stage. Among the pupils was a little Jewess, fourteen years old, plain looking and poorly dressed, and as it was his fate to take the same omnibus with her, politeness demanded that he escort her to her door. This he hated to do, as she was a most hopeless-looking creature and he was cad enough to be ashamed to be seen with her. One day in class, the teacher asked her to deliver a line of Racine, and said:

"Shall I give it as I was told to, or as it should be rendered?"

Very amused, he replied: "Mademoiselle will be good enough to give it first as she has been told to give it, and afterward the class will be delighted to hear her improvement."

She obeyed, and Professor Lainey added: "For the first time I understood Racine."

Continuing, he said: "I saw no more of her until I was an art student in Paris. One night I went to the Théâtre Français, and there upon the stage appeared the little Jewess of my class. She was none other then the divine Sarah!"

Poor, plain, and of a despised race, even as a child her brain had begun to work. Like Christ, as a boy before the elders, she told *them*, not they her.

Professor Lainey had been in Fontainebleau during the Franco-Prussian War and remembered the invasion of Barbizon. The *franc-tireurs* (citizen troops), of which he was a member, were a constant bother to the Germans. One of their pranks was to stretch a wire across the road, just the height of a rider, and they finally succeeded in decapitating an orderly. The Germans decided that some one must hang for it, and, being unable to find the guilty one, they chose a dozen men and told them to draw lots. Not liking to kill one of the prominent citizens with whom they had been playing cards all winter in quite a friendly manner, they put on the list a man whom we call a "natural," then winked and walked away. But they reckoned without the French nature. These men refused to sacrifice the poor half-wit, and said:

"Hang all or any one of us. We will not choose."

France is still covered with the evidences of monarchs, and one of the best reasons why kings no longer rule and the Third Empire went to pieces still remains in Fontainebleau Forest. In walking about, one has to use the utmost care, as one is constantly catching his foot and taking a "header." All around, underneath the brush and now entirely covered by it, are paths of asphalt, miles and miles of them, literally riddling the whole woods. These were laid by her generous spouse so that the Empress Eugènie could follow the boar hunt in her Parisian shoes and not wet her feet on the grass!

III. Montreuil

The history of France could be told by the wall which surrounds the village of Montreuil. Originally encircled by a Roman structure (the bricks of which still show a few feet above the ground), every succeeding dynasty has added its touch, each a different material, until the wall has become as expressive of the past as a patchwork quilt. There are several layers of soft stone, one of granite put on by Vauban; the top must have been added many years ago, for there are large trees growing upon it. The town was besieged thirteen times by the English, but was never taken.

During one of these seiges, there was a drought inside the wall, and they were forced to brave the enemy and get their water from one of the many springs out upon the hillside. Thinking it better to save the fighting men for sterner duty, it was decided to let the clerks and those who wrote in the books go for the supply. There was one *petit clerc*, noted for the beauty of his singing in church, who was beloved of a girl of high birth. These two met but seldom, as their affair was not approved by the young woman's family. One night the clerk's name was on the list of those who must go outside the gates. His sweetheart found it out and, stealing the message before it was delivered to him, she put on boy's clothing and took his place. That night the English lay in wait and killed a dozen or more water carriers, throwing the bodies into the spring. This was supposed to have stopped the flow of the water, and to-day the inhabitants will show the sink in the side of a hill which used to be this spring. I have always wanted to dig down and see if a girl's skeleton were there.

Standing on this wall, I could not help being hypnotized by the surroundings into a feeling that it was not the nineteenth, but the fifteenth or sixteenth century. I could see, with my mind's eye, coming up the valleys toward the walled town, a long line of men and laden beasts, a troop of soldiery returning to their nest with the spoils, the loot raped from the countryside; for as neither printing nor powder had come to their aid, the countryfolk were robbed of everything they had but their shift and their pickax. Led, perchance, by Sieur Johan or my lord high bishop, they bore upon their saddlebows beautiful maidens with streaming hair, their heads drooping and their hands tied behind their backs.

At the end of one of the streets of Montreuil, quite a distance down, there is a church which seems to be covered with lichens, but on nearer approach they are seen to be bullet holes—mute testimonials to the sufferings the people have endured during the ages—for example, the result of the French Commune.

I slept in the inn made famous by Laurence Sterne. It was here that he stopped near the beginning of his Sentimental Journey and hired his valet. On its wall in large copper letters were the figures 1640, indicating that it had been built in that year. It was a fitting place to stop on a quest of romance, and, indeed, one could not be surprised at any strange adventure that might overtake one in such a memory-laden setting. Even the bedroom (I wondered if it were the same that Sterne occupied) was of a charm and quaintness that was conducive to the most extravagant dreams. The furniture and fixings breathed of the long ago, and all about in convenient nooks and crannies were bits of old brass for which any collector would give a king's ransom. But best of all (and these were evidently placed so that they would be the first things upon which the sleep-laden eyes of the lodger would rest when he was awakened by the early morning noises), was the decoration around the foot of the bedroom wall. In solemn procession, and reaching to a height of about five or six feet, were illustrated the gods and goddesses of Olympus! I have always wanted to do a room like this.

IV. Grez

Grez has been immortalized by the artists that have stopped there. The bridge, built over the river Loing, which was so much like the Concord that it was a constant delight to me, has been painted times innumerable, but it is so charming that we never tire of seeing it on canvas.

The story of Grez is the story of nearly every French village, and one has only to notice the way it is laid out to visualize its history. There is one central street upon which the houses face so close together as to form a solid wall on either side. In the back of this phalanx of stone the whole life of the community goes on. Here are the gardens, many of them sloping down to the river, where are the stones upon which they wash their clothes; here the children play, protected from all harm. The cultivated fields lie away up on the hillsides, as do the pastures, but in olden times, before the last ray of the sun had left the sky, every evening would see each inhabitant of the village back in his home, close to his neighbors, protected not only from the roaming wild animals, but from the lord upon the hill as well. The wolves were the scavengers and nightly used to clear the little street of all its refuse, so that anything thrown out of the window (and everything was) had disappeared in the morning light.

I passed many months in Grez. Here again I met the trail of Stevenson, only too late. He had started the habit of going there, and I saw the actual garret room which he speaks about in the *Treasure of Franchard*. It was here that the mummer died—while the big shadows were dancing about the walls—and left the boy to the doctor. The same landlady was bustling around the inn, and during my stay, as business was none too good (or else she was a generous provider and therefore a bad manager), we had to give her our money beforehand or there would be no dinner.

John Runciman was one of the bright, particular lights at the inn. He was a very unconscious man with a brave brain and would quietly say anything he pleased. He was also a musician of no mean attainment and could sit at the piano with his back turned to the keys and play Chopin well enough to suit *me*. He had the audacity to write the musical criticisms for the *Saturday Review* (Frank Harris being the editor at the time), and all the time he was living in the Fontainebleau Forest! I asked him how he could manage to satisfy his readers without having heard the concerts.

"Oh," he replied, "one conductor always plays too fast, and a certain soprano invariably breaks on her high C. Besides, I know all the music, and the public does not want anything new in the way of criticism."

Runciman once showed me a magazine which he had saved, with an article by Stevenson telling how he had written *Treasure Island*. He was down in Bournemouth for his health, and at the same place was a little boy who was dying of tuberculosis. Stevenson composed the tale for him and got him to draw the map of the island as he had imagined it. This he sent with the manuscript, to London to the publisher. Through some carelessness in the office, the boy's drawing was lost, and, although Robert Louis Stevenson tried to do it from memory, he declared it was greatly inferior to the naïve child's fancy.

I hesitate to tell about something that I have always thought very beautiful, and that is the song of the nightingale, but I remember some typical Gopher Prairie people coming to Grez and, doubtless, being disappointed at the abandoned street, the dogs, and the hens, when remaining up especially to hear the songbird, said that they had been awakened many times by that sound, but had "always thought it was the croaking of frogs."

However it may have sounded to the Middle West, it was sufficiently beautiful to my untrained musical ear to make me journey back to Grez twenty years later to hear it again. You can take a scientific or sentimental view of the flight of the queen bee, and I prefer to hold with Maeterlinck.

No birds in the world make real music except the nightingale and the wood thrush. The remainder whistle. Shelley's lark is the ideal of the going to heaven and disappearing, but there is no song. This little bird in our dark wood coppice used to come out and sit on a garden post at night and commit suicide from love in such a way as nearly to tear his throat apart. Look out how you take it seriously, though, for the next minute after you are sure the life has gone out of his body he is fooling you by gurgling such sentimental poppycock as "I took you away and made you love me." All the way from Hamlet to Pierrot, it is music burbling through blood and tears.

V. Stuttgart

It is a far cry from Paris to Stuttgart, but my only experience of Germany is in this town, and there are several things about it that I like to remember. The greatest impression left to me is the music, everything was permeated with it. I have never been able to perform on any instrument, and my only claim to singing is that I could yell louder than anyone else in school, but some how I have always felt the rhythms inside, and the wonder to me was to see a whole race of people who were musicians. In the later afternoon the workmen come home from their work in the vineyards, fifteen or twenty of them in one group. They fall into singing quite naturally, each one taking the part best suited to his voice, while away down the road another group will take up the melody, fitting in perfect harmony, until the whole has formed a large chorus, singing in accord. I often think it is a pity that we do not have something like that, but I suppose that these songs must be the growth of the soil—and we are too young.

Many years ago—I do not know how many—a citizen left a sum of money in his will, providing for music to be played from the cathedral tower at twelve o'clock noon. I do not know if he directed the kind of music it should be, but in my time it was provided by four stringed instruments. Just after the clock had struck the hour, proclaiming that the weary worker might pause and rest, this music would come down from the sky, as if some heavenly chorus were singing.

My host in Stuttgart was a scion of one of the aristocratic families, and I had a chance to peep into the gay German life of the period. We used to lunch quite often at the officers' mess of a certain smart cavalry regiment who were noted for their daring and bravery as well as for lavish entertaining. A most amazing habit that these genial souls indulged in struck horror to my very marrow. At regular intervals, as a test, they were required to ride a distance of twenty miles.

Tied to the saddlebow was a magnum of champagne, and they must drink this on the way, the one reaching the end of the journey first being considered the real male of the crowd. This was not so bad, but they did not hesitate to run down peasants and kill them without compunction. Their foolhardiness and utter indifference to the lives of the country people was an ingrained part of their natures, and no one seemed to think anything about it. It was considered a huge joke if one of the cavalry officers was found later thrown from his horse into the bushes and dead drunk.

Employed by my friend as a tutor for his children was an unfrocked French curate, and he was always arguing that the German women were plain. I was asked as an artist to judge. At four o'clock in the afternoon, we went out to the promenade and watched the beauties of the city pass by. From that motley crowd I was able to pick out only eight who were at all pretty. Of these, they told me that two were American, two English, one Swedish, and two Viennese, while only one of the whole galaxy was from Stuttgart.

Chapter IX: First Decorations

COMING home—somehow it did not seem as if it could be a reality. I had begun to feel quite American when my fellow passengers started calling me "Colonel Cody." In Europe I had passed easily for an Englishman and sometimes a Swede, it being very foolish to admit a residence in the U. S. A. unless one was prepared to be cheated on every hand. But as the boat neared American soil I felt my patriotism rising every minute. Thirteen years is a long time for a man to be away from his native land.

A Canadian on board the English ship became a kindred spirit—we "Westerners" finding it necessary to form a close alliance. He and I played bridge every day with two men, one from Glasgow and one from Liverpool. During a heated conversation, one of them made the remark that we were getting quite cocky over in the States, adding that England would "have to be sending some ships and men over to settle America before long." At that, a little voice piped up (the Canadian's) saying:

"What! again?"

The steward was sent for and drinks ordered, for the British *do* know how to pay when they are beaten.

At ten one morning, when the first pilot boat loomed into sight and I leaned over the rail and saw these men in oilskins busying themselves about the craft, my calm, joyous attitude suddenly deserted me. The thought had burst into my mind that this boat must have put out from New York and these men were

Americans. My heart came up in my throat and I had to go below. At four o'clock that afternoon we docked, and as I walked away from the ship, all the familiar sights and sounds coming upon me with a rush; I stopped and, utterly unmindful that I might be run in for a lunatic, kissed the post of the Ninth Avenue Elevated. Homesickness and love of my native land, qualities I did not realize that I possessed, had taken hold of me.

New York had never been my home before, so I did not know it well enough to recognize much change; but from '91 until the present day the city has altered beyond recognition. A Dutch banker once told me that if the money that his countrymen paid the Indians for the island of Manhattan had been put out to interest, it would be sufficient to purchase the land to-day. I wonder if that be true?

Most of the life of those days centered about Union Square, with tentacles reaching down to Washington and up to Madison Squares. On the Seventeenth Street side of Fourth Avenue was the Clarendon, and, opposite, the Everett House, that famous rendezvous for politicians. On Twenty-third Street was the Academy of Art, which housed itself in a building evidently copied from the Doge's palace in Venice, while next to it was the Lyceum Theater, upon the stage of which most of the famous actors of the day played at one time or another.

Niblo's Garden, in what would be downtown Broadway to-day, was another famous amusement place, but of a different character. The owner had a large private box which was always filled with parties of friends. It was practically on the stage, and one could reach down and touch the shoulders or heads of the chorus girls. Behind it was a reception room, and a bathroom with a stairway which led to the green room, and here many gay suppers took place after the show.

A little beyond Seventy-second Street near where the Natural History Museum was being built, I picked mushrooms on the hills occupied by squatters and goats. Up at Nineteenth Street and Fourth Avenue, near where the Unitarian Church now stands, was an open lot which was used for a circus, and I remember at one time it was occupied by a panorama of the Siege of Paris. On the corner of Nineteenth Street and Broadway, in the midst of one of the busiest parts of the town, was a quiet dwelling, occupying almost a whole block of land. Here were green trees and shrubbery with grass, and in the "back yard" they still kept chickens and a cow! This was the home of the Misses Goelet, who had lived here all their lives, and even the influx of business, theaters, etc., could not make them sell and give up the home they cared for.

Delmonico's was on Twenty-sixth Street. It was one of those landmarks that always kept pace with the trend of the times. I can remember only one very distinctive restaurant at that time; it was named the Au Petit Vefour and was run by Henri, who used to cook for the Stomach Club in Washington Square. Like all French places, it was not particularly smart, but the table and service were always immaculate. Henri went down to the markets every morning at six o'clock, digging down to the bottom of the boxes of fruit and vegetables, and feeling of the chickens until

First Decorations

he managed to bring home the raw material which he and madame between them prepared in a style fit for a king. Calories, vitamines, etc., had not become popular, and I do not believe Henri ever heard of them, but he could serve, by instinct, a balanced ration accompanied by the proper wine. When you got through, however, it cost as much as Delmonico's.

It is hard to picture New York without subways, and to think of the tired workingman reaching his home after a hard day's work by the aid of a lumbering horse car. It seems almost incredible that so many changes have taken place in thirty years. The horses of the Fifth Avenue buses were the butt of many a joke in *Life*. One crossed by ferry to Brooklyn, and the city was just beginning to dig the trench on Broadway for the cable car, announcing with a loud voice that it was the first cable in America. It did no good to tell them that I rode on one in San Francisco in the 'seventies.

Of course, there were no traffic laws, as these are quite recent, and this made the streets seem more crowded than they are to-day and therefore harder to cross. There were one or two policemen at the most prominent corners, but these seemed to have been chosen for their great physical beauty rather than to aid traffic; vehicles could go right, left, or backward if they desired.

The Tenderloin (which word originated from the remark of a police captain that he would take it as his beat—"the best part of the animal" from the point of view of graft) was in one section. Due to some misdirected effort it is now scattered over the city. The days of Chicago May are gone—she with golden hair, pale-blue eyes, looking fourteen, but really twenty-five—dear, pathetic creature for whom everyone was sorry. No longer does she beg the unsuspecting clubman to "take her home and let her warm herself for a while by his fire," only to bawl him out in the vilest language if he did not recognize her when, dressed in his "long and high," he dallied up Fifth Avenue, making Sunday calls. These days are gone, yes, but is it any better, I wonder, to have a gambling den, a blind pig, or a house of prostitution tucked safely away behind the portals of one's most respectable apartment house?

William A. Coffin originated a plan for the improvement of New York which was said by prominent architects to be practical and paying, but could not be carried through in a democratic country—there are many arguments in favor of dictatorship. The human race will not economize for its grandchildren unless forced to, and it will seldom vote "yes" for a project that will not benefit the present generation. To fill in the East River from Brooklyn Bridge to Fiftieth Street was the idea, and so broaden the land and make a space to spread. The Fall River Line would have to unload farther North, but there is no particular reason why the shipping should concentrate itself at the Battery. Another argument against it was that the good health of New York was due to the fact that it was surrounded by water. This may be true, but it does not seem to me that the East River carries away any refuse. The development of the airplane will most likely make this unnecessary, however, as mankind will take to the hills and the valleys will cease to have value.

New York is always symbolized for me by the steam that rises from the housetops and looks so much like the plume of Henry of Navarre. It is not black and dirty as is the smoke of so many European cities, but diaphanous and variable, like the Latin races of which one element of the population is composed. However, it is always and steadfastly anchored to as solid a foundation as ever existed—that of the English-speaking peoples.

I had hardly had time to renew my acquaintance with the greatest metropolis of my country when I was called away to another large city.

To Chicago must be given the credit for the first public mural decorations in America, and with her, Frank Millet (in whose brain was born the original idea), backed by that most unusual genius—Daniel Burnham. Millet was the director of fine arts for the Exposition of 1892, and one day, after a meeting, the whole committee went over to the Manufacturers' Building, where he was asked what color he wished to have the ironwork painted. He wanted to know what the matter was with the present color—it was that reddish gray, or crushed strawberry, the color of iron as it comes from the foundry.

"Do you, as color man, stand for it as it is?" said Burnham.

He said he did.

"Well, you have saved us twenty thousand dollars."

At the next meeting Frank arose and demanded the money he had saved the committee, saying that he would bring eight of the foremost painters of America to the fair and have them decorate the domes of the

Manufacturers' Building. And so came the change from Italian workmen, who had formerly smeared the walls with bad copies of their old masters, to American artists (not experts in mural work, it is true, but full of enthusiasm and fresh, original ideas). I was on the point of starting back to Europe after doing a stained-glass window for my class in Harvard, when I received a hurried call, and in spite of the fact that Mr. George B. Post, the architect, upon being asked which of the Chicago decorations he liked best, said, "Simmons's—for if my building will hold that up, it will hold up anything," I feel that my career as a painter was entirely changed at Chicago.

Olmstead originated the plan of the fair grounds—that charming idea of letting in the waters of the lake to form canals instead of streets and making a modern Venice. In the moonlight it was a veritable fairyland. But the guiding hand in all things was Daniel Burnham, the director-general. This able, handsome, and dignified man, always undeniably a male, was as representative an American of the period as one could imagine. He was large, of the Grover Cleveland type, but with unbounded energy, one who worked while he worked and played when he played. He could accomplish more in a day than any ten men, and one reason was that he began early. Much to the consternation of some of the directors, he used to call the meetings at seven o'clock in the morning, and there was a great row if everyone was not there. These directors were not an easy group to handle, and the presiding genius was often in need of a high hand to keep them straight. For example, one of them, much puffed up by his position and thinking to give it a fitting setting, bought an old-fashioned tallyho and four, with all the appurtenances, and came to the meetings (the great horn announcing his approach) but—riding *inside* his coach!

Cockroach Ranch—called so because they indulged in the best North American manner of spoiling food—was the dining and meeting place of the artists of the Exposition. Here, in a big, bare room, looking like a railway station, with a long table in the center presided over by Elihu Vedder as our *doyen*, we met and talked of all manner of things, while such people as actresses and diplomats on a visit would sneak in to listen to our extravagant conversation. In fact, we bragged so much at night about our work and then at lunch the next day admitted it was rotten, having seen it in the "cold, gray dawn of the morning after," that Bauer, the sculptor, said to us one day:

"You fellows remint me of a painter-man I used to know in Chermany. He vas joost like you. He vould paint anythings, nothings—for money. One day a fellow, he comes and says:

"'Vill you paint me somethings?'

"'Yes, I vill paint you somethings.'

"'I vant a sign—a white horse for my inn.'

"'I vill paint the sign, but you better haf a red lion.'

"'I don't vant a red lion. "White Horse" is the name of my Inn.'

"'Then you had better change the name of your inn, for if I paint you a white horse, it vill look like a red lion.'

"Now my frient he could paint nothings but red lions."

Which all goes to show that you cannot escape your

personality, no matter how much you try. For years after would be heard coming from a group of painters:

"When I got to my studio this morning, there was a red tail sticking out of the door and I was afraid to go in."

It was Robert Reid who started us making caricatures. When Elihu Vedder left us to go home, he drew a picture of a dodo with these verses underneath it:

> There was an old dodo of Rome
> Who said, "If I'd but stayed at home
> With my Omar Khayyam
> Such an artist I am,
> I'd have painted a hell of a Dome."

The result was that everyone started to imitate him, and we had over a hundred humorous drawings. I remember one of Proctor, the sculptor, sitting on a dead grizzly with the caption, "He shoots 'em, he eats 'em, he models 'em." A wealthy man, whose name I shall not mention, offered to buy the whole collection. We told him they were not for sale, but that we would give them to him for the drinks and smokes, promptly bundling up the whole lot and sending them to him. But we reckoned without our donor's Scotch blood, and the forty or fifty of us were presented with two bottles of rye whisky and one box of poor cigars! Not to be outdone, we set to work and made a far better set of drawings, giving them to Daniel Burnham. The millionaire felt greatly outraged.

One visitor to Cockroach Ranch whom I remember very well was Eugene Field, the writer. I first met him in a Chicago club, and upon presentation he greeted me with these words:

"You get out of this town; you are spoiling my game. Everywhere I go, I am taken for you."

He was slightly shorter than I, and bald-headed, so that I could not see the resemblance. But as I have been mistaken at various times for Sol Smith Russell, Forbes-Robertson, Maffit the clown, and William Gillette, nothing surprises me. I once told Gillette about some one taking me for him in London. He said:

"That is not the worst of it. By God! I have been mistaken for *you!*"

The truth is that I am a perfect Yankee type and might have posed for the original Uncle Sam. When Robert Reid was painting his decoration for the Boston State House, he had a portrait of each one of the judges to put in it, and I could have posed for any one of them.

The army officers who were stationed at one place or another about the fair grounds or who came to Chicago as visitors always managed to drift in with us artists. They were a jolly crowd, and there was one or more in at every one of our frivolities. There was one colonel— I cannot think of him by name, but as the man who always began a story or an address with, "As I was about to remark when rudely interrupted by the gentleman on my left. . . ." We had a joke which we tried on each newcomer—namely, that of seizing our chairs, straddling them, and running madly around the table striving to ride him down. We tried it on the colonel only once. He immediately grabbed his chair, did not join us, but jumped with it upon the table, riding down the middle and smashing everything as he went.

One officer, an impulsive, big creature, had been colonel of an Indian regiment, and another was the commander of the Buffaloes. I asked them to compare the character of the two races as soldiers. I was told that the negro was perfect, if led by a white man, but an officer could never make an intimate friend of one. On the contrary, the Indian was not perfect until he was in a fight, and then the white man must know enough to let him alone. An officer always made intimate friends among them, and he could eat and sleep with them as he would with his brother. The Indian is an inbred man and can be the friend of any other inbred man (aristocrat).

One night I went with Captain Maney to the Electrical Building; he had charge of the comfort of the ten thousand troops quartered there. As we entered, three noncommissioned officers came up, saluting, to ask for instructions. One was an Irishman—an alien; one was a negro—a freed slave; and the third was an Indian—an aborigine. The colonel himself had been an officer of the South in the Civil War and was a pardoned rebel. This could never have happened in any other army in the history of the world, unless perhaps in ancient Rome. They might have had the freed slave, the alien, and Cataline (the rebel), but I don't think they could have produced an aborigine soldier.

We artists of the Exposition were given a very smart banquet by the Chamber of Commerce of Chicago. This brought to mind a story which I told to Mr. Armour, much to his delight. A young girl calls on a woman friend and talks to her little boy, who is taking care of his baby sister in the carriage. She says to him:

"JUSTICE"
Center Panel by Edward Simmons, Criminal Courts Building, New York

Copyright by Edward Simmons; from a Copley Print
Copyright by Curtis & Cameron, Publishers, Boston

"Won't you give the baby to me and you can come and see her at my house?"

"No," he answered, "she'd starve to death. Your dress buttons behind."

To me the baby is the fine arts, and it has always seemed that America's gown buttons behind. Heretofore, the guilds of Europe and certain business men have done so, but I believe that this banquet was the first time in the history of mankind that commerce has ever honored the fine arts.

Often after the day's work was done we would go out to the Argo—a club in a real ship tied to the end of a long wharf. Our hosts were the brains of Chicago—a famous architect, great manufacturers, a noted editor, and among others a banker who afterward sat in the Cabinet at Washington. One started down the railway tracks—no path—cars shunting across the way. Finally, one saw the ship looming up. As one neared, noises came of the tackle; they were evidently coaling. Once close in under the belly, a big port opened very much like the holes in the bows of the lumber vessels at the wharf in Bangor. A stair before one, stewards, a warm welcome from the hosts. Then a great waxed floor, a perfect table, and a perfect dinner. Music, dancing, when some one would say:

"How about the lake?"

All would start for the bulwarks, and there below lay the "detachable *Argo*," a small clipper steam yacht. The moon, dancing lights, coming and going (Chicago was the biggest port in tonnage in the United States), there was never anything like it!

This fair at Chicago, of which Besant, the writer, said,

"No Roman Emperor ever saw such pomp," was for the world at large an advertisement of what we had to show them; but the *Argo*, with its pleasures of sight and sound, good wine, beautiful women, congenial company, was an expression of our hosts' (the Argonauts) private pleasures. One would meet a band of foreign commissioners, their decorations gleaming on their breasts, bowing over the hand of the daughter of a Senator, Governor, or humble voter. No European country with its years of bacterial history could have produced this group—an emanation of the humus of our great virgin forests with a soil as yet undefiled.

For me, coming, but for a short time while in New York, straight from France and England, and who had not seen my native land for thirteen years—for me, blue and lonely, five thousand miles from family, Chicago had been a shock and a horror. And then from it this flower, this *Argo*. I felt as if Munkittrick must have had the same situation in mind when he wrote his quatrain "To a Bulb."

> Misshapen, black, unlovely to the sight,
> Oh, mute companion of the murky mole,
> You must feel overjoyed to have a white,
> Imperious, dainty lily for a soul.

Incidentally, the *Argo* had its right and proper shipwreck, I am told. One winter a boat, driving before the storm, ran into its bowsprit and was very thoroughly destroyed.

Chicago gave me a taste of the joys of decorative painting, and I resolved in my mind the idea of devoting all my energies to it. Painting pictures to be hung on the wall by strings, generally badly placed or in the wrong light, was not satisfactory. Also, one had to be subsidized in order to wait for sales. But given a certain space to beautify, a space one knew about beforehand (the light, height, and color of the wall), and where one was reasonably sure his work would remain permanently—that was worth doing. While I was pondering on the subject, the news came of the competition for a prize given by the Municipal Art Society, in New York, for the decoration of the Criminal Court room.

There was no money prize except the payment for the work ($5,000), but the proposition was very unusual and one to be sought after. I heard of the competition only on Friday, after everyone else had sent in plans, and the contest ended Monday. Two days and three nights! I never slept from the time I "hit" my studio Friday afternoon until three minutes of nine on Monday morning, when I ran from Fifty-fifth Street to Fifty-seventh Street with my sketches in my hand to present them to the jury. At the last minute there were complications. I had to have the drawings photographed and reduced to the correct scale, and then there were the frames. At eight-thirty the latter were not ready, so I took the workman's tools out of his hands and finished them myself. All this time I had kept my faculties going by a combination of green tea and absinthe, drinking first one and then the other while working at a feverish heat.

Thomas Dewing had said that a criminal court was a butcher shop and could not be decorated; that the only thing was to put a crucifix over the head of the judge and say to the prisoners, "There, damn you, look at that!" It was a ticklish business, for these poor devils come there, go over the Bridge of Sighs to the Tombs, and we never hear of them again.

I decided that that being so, no brilliant color scheme was quite fair; one could not flaunt before these men roses and sunshine, so I adopted the theory of purple and white. Not all the contestants thought my way, however, and when the sketches were assembled and exhibited, there were one or two ridiculous ones. One man had suggested the first execution in New York City—three Indians hanging by the neck to a gibbet. Cheerful prospect for one expecting a sentence to the electric chair! A woman from Brooklyn sent in a bright little thing of birds, fountains, and babies playing about. Just as indecent as the one in the opposite direction, although I suppose the poor lady's idea was to show the condemned man what he was leaving behind.

Next was the question of composition. I decided to have three panels, the one in the center the tallest, so that it would not be obscured by the judge, and that the subject should have to do with His Honor and *not* the prisoner before the bar. Consequently, I put Justice in the middle, and what a fair-minded judge should be thinking of on the two sides. Artists have many limitations put upon them and are not always the free creatures often imagined. In this case, my classifications were as clear as any botanist's. As to family, she was a Justice of America and carried the flag. In the Middle Ages she was always represented as being blind, but in a glorious democracy she should be clear-eyed. As to genus, she was of the state of New York and therefore should bear its coat of arms; as to species, she was of the city of New York and should bear *its* emblem. In one hand, she carried the scales for weighing the facts offered, and, as either innocence or guilt must predominate or there is no decision, the pans were uneven. In the other hand she carried the crystal ball, emblem of truth, surmounted by a cross, for she was a Christian Justice. In order to complete the scheme and carry out the composition, I placed two little boys to the left and right below and looking up at her; one was offering her pigeons for innocence, and the other the sword, if she needed it, for condemnation. Behind her was a bronze door. The Temple of Janus opened its doors when war was declared—also the feeling of a closed door suggests that unfortunate companion of Justice—Punishment.

The left panel was my idea of the mental qualities that a judge should consider. They are called to-day—Liberty, Equality, and Fraternity, but I did not so name them. I meant to suggest two people thinking of themselves and one thinking of the others. The first was Liberty, who had broken his chains—the physical; the third was the Scientist who was absorbed in facts only—the mental; and the second, between the two, was Brotherly Love, who was bringing them together. The judge should think to what class a man on trial belonged. A free, thoughtless soul should not be condemned for not remembering facts, a scientist for lack of imagination, or the middle figure for forgetting himself.

On the right I put the Three Fates because the judge also was born and must die. Michael Angelo (if he made the panel—there is a question as to the artist) has painted them as old women; Hesiod has stated that they were of different ages. I figured them as

Birth, Life, and Death. In the laughing young woman's lap I put a child playing with the thread of human life which issues from his navel; next a grave, middle-aged woman who measures the thread; and third an old hag who cuts the cord—Clotho, Lachesis, and Atropos.

The color scheme of the whole room was left to me and I did the best I could with it, also outlining the panels with gold bands. Alas! as years went on, some politician, instead of leaving time to mellow it to a beautiful tone, has seen fit to retint the walls and—worse and worse—he has large plates with labels to each picture. You may as well write "horse" under a drawing of the animal as to put "Justice" under my panel. If a decoration is not intelligible to a Chinaman, there is no reason for putting it up.

The Municipal Art Committee had a grand unveiling of the work, with Joseph Choate to make the address of presentation and the acceptance for the city by the District Attorney. Mr. Choate arrived early and got quite a few data from me. It may have been something about my manner, but I think it was his own disposition—which encouraged, became malignant, like the clown that slaps the face of the little boy who cries when his red apple is stolen from him; he spied me in the farthest corner, where I had retired to be out of view. Then, in his oiliest and most oratorical manner, he declaimed:

"Greece had her Apelles, we have our Simmons; Rome had her Michael Angelo, we have our Simmons; etc."

The crowd applauded, but he knew that I would get the sting; it was as if he were speaking to me alone and I never forgave him.

"THE THREE FATES"
Right panel by Edward Simmons, Criminal Courts Building, New York
Copyright by Edward Simmons; from a Copley Print, Copyright by Curtis & Cameron, Publishers, Boston

Chapter X: Democracy and the Fine Arts

MONEY, commerce and the Protestant faith have been drawbacks to the progress of the fine arts in America—the last do not believe in beauty, as do the Roman Catholics. Better than Mohammedanism, though, whose Koran does not allow the right of man to copy even the meanest of God-made creatures, the Eastern art is a constant struggle between religion and the desire to make representations of living things. Autocracy's motto—*"væ victis,"* or to the devil with the hindmost—is the proper one for the fine arts. The taste of a whole community is the dead level of mediocrity, and a proof of the scant attention paid to art in America is the place given it in the newspapers—before the fashions and after the dog fights.

Last week a statue of General Grant was unveiled with much celebration. Although the sculptor who made it had spent fifteen years of his life doing the work, there was no mention of his name in the account in the papers, but the wives of the Senators and Congressmen present were featured by photographs in the Sunday supplements. In France it is different. The committee would probably be mentioned first, but the artist's name would come second. Public opinion rules, and the arts will come back when the people want them; and then the fact will be recorded on that thermometer—the newspapers.

Most of our organizations, in my opinion, have been a complete failure, due to this democratic idea. I was in at the beginning of the Institute of Arts and Letters.

Holbrook Curtis came to me one day, telling me of the proposition and that I had been chosen as the member of the initial committee to represent painting, sculpture, and architecture. The little group who met to start the society consisted of William Dean Howells, Charles Dudley Warner, Marion Crawford, Johnson of the *Century*, Doctor Curtis, and myself. Alas! the literary element prevailed!

I was asked to hand in a list of those whom I thought worthy of becoming the first members, so brought into the next meeting the names of Whistler, Sargent, and (*ex officio*) myself to represent painting; Charles McKim for architecture; and Augustus Saint-Gaudens for sculpture. To my astonishment, a list of more than a hundred writers was offered to me. I objected on the ground that to belong to this Institute was a prize, to be given for extraordinary merit; therefore, the greater the number the less the honor. There was much talking and arguing, during which I could see I was becoming exceedingly unpopular among those who believed in the "American advertisement" point of view. Finally, Marion Crawford, who had hitherto kept silent, said:

"Oh, Simmons, leave these people to stew in their own juice. Our host here has some very good Scotch whisky. Come with me and we'll sample it."

Later I was given a list of more than a hundred names of painters, to mark those of which I approved. I refused and stuck to my theory, that only a few should have the honor—and I automatically became an outcast. I never had anything more to do with them until I was invited to read a paper on the fine arts at one of their meetings. But, if asked to-day, I could not tell whether I belong to the organization or not.

This experience being so disappointing, I was always loath to join any group of artists. It seemed to me that it was impossible to have it work out successfully, as the purpose on the surface of things was never the real underlying one, and it was impossible to mix democracy and the fine arts. The Ten American Painters was started quite by accident, and when the too-human elements began to enter, it died a natural death. We never called ourselves the "Ten"; in fact, we never called ourselves anything and it was our purpose, at first, to have twelve. We were just a group who wanted to make a showing and left the society as a protest against big exhibits. At our first exhibition at the Durand Ruel's Gallery, we merely put out the sign—"Show of Ten American Painters"—and it was the reporters and critics speaking of us who gave us the name. In the original group were Twachtman, Dewing, Metcalf, Reid, Hassam, Weir, Benson, De Camp, Tarbell, and myself. After the death of Twachtman, Chase was voted in to take his place. We had asked both Winslow Homer and Abbot Thayer to join us. Homer replied that he would have been mighty glad to be a member, but that he never meant to paint again, that he was tired of it all; and as far as I know he never did. Thayer accepted with enthusiasm, but later wrote: "Tell the boys I must decline. The poor society needs me too much."

The first few years we divided the wall into equal spaces and drew lots for them, each man having the right to use it as he saw fit, hanging one picture or a number of pictures. As long as we adhered to that idea all went well. But then objections came in. I, being a mural decorator, had large work, and those members with small canvases naturally did not want them hung next to mine. This, of course, restricted me in my showing. At last, to save controversy, we left the hanging to the dealer, and he placed those which sold the best in the choice parts of the room and the others elsewhere.

We left the society as a protest, not believing that an art show should be like a child's bouquet—all higgledy-piggledy with all the flowers that can be picked. We were accused of starting as an advertisement, and, indeed, it proved a big one, but there was no such idea in the mind of any one of us. Many others took it up, and a group followed us, calling themselves "The Eight" in an attempt to boil the egg over again. When the wives of our members "butted in" and made the proposals of sandwiches and tea and finally wanted us to have music at our openings (music with painting is like sugar on oysters), we struck. The "pep" and enthusiasm of youth started the Ten American Painters and age has finished it. Peace to its ashes!

It is years since I have acted on a jury for the choice of pictures for an exhibit. I do not understand the politics of the affairs and always get myself much disliked, for one reason or another, so I gave it up long ago.

American juries *never* have full authority. They are always dominated by some bugbear of politics or obligation, and I always found them very disgusting affairs. In Paris, in 1889, I was chosen as a member of the jury for the World's Fair. The United States government, through our ambassador, issued a statement that our acts would be absolutely final, and we had every hope of making this show a beautiful affair. We had the money and we had the painters, but we reckoned without democracy and—Rush C. Hawkins, the commissioner. As Whistler afterward said, "How intensely American to appoint a colonel of dragoons at the head of art!" The first thing that he did was to beautify the room—without asking the advice of any of us, of course—and the result was a triumph. The *pièce de résistance* of the occasion was a great big ripe red-plush tomato, or rather something that looked like one tomato on top of another, plunked right down in the center of the room, ostensibly for the people to sit on. It must have cost thousands!

Mr. Hawkins's next act was to "invite" a number of prominent painters to exhibit their work and then send them before the jury. Whistler was one of these. He had been invited by the Prince of Wales to send to the British exhibit, but had been patriotic enough to prefer to be represented in the American section. When he found that he had to go before the jury, he promptly withdrew his pictures—a portrait and twenty-six etchings. The voting was such a farce. We had handed the black-and-white section over to Stanley Reinhart, telling him to do as he pleased. When the question of the Whistler etchings arose, a prominent member of the jury insisted that we all pass on them. I objected, as I could see that the etchings had been carefully chosen as a group and all should go together.

A half dozen men were on my side, but we were overridden, and the spectacle of those artists having these etchings by Jimmie Whistler passed before them, one by one, and choosing five or six from this priceless collection (when they had accepted all of Abbey's and Reinhart's without discussion) was ludicrous. The result was that Whistler sent all of his work over to the English show, where it was one of the cards. I was so ashamed of my country!

Speaking afterward to the prominent member of the jury who had insisted upon this farcical voting, I forced him to give me his reason. He said that he did not like Whistler, and would not vote for anything by him, anyway!

There were many other reasons why we did not have a good show. One was the number of jurymen who had favorite pupils and must have a place for their work. Most of these we succeeded in eliminating, but they crept in in spite of us. I remember one man telling us of a beautiful girl, one of the capital F's of the F. F. V.' s of Virginia (whose family had been stricken with poverty by the Civil War), now supporting her invalid mother by her art—not a word about the merit of the work. We had rejected a portrait by the young lady, but took it back, not on account of the story, but because it was so offensive to see this particular juryman weep about it.

Then there were the indignant American citizens who appealed to the ambassador over our decisions. The United States government had given us the final power of acceptance or refusal, but overrode us in a number of cases. A noted American sculptor, whose position socially was unimpeachable, but whose work was fundamentally "rotten," had gone so far as to have his several groups of large statuary placed where he thought they should eventually rest, and there was consternation when we refused them. A member of the jury tackled Alexander Harrison and myself on the subject one night with the argument that we were in duty bound to recognize the work of a man so highly placed socially.

Harrison replied: "You may think that in talking to Simmons and me you are speaking to two gentlemen with social position. But you are not; you are only talking to two Puritans. We do not think it is right."

But the American government stepped in and the sculpture was duly accepted.

In another case the ambassador came to us with a pathetic appeal for protection, asking us to reconsider our opinion of a portrait we had rejected.

"The lady who painted it sleeps on my doormat," he said, "and she's got to be removed." With laughter we took it back.

Once in Philadelphia I was one of a committee that was to decide a competition for the decoration of one of the public buildings. It was a great plum, for in addition to the actual payment for the work, the winner was to get a prize of two thousand dollars for his proposition. All through our meeting I felt a strange and subtle influence at work, although I must confess I was not approached or asked to use my vote in any way for any contestant. Edwin Abbey had sent a sketch, very good, but the charming part of it had been done by a young architect in London and it was very doubtful that it would keep its beauty if carried out in a large design. The majority decided for a younger painter, and the award was given to him. Right after the decision there was a large reception at the home of George W. Elkins, who, if I mistake not, had given the prize. I shall never forget his look of surprise and then chagrin as we filed in and announced our decision.

"Why," he said, "I thought it had been all arranged that Abbey was to have it."

Needless to say, the young artist never got a chance to carry out his work, although they were obliged to give him his prize money.

Speaking of competitions, I once entered one for the decoration of a prominent New York hotel. There were three members on the jury. I lost, in spite of the fact that all three of them came to me, separately, and told me in strictest confidence that he had voted for my proposition.

Some of my most humorous experiences have happened when working for women. Two or three things almost always occur. Women either insist upon having the kind of work their social set considers the fashion for the moment, or they try to control the color scheme, or the composition, and always the meaning. A well-known interior decorator and I spent the better part of two years in attempting to make beautiful the reception room of a magnate's wife, only to have our efforts frustrated at the last moment. She hung up two pairs of very handsome damask curtains of a deep orange color lined with cold pink. The windows faced to the south and the light coming through them made an effect of rotten eggs—for the rest of the room was lilac, ivory, and old gold. When we remonstrated we were met with:

"Now I have you artist men! At the sale, when I bought these, Mr. Whistler bought an identical set. I suppose that his taste is as good as yours?"

It was useless to explain that Whistler had a very different setting for his. This same lady was almost inclined to treat me as a workman and seemed rather put out when her husband invited me to luncheon. The only reference she ever made to my painting was to say that it was a pity my name was not "Simoni." It would make such an interesting signature!

Once I was directed by a spirit as to how to paint a portrait. It was out in the Middle West. Not quite so bad as the woman in London who used to have interviews with one of her children born dead. In this case it was the ouija board that operated every night and gave me my instructions for the next day as to how to get the right expression upon the face of this elderly woman who was sitting to me. A brother, born four years before herself, had died at the age of five, and in that other life, "over there," he had kept in touch with the march of events down here. When his sister journeyed, he journeyed with her, miraculously learning the language of each country in which she happened to stop, so that he could send her messages with a foreign flavor. He told her what to do when she was ill and how to meet every problem of life, but with all this vast knowledge he could not, or did not, tell her how to keep young; and I had just as hard a time disguising the wrinkles on her cheek and the cords in her neck as if she had been an ordinary human being with no little brother guiding her from another world. I could not but think—what a dull heaven to live in—so irrevocably tied to this earth. This spirit was at the beck and call of his sister, doomed to follow her every thought and action, with far less freedom than if he had remained a poor mortal. I would rather sit on a cloud with a ready-made halo about my head, and at least have time for contemplation.

Now that I am on the subject of women—I do not mean to criticize harshly (I have loved them all my life), but one thought leads to another. There is the case of Mrs. McAllister. Of course, that was not her name, but it will do as well as any other. Virgil Williams and myself were once invited to her house in San Francisco to see a statue she had made. We were told beforehand that this woman was one of the few beings who disproved the theory that starving in a garret was necessary to be a success in the fine arts. The death of her husband left her enormously wealthy, and she decided to show her talents. First she wrote a best seller; then she composed a concerto; then she painted and finally, probably holding the belief that all the arts are interrelated, she tried her hand at sculpture. This, a statue of Eve, was the object we were asked to view. Williams, after looking at it awhile, said:

"Happily, Mrs. McAllister, we have both been married, and so I can speak most freely. You have evidently forgotten one thing which is more important than you think. You have neglected to put in the navel."

"Oh, not forgetfulness, Mr. Williams," cried this ultramodern woman (psychoanalysis and sex discussion were not so free as they are to-day). "In consulting with my spiritual adviser, the Reverend Mr. McCann, we decided that as Eve was not born of woman, a navel was unnecessary."

It has always delighted me to see William Hunt's hesitation about that sort of thing in his fine work for the Capitol at Albany. If he did really put breasts and a navel on the figure at the stern of the boat, they, like the decorations by the magician painter of the story, are not to be seen by vulgar eyes. Oh, those inhibitions of Boston! As my uncle George used to say, "Edward, anything but the physical or the material." I was too young then to realize that in talking so much about it he proved his taste for it. But I am unkind; blind men should not be called to account for the spots on their clothing.

Women are generally utterly ruthless where their vanity is concerned—equal suffrage is doing away with this, however—and will sacrifice the poor artist to its desires. The Ten American Painters were having a retrospective show in Philadelphia. Naturally, we were trying to get hold of all our good work, so I asked a society woman who owned one of my best paintings to lend it for exhibition purposes. She replied that she was having a tea that week and it would make a spot on her wall to take it down. This was quite a contrast to Andrew Carnegie, who not only gladly lent me a marine he had purchased some years before, but had his agent box it, insure it, and send it all at his own expense.

Portrait painters have the hardest time, though; as every woman wishes to see herself idealized or as she was twenty years before. Poor Meissonier was asked to paint in Paris, a portrait of the wife of an American millionaire well known for having made his money in the gold-strike days of California. I knew the lady and I saw the portrait. It was admirable in the sense of being a perfect likeness and bringing out all of her limitations. She looked like a cook and he painted her like a cook. She refused to pay for the work, saying that it was utterly worthless; consequently, Meissonier took her into the courts. In France, the artist has a better show than here, and he won. The lady paid the bill, but announced that as soon as she got home she intended to burn the portrait. Whereupon Meissonier's counsel asked that the court forbid this, as such an act would establish a bad precedent. It would lie within the power of a wealthy man, wishing to revenge himself, to buy up all the work of a client more than seventy years old, and, by destroying it, render the artist's life a vain and useless thing. The court took his view and forbade the lady in question to injure the portrait. In spite of the fact that she declared she would disobey, I saw the portrait twenty years after.

When the fine arts and literature meet, many interesting things happen. We have our critics. Some of them are wise and some of them are dull, but not many of them have the slyness of Mr. Emerson when he answered Daniel French's question as to what he thought of the bust the sculptor had just finished of him, "That is the face I shave." A queer thing—the literary mind. I objected once to Gilder because he was criticizing a picture, saying that it was not fair, as he was not a painter. He replied that he had heard me discuss a sonnet.

"Yes," I maintained, "but I have used the English language since my earliest years. I am therefore a professional. You are not a painter. You may say that you do not like a picture, but you may not say what is the matter with it, as you did."

Every time I think of Gilder I recall something he once told me about the dead Lincoln. He had gone to view the body and was one of a long line of people passing about the form as it lay on its bier, and was much impressed by the august and noble smile on the dead President's face. So much was he affected by it that he turned to a man standing beside him and mentioned it.

"Yes," the man replied, "We rather flatter ourselves on our smiles." It was the undertaker.

It was surprising to see, after that, a sonnet by Gilder on Lincoln's smile. Sometimes an editor's sense of humor becomes a trifle dulled. I sat and heard a number of them discuss perfectly seriously whether the word "hell" should be allowed in its entirety, printed "h—l," or cut out altogether.

I was once foolish enough to contract to make some covers for a well-known magazine. All went well as long as I was allowed to choose my own subjects, but when the editor got the brilliant idea of taking characters out of the Bible and drawing them as modern men, I struck. Take David, for instance; what financier would care to be represented in such fashion? If the gentleman were alive to-day he would be in jail.

The editor threw up his hands and said, "But he is in the Bible." Of course it ended by my displeasing him.

I was called up on the telephone one day by Mr. J——, editor of one of our yellow publications. He said his magazine was considering an article on Decoration and told me to forward, without delay, permission to publish a reproduction of my "Justice," upon which there is a copyright. I asked what there was in it for me. He was astonished that I did not realize the enormous advertisement it would mean for me. I answered that as *Harper's*, *Scribner's*, *Century*, etc. (at that time) always sent me a check for seventy-five dollars when they reproduced anything of mine, I though a thousand would just about pay me for dropping to the level of his magazine.

This same gentleman had, in addition to his other interests, once owned a string of grocery stores. Guy Wetmore Carryl told me this. It appears that he sold a story to the magazine, and this thrifty editor (later finding no use for it) wrote to Guy and asked him if he would take it back and return the cash he had received. Guy refused. Then the editor wrote and asked him to try to sell it to some one else and "cash up." This was too much. Stopping at one of the editor's grocery stores one afternoon, he bought a can of tomatoes which he took home and opened, chose a tomato, bit into it and put it back into the can again. Then wrapping it up, he left it on the editor's desk with this note.

DEAR J—— :—I bought this can at your store and do not like it. Won't you be good enough to try and sell it for me and send me the money?

Needless to say, they did not speak after that.

The American idea is frequently to honor a foreigner because he is a foreigner and not because his work merits the praise. Change a good old Yankee cognomen into something that sounds like Italian or Russian, and the singer is assured a far better hearing. The same in painting. If a third-rate Italian should be in competition with Sargent for a public decoration or a portrait of a President, the Italian would probably get it. About the year 1894 Charles McKim, the architect, was getting ready to beautify Washington and have it cleaned of all its horrors. He died before he accomplished his purpose, but he made a beginning, and that was to decorate the interior of the Library of Congress.

There was a great question in mind as to whether I should join the group of men who were doing the work. The United States always paid less than anyone else, and I was tempted to take more profitable work. I could have accepted any number of orders and hired assistants to carry them out, but I have always felt this was unfair to myself as well as to the public. A decoration is a creative thing and, as such, can be carried out only by the mind that conceives it.

In the Library of Congress I was given one of the rooms to the left of the doorway on the first floor of the building. It is called a curtain corridor. There were nine semicircular panels, nine feet in width at the bottom; therefore the radius was four and a half feet. All such tympanums are stilted, making this radius in reality about four feet ten inches. The argument was, how to get the human figure into a space so low.

I did not want to make them half size or even under life, and my decision proved very wise. Elihu Vedder made his figures undersize and the result was that the rest of us dwarfed him. My choice of subject was the Nine Muses, and I resolved to make them sitting down. Terpsichore, the Muse of Dancing, sitting? I contrived to bend her over so that she just squeezed in. There is an old work of the early Greeks in bas-relief of Terpsichore that is one of the most beautiful compositions I know of. She is bending down and arranging her sandal. If I had not been fundamentally opposed to that class of theft, I would have used the idea; but a copy of anything, no matter how great, is never so good as one's own conception. It is always unwise for an artist to have the classics about him at any time, and he should *never* have any of them near by to influence him when he is doing compositional work.

There were thirty-six pendentives in the domes of the ceiling, which I decorated with little figures, using no models, but painting directly upon the walls, composing as I went along. I shall never forget this experience. It was in the summertime, and a hot spell struck Washington. Anyone who knows the capital will realize what this means. I was under contract to finish it at a certain time, and here I was working in these little sealed domes (which never were and never could be ventilated), while the thermometer was so high that eighty people died one day from sunstroke. It was mephitic. I was so terrified that I almost lived on milk and limewater.

Right here I would like to say something about

health. It is important, perhaps even more for an artist than for any other class of person, to keep himself in trim. Burning up tons of nervous energy, living perhaps a precarious existence, it is necessary that he take himself in hand early in life and learn about his own body. We are not all constituted the same and what is one man's weakness is another man's strength. In my own case, I was practically an invalid up to thirty, when I made up my mind to overcome my ailments. Artistic effort needs a tremendous amount of vitality back of it to carry it out, and the sensitiveness which accompanies the creative temperament is easily a prey to small discomforts. Learn your limitations and you can correct them beforehand. Knowing my stomach was my weak link, I treated it with care during the heat at Washington and came out with no disaster.

Several amusing occurrences of that summer come to mind, showing how many contacts an artist has with different walks of life. I was approached by the delegate of a trades-union—a man with dirty fingernails and collar, black sweeping mustache, fat, sweaty, and insolent—who asked me if I were a member of the union.

"What union?" I inquired.

"Paperhangers."

My assistant did belong, and the other four men working on the walls were furnished by the United States government. He looked rather foolish when I suggested that he call them off the job. He started to leave, when he turned around and asked:

"Why don't you belong to the union?"

"I've never been asked," I replied.

"Well, I ask you."

"I accept," I said, "but I will not lose money by joining, though. I am making forty dollars a day. What class can I go in?"

He departed.

Another day, I was up on my scaffold, when my assistant came up and whispered in my ear that there was a man down below who wanted to "lick" me. I called down to him and he said he would like a word with me. He was a burly Irishman, and I was not anxious to start anything with him.

"Did you do that picture?" he said, pointing to my figure of Melpomene, "and who is it?"

I told him that one of my relatives had been the model, and something in my manner made him see that I was telling the truth. Then he broke down and almost wept.

"It's the image of a daughter of mine who went wrong two years ago."

When my work was all finished except a little varnishing on one panel and I was feeling very proud of the effect, I was honored by a visit from Mark Hanna. He was showing some ladies a ound the building. Rushing in at the head of his party, he gave a cursory glance up and down, and then hurried out, saying:

"Come on; there's nothing here."

Just so much notice does politics give the fine arts.

"MELPOMENE."
Panel by Edward Simmons, Gallery of the Muses, Congressional Library, Washington
Copyright by Edward Simmons; from a Copley Print, Copyright by Curtis & Cameron, Publishers, Boston

Chapter XI: Stanford White

THE slow but steady progress in America toward a sense of beauty is due more to the architects than to any one class of people. The definition that an "architect is a business man with a slight artistic leaning," is not such a bad one, and the combination of the two qualities has proved most happy in many cases. I think we must grant some of them more than a *leaning* toward the arts, though, and give them credit for a certain "taste" developed in our country during the last part of the last century. I have heard a prominent architect declare the Woolworth Building, built by Cass Gilbert, to be the most beautiful example of the Gothic ever done in America, and yet it is also a good business building. This shows that any type of architecture can be made practical. As to the interiors, we might still be in the Victorian Age, if it had not been for these men showing us how ugly it was.

As soon as I returned from Europe, I was put up at The Players, and after my two weeks' card, given me by Alexander Harrison, expired, I was proposed for membership and duly elected. My sponsor, besides Harrison, was Stanford White, and during my time as a guest of the club, I got to know this very simple person (who was a child and an artist and never became an adult) as well as I did in later years. The three men of the architectural firm of McKim, Meade, and White fitted together perfectly. I once asked Meade what he was doing in that gallery, and he said that he was the water which makes the chemical reaction of acid and alkali lose its power for harm—he kept the other two from being crazy artists.

Stanny always looked to me like Vercingetorix. I used to say that his proper clothing was a wolfskin and a battle-ax, and that he should let his hair grow long. This hair, which was bright red, was accompanied by the usual white skin of that type of person, so that in swimming he looked (he was very tall) like a great white tallow candle. He was as strong as a prize fighter, but, like most men of that character, he never used his physical power. Unlike most big men, he was always in a hurry, dashing about here and there and with his body always slightly bent forward—he took very short steps—trotting along the sidewalk like a busy little girl.

Red hair, of course, means a violent and ultra-passionate disposition, but Stanny *never* lost his temper. A delicate sensitiveness combined with a tenderness that would not be understood by the ordinary human being. I have seen him turn the color of castile soap if he had to do with any deformity or suffering. We had a mutual friend, a lovely boy, a humpback, who died never knowing that he caused horror to Stanford White. To shake that thin wasted hand would cause him to turn away his face with a green, seasick expression, but he would do anything rather than hurt the boy's feelings.

One day I went out of the club with Stanny—or rather, I rushed out—he did not *go* out of anything, but ran and slammed the doors—when we came across a professional beggar who was well known to both of us as always being just a "quarter" shy of the fare he needed to get to New Rochelle. He had probably been on his way to New Rochelle for the last twenty years. Stanny, as was his custom, grabbed a handful of silver from his pocket and thrust it into the astonished beggar's hand in an embarrassed way. I said:

"I suppose you know that you are not really doing him any good. They say he is rich."

"Oh," he answered, "you don't understand. Do you suppose I was trying to do him good? I was only trying to justify my own existence."

Of the most impetuous, impulsive, lovable nature, with him to think was to act. I once tried to chaff him about the way his child was being brought up. My boys, about the age of his, were always out in Gramercy Park. They had said:

"We are always together unless it rains, but if Larry White gets his feet wet, the nurse makes an awful fuss and takes him home. And she never lets him go on the grass."

I told his father. There was a roar and a bang and Stanford was gone out of the door. In a few minutes he was back, saying:

"He'll play with your boys to-morrow."

"What did you do, scold the nurse?" I asked.

"No; I fired her."

Stanford White was a real artist, one of the kind that could no more help doing beautiful things than he could help living. Practically a boy when he did it, I saw a frame in his home that he had carved for Mrs. White during their engagement. It was a most delicate and complicated pattern—I have the impression that it was of flowers and figures—but it gave the effect of one of those Chinese openwork ivory carvings, and formed the most exquisite setting for a small portrait by Thomas Dewing, something that Meissonier could never have done, as he had not Dewing's sense of beauty.

I believe that Stanford set the fashion here of building to our latitude. We had formerly copied the British in our homes, using red brick or brownstone, with small windows, reps curtains, and nailed-down carpets of warm dark brown and scarlet—the stuff of the north for New York City, which is the latitude of Madrid. The change was to blond brick, marble, or Missouri limestone for the outside; and stone or polished floors, Turkish rugs or mats for the inside, with a decided lightening of the color scheme, so much so that a great "gag" was to call the firm "McKim, White, and Gold." To show that most of their tendencies were for light interiors, a remark of Stanford's can be quoted. He told a woman, for whom he had just finished an ivory-colored room, when she asked him what to put on the walls, "Oh, any color as long as it is red." Any painter knows that, given white as a background, the only color one can trust the average citizen with is red. It takes an artist to put blue and white or green and white together; and some one with a Whistlerian feeling to put black and white together; but a child can use red and white.

Nothing could be more different in style than the buildings Stanford designed—the Madison Square Garden, the Metropolitan Club, Doctor Parkhurst's Church (which has now been torn down), or any of his business buildings, are each made for the things they were to house. His personal tastes were absolutely under the control of his artistic feelings, and his sensitiveness was so great that he could lose his own personality. When he fitted up his own house in Gramercy Park, the music room was not his, it belonged to his family and their friends, and he made it more beautifully classic than anything I have seen in North America. A flight or two up was his own room. Vercingetorix in his cave with all his spoils piled up around him! Everything he cared about (and he wanted it at once) and a heterogeneous mass of priceless books, paintings, draperies, all in a careless disorder, was happiness to him in his own den.

I was in The Players when Stanny returned from his trip to Virginia, having been asked to restore the principal building of the university, which had been designed and built by Thomas Jefferson. As we sat together over something to drink he seemed to be puzzled, confused, and silent. I asked him what was the matter. He started and came out of his mood, saying it was the job down South. "I've seen *his* plans," he said, speaking with great deference. "They're wonderful and I am scared to death. I only hope I can do it right." This left me with a conception of the greatness of Jefferson in another rôle of which I was ignorant—his architectural side. He is constantly impressing me as our first American—an artist and, like all the big ones, a true democrat. He represented the ideas of to-day and was farsighted enough to know they were coming.

I saw the Metropolitan Club built; in fact, I painted

the library ceiling. I remember, in looking it over one day, I threw a lighted match among some shavings and, in a panic, ran to stamp it out. I was told I need not be afraid, as everything was fireproof. Stanny had bet a large amount with Ogden Goelet that he would have the club finished on the specified date. Just at the last moment the workmen struck. The mantelpieces, of which there were a large number, had not been polished in the state of New York and the unions demanded that they be done over again. There was no time the night before the limit expired, but I knew Stanny had a plan, so I went up to see the fun.

Stanny and the contractor had a line of boats filled with the necessary materials waiting at the North River, and another line of carts and workmen to bring them up. A thousand men and women were waiting in the street—masons, handy men, scrub women, and what not. At six o'clock sharp every trades-union workman had left; then in came the army. The first ones, bearing huge rolls of paper, unrolled them on the floor from the door to every fireplace. Women with mops stood at attention, to clean up if anything dropped. Out on the street, the carts came up to the door, one by one, each in solemn rotation, depositing its contents of the grates, cement, bricks, or some material necessary to the completion. These were whisked up by the workmen and borne in to their rightful places. A continuous procession upstairs and downstairs which reminded one of an army of ants building themselves a new home. All this time the women with mops were waiting, lest a bit of something drop on the new polished floors or splash against the walls. So carefully was the whole affair planned, however, that not a thing was marred, and at 9 A.M. the next morning Stanford White handed over to the committee a finished building. He won his money from Mr. Goelet, but with his customary generosity bought a beautiful piece of tapestry and presented it to the club.

Stanford was accused of shamefully copying when he built the Madison Square Garden. It was supposed to be an exact replica of the Giralda, in Spain. I have never seen the Giralda, but I have seen on the right and left of a page, in juxtaposition, a photograph of both buildings. I do not see a resemblance striking enough to comment upon. When one thinks of how Shakespeare and Dumas, and, in fact, almost every great man, has borrowed, the question for the fair minded is whether the thing borrowed has been changed by the personality of the borrower, which, if he be of any value, must overlay and extinguish that first personality and give an entirely new impression. Remember the lines, "He winked at Omar down the road . . ."

Mrs. Van Rensselaer wrote a long article somewhere about the Madison Square building and gushed about that rare quality in the architects who would go so far as even to vary the color of their bricks in constructing the tower, so as to give it variance of tonality. This seemed to me improbable, and one day I asked Meade about it. He said it was "rot," that if one of the brickmakers had not gone bankrupt, the tower would have been the same color all the way up. I commented upon the hideous color of the combination of brickwork and terra cotta produced both in this building and in the Herald Building at Thirty-fifth Street. Stanny told me not to be silly, but to wait until they were twenty years old. Remembering it the other day, I looked, and, behold! the tonality and color in the Madison Square building had come together like smoothing velvet.

The first attempt at the statue on the top failed by reason of the fact that the drapery which flew from the shoulder, and served as a tail or rudder, did not accomplish its purpose of turning her arrow into the eye of the wind. Saint-Gaudens (the sculptor) and Stanny spent some thousands of dollars in taking it down and making a new one. The second worked as a weathercock, but, alas! it was not half so beautiful. To-day the drapery over which they spent so much time and money is gone. So much does America care for its art and its artists!

One should not judge Stanford White's ability as an architect by the Washington Arch which stands at the foot of Fifth Avenue. The temporary arch which preceded this one was put up in lath and plaster—staff—to celebrate a memorial occasion, and was rarely beautiful in structure and proportion. The city fathers asked him to reproduce it for permanence in marble. He told them it could not be done, but after much argument he gave in. I suppose it was a question of bearing power or stress, but he did not succeed. Very few men have ever been able to alter—to their own satisfaction, or to that of the public—their first inspiration. A "dub" can; an artist can't. The Washington Arch stands to-day, as many other buildings in America do, a monument to the interference with an artist's dream.

Trinity Church in Boston is another example of the same thing. Richardson's original idea might have been a masterpiece, but, long after it was wise to change his plans, the city authorities decided, either from economy or from some other good reason, that, as the building was situated on made land, it would not stand the weight of the tower. They made him cut out fifty feet in height. You might as well cut out two inches from a woman's neck. Also, it is not fair to criticize our own Grant's Tomb. The architect's plans were, I am told, that one should see a building of stone capped by a great mass of bronze figures on the top and one group on each of the four corners. The best modiste in Paris might plan a hat with four large bunches of blue flowers. It is not fair to call the hat her creation if you remove the bunches. Those in power, again probably from economy, considered the tomb of the President good enough as it was and did not add the bronzes.

Now in the days of the great men in art such things were generally in the hands of a dictator—pope, king, or Mæcenas—and the people had nothing to do with them—except like them. Whistler says that the warriors, on returning from battle, did not care pro or con whether the artist-man, who stayed at home, had carved their goblets or not, as long as they were just as good to drink out of. I suppose one worships in the Trinity Church just as well, but I do not believe that Grant receives the honor that the building as it was planned would have given him, in the mind of either laborer or lord.

This time was quite a social period in my life. Good

plays, good music and much of it—there was a spontaneity in the New York folk that has never touched me at any other time in America. I was strong, though never muscular, with the vitality of five men; and to work all day, run to the club in the late afternoon, dine well, and then be in the company of congenial friends most of the night, did not put a dent in my surplus energy. Stanny was the great driving force of all our entertainments, and as he was the type of man who always paid for everything and shoved anyone aside who tried to get in first, my lack of money did not make much difference. It was in 1893, I think, that he made me a member of the Vaudeville Club. In those days, that large space to the left, in the second tier of the Metropolitan Opera House, was given up to men only, and behind was the bar, a set of rooms, and a small stage. Here a member could meet a friend, have a drink, go in and hear what he wished of the opera, and come out when he felt bored. After the performance there would be a supper and a show given by the leading vaudeville people from Broadway. Relaxation after the music, good food and drink, and much talk and fun. Such entertainers as Vesta Victoria would be on the program, and once we were honored by the presence of Mr. Sandow. The latter was quite a lion for a time. I remember him, in evening clothes, coming into the box of a lady very highly placed socially. He seemed to be paralyzed by the attention given him. When he said good-by, and evidently wishing to return his social obligations, he handed each feminine occupant of the box a ticket to his private performances out at his quarters, where they "could see more of him."

I remember one dinner party which was much criticized, but in reality how very moral and dignified it was! The guests, all men, were socially and artistically of the best set of the town. We wanted a "blowout" and we did not propose to be limited by New-Englandism, politics, or anything else. There were fifty men; everything was in perfect taste, arranged by the best artists in America. There was remarkably good music, made by a colored orchestra, and—*mirabile dictu!*—no talk, no speeches, and no toasts. Every man at that dinner knew that his next-door neighbor would be a treat to talk to and a man on his feet would be an interruption. Two girls—models—in exquisite costumes, one blond and one brunette, poured the drinks, each one serving the colored wine which corresponded to her complexion. At the dessert, solemn servants came forward, bearing a huge six-foot pasty which was placed in the center of the great horseshoe table. The negro musicians began to sing, in that inimitable manner and rhythm of their race.

"Sing a song of sixpence, pocket full of rye,
Four and twenty blackbirds baked in a pie—"

At the next words,

"When the pie was opened—"

one of the artists leaned forward and skillfully broke the crust, and myriads of canary birds (blackbirds not being obtainable even by Monte Cristo) outpoured and flew to every corner of the room, just as a charming young figure of a girl, draped from head to foot in black illusion, with a stuffed blackbird upon her head, arose from the dish. It was so new, original, and pretty, that comment upon it is absurd. The society of these men was so good, so envied, and so far above the average "low-brow" that it was preyed upon (probably more than other class at any other time in the social history of America) by the jealous and the criminal, and blackmailed to an extraordinary degree. It just naturally broke itself up; Beauty is sensitive and would rather disappear than run the risk of unwelcome publicity.

Referring to the character of Stanford White, his right hand never knew what his left was doing. I think he more nearly fitted Emerson's definition of the word "gentleman" than anyone else I have ever known. It runs something like this: "A gentleman is one who never brings his mental or physical troubles from his bedroom; if he cannot leave them behind, he stays with them." If the word can be divided into its two constituents—"gentle" and "man"—Stanny was certainly both, and I think "gentleness" (the opposite of "weakness") is possibly one of the words which implies that we are now some distance from our ancestors, the cave dwellers. He may have had troubles of his own, but we never knew about them, for he was always so busy doing something for some one else that he hadn't time to talk of himself.

He pulled me out of many a financial hole, doubtless sometimes with much work for himself. It is not always easy, even for rich men, to get sums of money on the spur of the moment. Once he lent me three thousand dollars on an order I was carrying out, and when I paid him, he returned me the interest money the next day, with the words: "I give you this on one condition, that you use it to go over to Europe and visit your family. You need a vacation." Dear old Stanny, it wasn't the money help that he gave his friends that made him so charming, but it was the little things that require so much delicate thought. I do not think he spent ten minutes a week thinking about himself.

One memorable Easter Sunday (the Ten were to open a show next day, and we were hanging our work) Stanny appeared. I had two marines which he liked, but he was greatly taken with a portrait of my grandmother which was not yet framed and was leaning against the wall in the corner. I had intended to get some inch-and-a-half molding for it. He could never bear to have a work of art improperly dressed. I can see now how he looked, beautifully groomed with top hat, frock coat—evidently on his way to some smart affair. He looked at me a moment, then grabbed the portrait and rushed from the place. Needless to say I followed. Outside was a fine equipage, his own, and, taking it, we ended at his office, where he had a floor stored with all kinds of valuable antiques, draperies, frames, statues, which he had chosen in Europe—not because they were old or only one of a kind in existence, but because they were beautiful—and brought over here. Keeping up his two characteristic gestures of scratching his head and rumpling his hair with one hand, and slapping his thigh with the other—his office force knew that if he ever did the two together it was time to flee—he dove into dozens of frames which were piled for at least fifteen feet away from the wall. Ignoring his clothes, he dashed in and was covered with dust in two seconds. In five minutes he had tried all the frames and found two that fitted the portrait. Telling me to take my choice, he turned around and was gone. I had barely made my selection and turned to go when a flunky from his Gramercy Park home ran in, out of breath, and grabbed the picture. When we got to the street there was no sign of Stanny or his carriage, but a large hired vehicle was waiting, ready to take me back to the gallery. He was doing that sort of thing all the time, but would have been very cross if anyone had mentioned it in public.

May I tell of a small matter which, until the death of both men, I have kept to myself? Once Stanny came to me acting rather strangely, and asked me if I would take a trip uptown with him. When we alighted at a studio building where many of my friends lived he asked me to show him the way to X's rooms—an artist I remembered leaving behind us at the club. It seemed strange that Stanny intended calling upon a man he knew not to be at home, but I kept still. Kneeling down on the floor, he shoved under the door a roll of bills which looked big figured to me, and we fled. In the cab outside, I inquired what it meant.

"You know he needs it. I have it. Why shouldn't I give it to him? But you must never tell."

I asked how much it was.

"Oh, I don't know."

The next day I heard X telling a friend that he had gone home the night before, ready to pack his things, as he was to be kicked out of his studio in the morning, but a most miraculous thing had happened. He had found a roll of bills under his door.

I never told, and he died without knowing who had helped him.

One could hardly tell about the work of Stanford White without including something of Augustus Saint-Gaudens, for America is richer by many works of art which are the combination of the genius of these two men. Saint-Gaudens was the son of a cobbler. I believe that if an exhaustive history of the clever people of the world were written, it would be found that a large percentage had been sons of cobblers. As a boy, I used to be fascinated by a certain cobbler of the town, and while listening to his words of wisdom I learned to make, entirely with my own hands, a pair of boots. He was a socialist and, I suppose, an anarchist, but the joy of life was in his heart and I am sure that fashioning a beautiful covering for the human foot is as near making a statue as anything could be.

It was funny to watch the French or the Irish crop out in Gussy. The French was always on the alert for something beautiful. I remember being taken by him and several architects up to a place in Cornish. They had found a charming view. After climbing away up to the top of a hill—mulleins, granite stones, and not much else in the foreground—I was told to look off over the landscape and rave. They called it "Too Good to be True." I can visualize a farmer, an old resident of the place (call him Haskins), coming in with the wood which he throws into the woodbox, saying to his wife:

"There, Mother, I bet you can't guess where that wood come from."

"No. Where did it, Jake?"

"From that piece o' land yer uncle Ezra left yer that Mr. Saint-Gawdeens and them dudes calls 'Too Good to be True.'" Great laugh from both.

But every year or two with Gussy the Irish would get on top. A day would arrive when the work he was doing would disgust him too much. Then he would fire his assistants, helpers, and everyone out and smash everything in the studio. He would spend two or three days loafing in the club and with his friends, then back again, clean it all up, and begin work, saying, "Now we can get ahead." The year that he was forty-nine he came to me, feeling very blue.

"Simmy, I'm out of it. I caught the model we had today in class winking at the fellows when I exclaimed a little too enthusiastically about her charms. The same thing happened to my master in Italy when I was a student, and I remember wondering how he could be so silly at his age." Then he told me how he had always jumped upon the platforms of the cars while they were in motion. That day, as he did this, the driver said, "Peart for yer age, ain't yer?" In the future he intended to wait until the car stopped and get on properly.

When he got these blue streaks he had the habit of coming down to The Players, finding me, and saying: "Now, Simmy, you must help me. Order anything you want, on me, but stay right here and talk to me." I suppose the sound of my voice was, for him, like Vergil's bees in the lime trees—a susurrus. The talk was anything and everything. Sometimes a discussion about a college education—as to whether Lincoln would have been the same if he had had one, etc., etc. I told him once about my discovery that every man, secretly and in his own soul, thought himself the ideal type of human being. An art class in Boston had been given as a subject for Saturday afternoon an ideal head of a young Greek. The results were placed on easels, and I easily picked out the author of each drawing from its resemblance to himself. Then Gussie remembered that in Italy there was a humpback in the class with him who made everything deformed.

In Chicago, where I went at one time to consult Daniel Burnham, I met Saint-Gaudens and McKim. To my astonishment, they had come to collect money to start an academy at Rome. They raised about one hundred thousand dollars, I believe, and this was the beginning. I always have been and still am opposed to formal organizations, and an academy seemed to me just another of the same kind. I couldn't see Gussie in this position and asked:

"*Que fais tu donc dans cette galère?*"

His reply was very logical.

"No, I don't, but when I was a boy I wanted to learn sculpture. If there had been an academy in Rome at that time, I could have gotten studio, materials, models, and all that I wanted for nothing. Let Chicago and everybody subscribe. Who are they, anyway? After one hundred years, the money will have been well spent if only one artist—say a Michael Angelo—is helped to get what he needs." He was willing to sacrifice the whole pig-killing town if one genius could be helped.

All the oil wells of Texas would not be worth, to our

descendants, one poem like the "Ode to a Grecian Urn."

If I had the task of taking to Europe one thing as the best work of art of America, I should take the tomb from the Rock Creek Cemetery in Washington, which was created by those three artists—Saint-Gaudens, Stanford White, and Henry Adams. Nothing we have made in this country as yet, whether paint, carving, or architecture, can equal it. This figure, an expression of the idea of death, marks, I am told, the last resting place of the wife of Henry Adams, but there is no name and no commemoration to any individual, no signature of artist or architect; it is universal and might belong to any one of us. A pilgrimage to this monument of a man's respect for the woman he loved is, of necessity, a sacred rite. One cannot pass gayly by in a motor car and give a careless nod of approbation, but one must alight (let us hope from one of those old-fashioned rickety open barouches, driven by the last of the negro coachmen) and proceed up the narrowest, most delightful little path, overgrown with shrubs and bushes, where at the top of a knoll and carefully concealed from common gaze is the Sphinx. Like the pilgrims to the ancient shrines, one wishes one had courage to go back and approach this beauty of all time and no time, upon one's bended knees. And her surroundings! How wonderfully the loving architect has framed her; no word and no talk about death. There she sits and speaks to everyone, and the message is the secret of his innermost thoughts—so much as he brings, so much does she tell, and no more.

One day in Paris the *Figaro* started a reporter out

to get the opinions of different intellectual men upon death. Some gave a column, some a half column, but when it came to Alphonse Daudet, he said:

"My idea of death?—*la mort?—psutt!—*"

There is nothing to say, and all I can think of when looking at the Rock Creek Memorial, are the words of Shakespeare,

>The Rest is Silence

Chapter XII: Fine Arts in Relation to "A Number of Things"

IT was during this period of my life that I did my best work; I had a good studio in Carnegie Hall, freedom from money worries, and abounding spirit. Also, my imagination was still fresh from the influence of Europe, and the Old World was enough in retrospect for me to realize its worth. One of the most interesting orders I received at this time was to decorate a room in the new part of the Waldorf Hotel, that addition called the Astoria. It was a long, narrow hall, the Astor Gallery, with boxes all around a dais at one end. The room was an attempt at the French of Louis Seize—bastard architecture, I think—fancy work and rococo with curves and bends everywhere. After my work was all finished I had to get up and paint over again the ribbon held by one of the Cupids. It was taut and I changed it to wavy, as it proved to be the only straight line in the whole room.

After I had submitted my sketches and they were accepted by the architect, I had to go and sign my contract at the offices of John Downey & Son. There was a large room full of stenographers and bookkeepers, with a glass place on one side for the boss. John Downey came out to greet me. As we sat at a big table, he pushed toward me a long document, saying:

"There's your contract. If you'll read it over and it is satisfactory, you've only to sign it and get your first payment."

I read it and reached for the pen to sign. He must have seen some doubt upon my face.

"Is it satisfactory," he asked.

"No, but I'll sign."

"Why, I drew that contract myself! What's the matter with it?"

"There is not enough time," I replied.

His eyes narrowed.

"Mr. Simmons, you have lived a long time across the water? Yes? Let me tell you something about American business methods. Never complain over here that you haven't enough time. If the job suits you, wade in and do it. If you can't finish it yourself, put on more men and work nights!"

"But there are things that can't be done that way," I insisted.

"Sir, I've been a contractor for twenty years in New York City and if there is anything you cannot do that way, I should like to hear about it."

"Well," I said, "I admit your business position, but I still believe that if you wanted a son and heir you would have to respect the old rule to wait nine months, and not put on more men and work nights."

Sensation among the blond typewriters!

The working of a business man's mind can never be guessed at beforehand. I painted two decorations for one of America's foremost financiers. In making the sketches I was mindful of the fact that he was a pillar of an orthodox denomination of the strictest type, and, while I suggested a group of dancing figures, I was very careful to drape them sedately with several layers of chiffon. What was my surprise when the criticism came:

"Mr. Simmons's idea is very delightful, but the figures are not nude enough!"

The late Andrew Carnegie was a good old-fashioned type of man who thought the God-given power to amass a large fortune was indication of an all-embracing good judgment and taste. I never met him but once. It was in '91, at a show of pictures of the Society of American Artists. I was presented to this short, stout little man. "Mr. Carnegie" meant nothing to me, as I had just come straight from England, and his fame had not managed to penetrate the shores of Cornwall. He was most indifferent, did not like the exhibition very much, and announced that he has purchased the only good picture, pointing to an unimportant landscape. Abbot Thayer's "Madonna" (which Clarence King said should have buckets under it to catch the dripping sentiment), a charming Thomas Dewing, a beautiful thing by Theodore Robinson, and others were all about him, so I ventured to tell the doughty Scotsman that he must be deeply ignorant on the subject of art. That naturally closed the interview.

For the Astor Gallery I chose as subjects women—which I like best to paint—representing the twelve months of the year and the four seasons, sixteen panels in all. How I labored over the color of the room, changing the tone every three feet all the way up, until it looked all the same! My idea was to make a background that would seem to be white, but against which a woman's complexion would be beautiful and a man's shirt front would tell. They have painted the whole thing over now, of course. My decorations are untouched, but it is no longer my room.

"JANUARY"

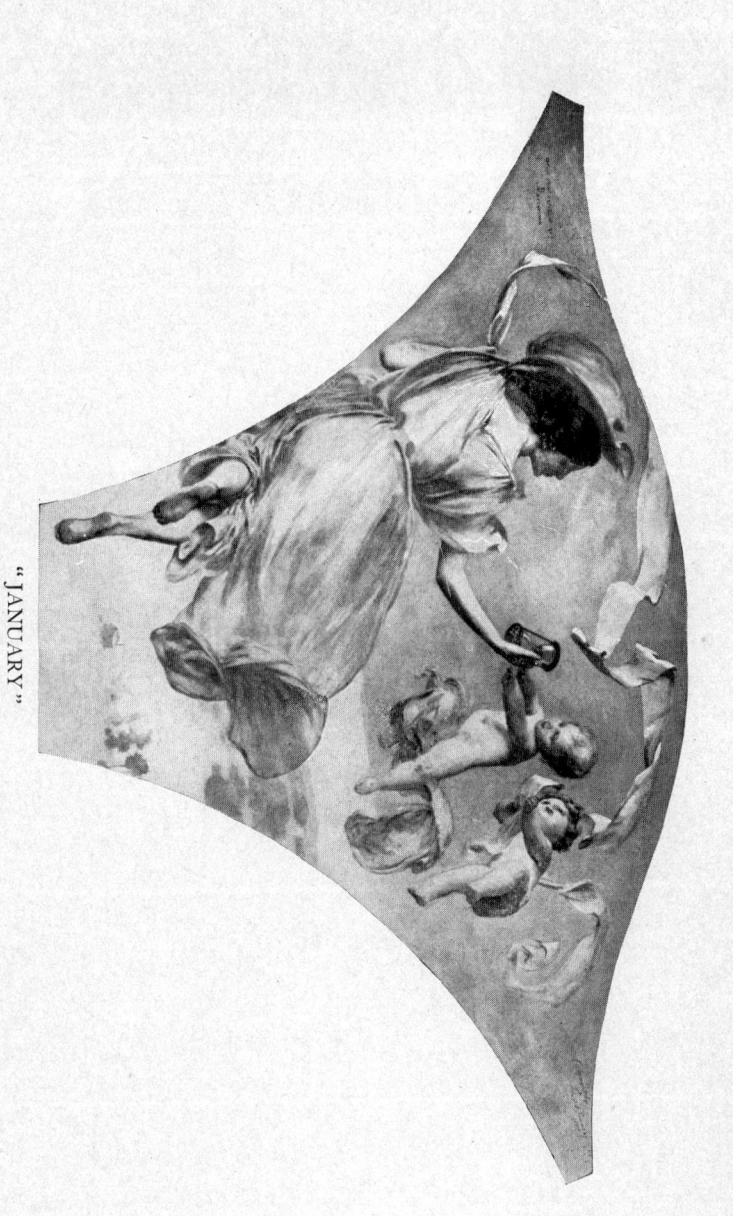

Panel by Edward Simmons, Astor Gallery, Waldorf-Astoria Hotel, New York

Copyright by Edward Simmons; from a Copley Print, Copyright by Curtis & Cameron, Publishers, Boston

People do not realize what these little things mean. The architects had given me the whole control, but even at the time I was doing the work I was greatly restricted. There were four little panels that were not in the contract, but sadly needed to be decorated. I offered to do them at my own expense and also to change the terrible red-velvet railing that ran around the balcony, but do you think the hotel authorities would let me do it? No; the opening was on a certain day and all the workmen *must* be out before then. Business before art every time.

I had to insure the panels twice—once to the contractor and again to John Jacob Astor, whose lawyer, by the way, demanded that all the artists working in the building hand over their copyrights to him, which they "had improperly taken out on Mr. Astor's property." We had a meeting, and the others decided not to do anything to antagonize him. I was furious and asked my friend, Luther Lincoln, what to do about it. "Oh, come away and take a walking trip with me to the Delaware Water Gap," he said. I went and I still have my copyright. To show that my rights in the matter are recognized by the authorities, the architect once wrote to me and, saying that Mr. Boldt had asked for permission to reproduce my panels in the *Hotel Guide*, and commanded me to grant the same. I answered and gave him permission to *buy* the photographs of my work from Curtis and Cameron, relinquishing my royalties. Mr. Astor, therefore, paid for the reproductions, so establishing my case.

This question of copyright is one that crops up all the time and never will be really settled until some artist has money enough to carry a case to the Supreme Court of the United States. Anyone who writes a book, a play, or music, and even those who make etchings and engravings, are protected, but the law does not apply to the painter or the sculptor. I do not believe that the Supreme Court would decide in our favor, for over here we are more apt to follow the English law, where the buyer, unless otherwise stated, retains the copyright, and not the French law, where the artist always has it.

After the decorators had been chosen for the work in the Appellate Court, the chief justice asked me to bring in some of my former contracts that he might see the form and make one for us to sign more or less like them. Then, later, he asked me to make one which I thought would serve. As the question was then vitally at issue about the copyright, I slipped in a small clause—"artist to retain the copyright." It came back to me blue-penciled, so I saw it would be no use. Later, the chief justice gave a talk at a lunch to which I was invited, and remarked that Mr. Simmons was "not only an able painter, but a keen lawyer." If it had not been for an accident, he would not have noticed a certain line that I had put into my contract, and I would have obtained a decision of the Appellate Court for nothing. That line would have established a precedent for the state of New York, and from that time all artists would have had and owned their copyrights.

James Lord was the architect of the Appellate Court. There was great trouble because he signed out the triptych to three men when it should have been given to one. He evidently wanted to give everyone a chance, for in the other part of the building he gave one frieze to five men. Our triptych was done by Blashfield, Walker, and myself. We were to do Justice in three forms, and as the work of Blashfield and myself was more nearly alike, we put Walker in the middle. I waited until Blashfield had determined the composition, the color scheme, and even until he had actually painted his background, and then, as far as I could, I followed him. After the canvases were completed and on the wall, I found that my two figures of small boys in the foreground were not in the right place, so I painted them out and moved them up four inches higher. Blashfield went even farther. He took out a woman's figure with her back turned and changed her completely, because he did not think she agreed with the general composition of the three. These changes were very difficult, as they were done under a different light, in a different place from the original work, and, of necessity (as the building was then in use), without the assistance of models.

A remark of Richard Canfield's on my panel is worth quoting. I have, in the foreground, a symbolism of a child pushing away the nose of a vulpine animal with his right hand, to protect a rabbit at his left. The great gambler said:

"By George! Simmons, I did not know you had so much intelligence as that. That symbolism of yours is very apt: Crime, Ignorance, and Stupidity. Is that what the Appellate Court stands for?"

At my first interview with Canfield I got a taste of the man I was to deal with. Clarence Luce was the architect who made the gambling house on Forty-fourth

Street, next to Delmonico's, and he came to me with a proposition to decorate it, saying that I was to talk the matter over with Mr. Canfield himself. I, of course, decided he would know nothing of art and it would be rather trying. I was mistaken. A short, fattish, powerful man greeted me and said, only:

"I want your best work. You know what that is and I shall know it when I see it. We'll talk the money over later."

This did not seem extraordinary to me at the time. Sad experience has since taught me to do nothing without a contract, but I have always found that with men of the character of Richard Canfield, nothing of the sort is necessary. In working for John Dunston, proprietor of the famous "Jack's" Restaurant, I would paint a panel in my studio, take it down to the room, and put it upon the wall, go directly to the office and get my money—no criticism of my work and no arguments—just a man's word, and as to the artistic part of it, he considered my judgment better than his.

Like Napoleon, when Canfield wanted anything done, he employed the best men and told them to go ahead. He became a great friend of Whistler's and has written one of the most interesting accounts of the painter that I have read. Whistler painted Canfield's portrait and doubtless found him a congenial companion—as who would not? He knew life, he knew human nature, he was an expert on guns and firearms and had killed his man or I miss my guess; and yet I must say that Richard Canfield was a man in every sense of the word and as much a gentleman as one who lives outside the law can be. He was the god of all the smaller gamblers and had helped more than one over the rough spots.

The house where fortunes were made and lost is standing to-day, and from the outside resembles nothing more than the ordinary, narrow, three- or four-story, brownstone dwelling place. In Canfield's time, Clarence Luce had managed to transform the interior until it was quite a gem in its way. Entering by the big swing door, one stepped into a small vestibule done in Numidian marble. In the ceiling were five rhomboidal panels of thin jade behind which were lights casting a soft glow, Oriental in its effect (one might imagine it to be Cleopatra's bedroom), and giving a thrill of mystery right at the start.

Before one was a solemn door and the usual grill with a bell. Upon ringing, a huge negro peeked through, and one was admitted if one were a friend. Behind this was a reception room, and here I painted Pandora and her box with a great smoke, interspersed with figures, coming out of it; while over the mantel of the room behind were Hospitality and her attendants. The gambling room was on the next floor, and on the newel post of the stairway was a charming little reproduction of the "Bacchante" by Frederick MacMonnies, of which Anders Zorn said to me:

"For the first time I see this lady where she should be—in a gambling house."

The architect had scaled everything down to undersize, so that in this narrow house things might look large. There must have been extra chambers in the walls, as in the daytime there was nothing to be seen of the tables or the wheels, and for aught one knew, it was a private home. The back room, where was served any kind of drink or food (even to cold partridge) that human ingenuity could conjure, was dark, of the dull colors of Spanish leather, and this formed a contrast to the room where the playing went on. This was light, with a carpet on the floor of terre-verte plush so thick that one's feet sunk into its depths without making the slightest sound. I saw that the only color must come from the faces of the men, the red spots on the table—and my decorations.

The spaces to be painted were two of those difficult cat-claw panels (spandrels) at one end of the room, and these were also undersize. I could not use a male figure, so made my "Night" and "Morning," taken from Swinburne's lines,

> When haughty Day represses
> Night's cold and faint caresses,

both from women models.

Along toward the beginning of my work things were not going well with me financially; so late one night I dressed in evening clothes and went up to see Canfield. He received me in the supper room, called the waiter to bring a decanter of rye (which he never corked, but simply covered with a fine linen napkin, thus allowing the fusel oil to evaporate), and then asked me if I had come to play. I answered that I should not think of doing so indelicate a thing while working for him. At that he nodded his head saying, "I thought not."

"I'm in great trouble," I said.

"Well, a man can't do his best work in that state. What is it?"

I made a clean breast of everything.

"The answer to all that is money," he said, calling his secretary. "Bring me a check for a thousand dollars," and then to me, "Now run away and do your best work."

In regard to questions of gambling debts, Canfield was inexorable if he was dealing with crooks (which are not always to be found in the lower strata of society, by any means), but for a young man who had made his first mistake he had nothing but kindness. A friend of mine was taken (when a bit alcoholic), by an older man, to Canfield's one night. After a short time he found himself in debt to the house for several thousands of dollars. He wrote out a check for the amount and went home. In the morning he realized what he had done and that he did not have anything like the amount to meet it. Bracing up, he groomed himself carefully and called upon Mr. Canfield. That gentleman had not yet breakfasted and seemed in no hurry to do so, for my friend waited several hours in the reception room. I suspect that the astute gambler was giving him a chance to show his mettle. When Canfield appeared, the boy (for he was very young) made a clean breast of affairs, saying that neither himself nor his family were in a position to meet the obligation, but that he was there to offer all he had—his skin. Canfield listened attentively, turned to his desk, picked up a paper, and said:

"Is this the check?"

My friend nodded.

"Well, don't ever do this again," he advised, tearing it up and throwing it into the fire.

I once asked Canfield about an account in the papers of a young man in one of our western cities whom he had sued for the payment of a bad check of $45,000. It seemed to me foolish, for of course he could not collect.

"Oh, I just did that to let you fellows know what a rotter the boy was, that's all," he said. "The night he lost it he had turned up at my place with his older brother and the manager of his father's business here in New York. When the young fellow began to lose heavily, my man came to me for instructions. I asked his companions what to do. They said to let him plunge, that the firm was good for it. Of course, the next day they refused to pay. That is why I sued.

"But a few weeks later they needed me. The young man had got into serious trouble which required a large amount of instant cash. It was early Sunday morning and there was at that time no place in New York where one could get money after banking hours. So the manager and the young man's brother turned up at my house, bringing with them a man whose name, on paper, was good for millions. Here was my chance. They needed $25,000 cash. I gave it to them in exchange for a check, signed by the brother and backed by the rich man, for $70,000."

I rather imagine that certain people had to leave for Montreal that morning and did not stay upon the manner of their going.

When politics and the fine arts meet, there is sometimes a clash. Senators and aldermen may be good lawmakers, but they are not always judges of decorative painting. The funniest time I ever had was in trying to decorate the Baltimore Law Courts building. La Farge and Vedder had both refused the order, and I could easily see why, after my own experience. There were seven rhomboidal panels in the entrance. The first suggestion made to me was to have a representation of Francis Scott Key finding that the "flag was still there." As he must have been below deck in a British war vessel at that moment, looking out of a porthole, the only way to do him would have been from the back view, while in the distance the flag would have been about the size of one of his ears. I might have been able to vary this seven times, but I doubt it.

Then they suggested Religious Liberty as a subject. My argument against this was that it is an idea of the mind and not for the eye. Pope Hildebrand, a most wicked man, would be a far more decorative proposition than Bishop Potter, though not representing Religious Liberty nearly so well. I tried to make a composition, but failed and gave it up. I did propose, however, that it could be done by taking the color red for the Church of Rome, raising the tone to a lively pink for the Church of England, then a very faint rose shade for Unitarianism. In this way the idea might be made to last out the seven panels, the last being one where only the pure in heart could see any color at all.

Brander Matthews once gave me the best illustration that I know of a purely literary subject that could not be painted. The ladies of New York presented a flag to a Negro regiment. The color sergeant stepped forward, as in duty bound, to accept it. He then should have stepped back, but, being a negro, had to say something. So, saluting, he remarked, "I'll bring these colors back or I'll report to God, the reason why." Now this is a fine tale, but how to paint it? One would have a negro and a flag; the remainder would have to be printed underneath.

Mistaking the subject for the artist is a great failing of a certain type of mind. This was true of Freddie Remington. He was a darling and we all loved him— one of those rare beings, a man without an enemy. When he began painting he was lucky enough to stumble upon a new field, one of great size, that had not been touched, and one that all America cared for. The West, the cowboy, soldier, and miner were virgin soil, waiting for his touch. Roosevelt, who did not know as much about painting as he did about roughriding, wanted to have a statue erected to him as the greatest American artist.

I do not believe the ordinary politician ever considers the fine arts seriously. To him beauty is something for Sundays or holidays, and he lets the women attend to it. At least, when we were in Washington some years ago, making an attempt to have the tax on art removed, I had a chance to judge the mental weight of one Congressman. I was asked to be one of the party (as one of the minor speakers only), for I could tell what I knew of the same matter in France and England. I was fool enough to say, in the course of my argument:

"This may not go down with the woolly West, but it should in the East."

Instantly a long young man, with a shock of dark hair falling over his forehead, rose and said:

"What's that, Mr.——" (turning to his neighbor to ask my name)—"oh, Simmons? What do you know about the West, if I may ask. How far west have you ever been?"

I think he took it for granted that I was born (like Sargent) on the other side. I answered:

"Three years under the shadow of Mount Shasta, Mr. Bryan."

I knew William Jennings by sight and judged that he had not ventured so far from his home town as I had. He was silenced by the chairman and there was a chuckle.

Anders Zorn told me two stories about Grover Cleveland, showing the extraordinary penetration and understanding of this statesman. While he was doing a portrait of the President, at one time he took the canvas and turned it upside down to look at it. To Cleveland's questioning he replied that he was doing it to see if he had painted the book too high in value, adding:

"What do you think?"

"I suppose you painters use the word 'value' to mean the importance a thing holds in its effect upon the eye of the beholder. Yes, I think it is too high but why do you turn it upside down?"

Zorn was interested. "Why do *you* think we do?"

"It must be to see it from a new point of view. To get a new conception of it all."

It was, but how keen of him to have thought it out!

Zorn asked Mrs. Cleveland what her husband's friends thought of the protrait. She replied that she did not know anyone who fitted that description, that he had many acquaintances, but no one that she could call his friend. It seems that the higher a man climbs, the farther behind he leaves his associates. Shakespeare must have been very lonely away up there on the mountain top.

There were two humps in the Monument Land near the Old Manse which were supposed to be the graves of British soldiers killed in the Revolutionary War. Hawthorne tells the legend of a boy who chopping wood there at the time of the battle of Concord, saw one soldier fall, and went over and finished him with his ax. When my dog Cuff used to start digging at this place, I always wanted to let him go on, just to see if one of the skulls was split. During this period of my life, no doubt aided by the usual school history, I formed a definite idea of the battle of Concord, and it was not until I tried to paint it for the Boston State House that I found out the real truth of the matter. And my enlightenment came from a Britisher!

I naturally started out with a composition of men in red coats, but, thinking it over, decided to be sure, so I wrote to Trevelyan, author of that wonderful history of the Revolutionary period, asking him where I could get information. A very courteous reply told me that he was in the country and that he did not have his books of reference with him, but added, "Why do you not go to that excellent library of yours, the Boston Athenæum, and consult the *Gentleman's Magazine* for June, 1775? You'll find what you want there."

I did find what I wanted, and a lot more. For instance, only one out of ten British soldiers at Concord were redcoats. Those who fought at the Bridge were the ones who afterward formed the "King's Own"—a flying wedge of two hundred men in dark-blue-and-black uniforms. Another little error of the poet Longfellow's is that Paul Revere may have been a very good silversmith, but he never got to Concord. He was only one of a group of men sent out to warn the countryside, and he, with many others, was caught by the British and sent back to Boston. And then the flag! Despite Betsy Ross, I shall have to confess that the Stars and Stripes turned up the first time at the siege of Boston and were carried by a body of Connecticut militia.

One of our well-known illustrators has made a drawing of Washington reviewing his troops under the famous elm at Cambridge (again the flag floating proudly in the breeze), the soldiers being carefully clothed in Colonial uniforms. According to the statement of the Rev. William Emerson, we find a blacksmith of Concord, during the siege of Boston, which was after the battle at the Bridge, carrying his own gun and wearing his leather apron. Also, Washington made a pathetic appeal to Congress for some form of shirt that should distinguish his soldiers from the citizens, saying that the only way he had to mark his officers was a red, white, or blue ribbon which they wore in their coats.

About this point in my reading I stopped and changed my entire composition, taking my cue from the letter which remains for us, from the American commander at the Bridge. He says:

"I then sprang to my feet, crying, 'Fire, fellow citizens! Fire!'"

Sprang to his feet? Where must he have been? Lying behind something. I had shot, fished, and traveled over this land all my life—it was only just across the river from our house—and there was nothing there in my boyhood behind which a man could have hidden. I looked this up and found there had formerly been a wall so that the market women during the spring freshet could walk dry shod in the days of the Concord River's overflow.

Considering the fact that I had never seen green grass anywhere near Boston on the 19th of April, it may seem strange that I put it into my decoration. Of course, I preferred it for my color scheme, but I actually found a letter from a woman of the period and of that date, saying, "I saw green grass waving out of my window this morning." It appears that that year they had an unusually early spring.

When I painted my second panel, I thought of the order that the Pope gave to Raphael to paint him putting out a fire by the power of God. The Pope naturally saw himself the principal figure and was disgusted when he found that Raphael had made him a little figure on a balcony in the distance, the artist preferring a group of maidens rushing around in the foreground with jugs of water as being more interesting to paint. Now my subject was War, and when I chose as my other panel "The Return of the Battle Flags into the Custody of the State after the Civil War," many people naturally expected that the governor and officials would occupy the prominent place on the canvas. The governor was an admirable man and did a great deal toward winning the war, but in actual fact

"THE RETURN OF THE FLAGS"
Panel by Edward Simmons, Boston State House

*Copyright by Edward Simmons; from a Copley Print
Copyright by Curtis & Cameron, Publishers, Boston*

he was about five feet high, "pot-gutted," bald headed, and not an attractive object from a painter's point of view. I did not wish to do a group of portraits, but a decoration, so I imagined myself in the park, looking up at the State House, with a line of color sergeants marching up the steps to present the flags to the governor and officials waiting above. As they were two or three hundred feet away from the gate, I had to reduce them to twelve or fifteen inches in height, thereby making lifelong enemies of several who were still alive. When the G. A. R. found I was not to do the officers, but the color sergeants, my trouble was by no means over, for the wives and relatives of more than a dozen sent me photographs of their beloved ones, some of whom were dead, some of whom had lost an arm in the war. Many of the likenesses were of the individual thirty years later than the day he carried the flag! *All*, of course, expected to be represented in the decoration by a life-sized portrait. I obviated this difficulty by making them march up the stairs away from one, as they naturally would have done, and a back view is not a good portrait.

The ceremony had taken place on a day in December, and it had snowed the night before; so the next question that arose was that of the army overcoat. I had seen many of them in my boyhood; all of the farmers wore them in the fields. I took it for granted that it would be easy to get one. I appealed to the G. A. R. of Boston, the G. A. R. of New York, and the G. A. R. of Washington, D. C. There were none to be had. Finally, I wrote to Sanger, a classmate of mine, who was the Assistant Secretary of War, and found that there were some in the army archives and that all I had to do was to go to Washington and look at them. They would even have them taken out for me to examine thoroughly. This, of course, would do me no good whatever. I must have one in my studio so that a model could pose in it. My home and studio were at East Hampton, Georgica Pond, at the time, and I was walking around my garden one day, feeling very low in my mind, when my man of all work asked me what the matter was. I was blue enough to tell anyone my troubles, and explained to him, with no idea that he could help me.

"Why, old Jackson wears a coat like that," he said.

I had no faith, but we harnessed up, drove several miles out, when, sure enough (I spied it at a distance), there was old Jackson weeding out his flower garden and wearing an original Civil War army overcoat. It was a beauty, stained by time and faded by the sun; a real work of art, but he thought me a great fool to give him an entirely new coat for it.

The last trouble was the flag. I found out that the maker of the flags carried in the war was still alive and had one in his possession. It was all battle worn and just what I wanted. After the panel was up the Boston *Transcript* published a letter from an indignant woman stating that I had no right to monkey with Old Glory; that as an artist I might have thought the flag would be better with gold stars, but that I had no right to paint them so. The original flags were upon the wall of the State House, about ten feet under my panel, and I replied to her, asking that she take the trouble to go and look at them and see that the stars were gold.

Also, as they had been given to the regiments by the ladies of Boston, the question was "up to them."

This United States flag is one of the most undecorative things that an artist has to use. Made like a crazy quilt, absolutely without an æsthetic excuse, even the Barbarians do better. It is based on the Washington shield, but is an exceedingly ugly arrangement of the colors. At a distance it looks like a sweet pea; pretty, but never dignified. We love it—not for its looks—but, as Desdemona loved Othello, "for the dangers he has passed."

I never understood Boston—or, in fact, New England—until I went back there after having spent years in Europe. There are many delightful qualities about the Bostonese type of mind, but their comprehension of the senses only through abstract matters limits their personal enjoyments. However, we cannot quarrel with them on some scores. Their love of music, for instance. I have heard music in three places in my life in such a way as to approach the indulgences of the Mad King of Württemberg. If one is not alone, one must have the sense of being alone; there must be no rustling of programs and no talking. Therefore the perfect way to listen to music is to have an audience composed of one's friends. You cannot tell a stranger to "shut up," but you can a friend; and you can also ignore him and thus establish solitude.

In the Vaudeville Club, in the studio of Augustus Saint-Gaudens, where every year he used to give a Sunday concert in memory of his dear friend Welles's birthday (as a rule it was a stringed quartet); and in the St. Botolph Club of Boston, I have really enjoyed music. We had the Kneisel and the Adamovski Quartets—the most wonderful music I ever heard. The man sitting next to me might have been anybody from a prince to Paderewski. I learned more about music and fell more in love with it than I had in all the remainder of my life because I got it under congenial surroundings.

Paderewski I never knew well, but have had the pleasure of playing many a game of pool with him. It was said that he ate nothing and drank only water during the day, if he was to play at night, a habit I can understand; for whenever I have had the problem of making what was to me a great composition, I have found it necessary to train for it by exhausting my nervous forces, thereby rendering myself simple in thought. So I imagine him drawing himself fine. After a performance he would arrive at the St. Botolph Club, wanting much food and, when he had fed, much fun. "Now let's play poker; now let's play pool." It was not the game, it was the sociability he wanted; because, once in it, he never knew when it was his turn to play, never could remember to ante, and talked all the time.

Paderewski comes nearer to being the traditional genius than any other modern—all the eccentricities with the real stuff underneath. They say he kept, in his younger days, a pet poodle to supply the requests he received for locks of his hair. And then the story of the cherry stones which a woman found lying on the corner of his mantelpiece one day and appropriated, and which she had set in a pin of clover-leaf pattern. Upon her calling the artist's attention to it, he remarked:

"That is one of the carelessnesses of my valet. It must have been he who left them there. Personally, I loathe cherries."

One of the drawbacks of Bostonians is the lack of a true sense of humor. The assistant professor of mathematics at the Technological School once told me that he comprehended infinity. A large order, but he was perfectly serious. While they are willing to claim such an advance in one direction, they sometimes seem to have no realization of the advance of the civilization of this earth. One of the younger members of my family —upon moving to Richmond, Virginia, two or three years ago—was admonished by an elderly spinster of Boston to "be sure and be kind to those poor heathens in the South." She meant the negroes!

Boston is a city apart. It has nothing to do with the rest of the country. Twenty years ago my mother, like all good Bostonians, stopping at the Murray Hill Hotel here in New York, said:

"Only think, Edward, there are thirty Cabots sailing to-day on the same steamer."

She was much shocked when I remarked, "I hope it is a strong ship."

Dr. Samuel Cabot's house was always a revelation to me. It was full of stuffed birds in glass cases. He was not without a sense of the ridiculous, however, for when he was persuaded to go to see a picture by his brother Edward (whom all the women worshiped for his artistic tendencies), he said about this painting— entitled "Peace"—of two birds building their nest in the mouth of a cannon:

"That's just like Edward; both his birds are male."

This desire of ignoring sex was paramount in many learned and otherwise delightful folk. I remember William Ware and had great respect for him, but I had to laugh at him. He was an architect of ability and a professor at Columbia, loved by his pupils, but the kind of man who had no respect for any idea that was not fifty years old—so that it was certain to be absolutely true before he taught it. He told me once that he had never been able to see any reason for women's existence. It must have been this side of his nature which caused him to go about with a small hammer and eliminate all evidences of sex from the newly arrived Greek masterpieces for the Boston Art Museum. He could not see anything incongruous in the fact that the fig leaves (cast by the workman in the Museum) were of a different color from the statues. Strange type of mind—and yet he had cleverness and a certain wit. My aunt had asked her husband to invite Professor Ware to dinner, but, thinking my uncle might forget the message, wrote a letter in addition. The professor answered both. The letters are records of brevity.

> Dear Sophy: Yours with pleasure, W. W.
> Dear James: Yours as to your wife, W. W.

Chapter XIII: The Players

THE mad progress of Big Business can almost be likened to a mighty cyclone which sweeps across the countryside with destruction in its wake, but here and there leaving, quite untouched, a farm, a fruit tree, or a windmill—delightful oases—which serve as the only record of a struggling civilization. Big Business in New York has wiped out the homes of the people and sent them in a frantic rush hither and thither in search of a place to live. Always there is that uprooting, due to the steady march of the threatening skyscraper up the island of Manhattan. As in the case of the cyclone, however, verdant places are left behind in this barren desert of commerce, little green spots which remain an eternal blessing and evidence that there were once normal human beings here who thought and had time to care for beauty. One such place is Gramercy Park.

I started one day to try to guess the origin of the name "Gramercy." Samuel Ruggles, the son of the maker of the park, told me that when his father had bought the land the squatters called it "Grommercy Crick" (there was then a small stream of water flowing through it) and the only word that sounded near enough to that was "Gramercy." I asked Carl Arendt, a well-known actor, what Grommercy meant in Dutch. At first he said, "Nothing," but later stopped me and said:

"You may have been aiming at *Kromme Zee*, which means *Crooked Creek*."

Like *Zuyder Zee*, I believe this is the origin of Gramercy.

The Park reminds one of certain places in London more than anything else. In fact, I have often seen moving-picture companies taking films down here which were afterward to be represented on the screen as taking place in the British metropolis. The garden is perfect in its miniature representation of the different seasons. There is one lilac bush at the southwest corner that always tells me of the approach of spring. One year it did not blossom and I felt as if I had lost a friend. The same gardener has been caring for the growing things for a number of years, and many a child has been intrusted to his care while the nurse or parent was busy elsewhere. He teaches them to love the flowers, to play on the paths so that the grass may grow, patches up the quarrels and broken heads, and is tsar in his little domain.

The plot of ground, with enough money to keep it going, was presented to the residents who live about the square, and most of the provisos have been kept, except that the donor required that no buildings more than four stories be allowed, and no house of other than brick or stone (barring wood, evidently). One or two taller ones have managed to creep in, but in general everything is almost the same as it was in the 'nineties, when I first landed in New York.

One Sunday in winter the son of the maker of the park was out walking with his dad, when along came a man with a gun, dragging a big animal. It was a wolf, and the man took them to the spot where he had shot it. There was a big patch of blood upon the snow. This is the place where The Players now stands.

Edwin Booth gave the house to the club, with the condition that he be allowed to make it his home as long as he lived. It is well known how the idea started on the yacht of Commodore Benedict and how that nucleus of clever folk grew into the institution we have to-day. It was not to be essentially an actors' club, but a place where the actor could meet his equals. One must be an artist or a patron of the arts to belong and, of course, this includes writers, architects, sculptors, and painters.

It is a very beautiful club. Stanford White is responsible for the architecture and gave his services gratis, as he did for The Lambs. Men coming from the Old World say that it is the only place in America that reminds them of home. The tonality of the rooms is like that of the very old houses of Europe; time has mellowed the walls as it does a bit of lace or tapestry. One of the ceilings that was a pale robin's-egg blue in '91 is now an exquisite velvet khaki. No man could paint it. Whistler would give up in despair the idea of even copying it. Like the quality of the hair and skin of a dear old face, it gives an air of good breeding, calm, and quiet over all.

The halls and stairways of the house are lined with photographs and playbills, with, here and there, a painting. Over the fireplace hangs that admirable portrait of Edwin Booth by Sargent which gives one an entirely new conception of the actor. On one of the walls is a drawing by Tom Nast, whom I knew well and loved dearly. It is a political cartoon which was the original, I am told, of the "Tammany tiger." Tom is the illustrator who disposed of the Irish-

American question forever by drawing a banner flying over the Capitol at Washington, on which were the words, "Erin go unum pluribus bragh." There are a number of unusually valuable mezzotints and wood engravings scattered about, and the biggest collection known to exist, twenty-six portraits in all, of the painter Naegle. Altogether there are five Sullys, an average Sir Joshua Reynolds, a remarkably good Gilbert Stuart, a beautiful Gainsborough in the earlier manner, while on one wall are two small panels by Benjamin West.

As to the books, there is a veritable treasure house—all the knowledge of the stage that one could possibly desire, with many valuable autographed copies and rare editions. The most unusual possession of the club in the way of printed stuff is the second, third, and fourth folios of Shakespeare's plays. The library room, arranged for ease and comfort, runs the whole length of the house. In the center are soft chairs and couches, with lights close to one's elbow. There is an air of rest and quiet which has often been found more conducive to sleep than weighty reading by certain of us who are in the habit of staying up till the "wee sma' hours." One memento that has always cheered me in my moments of financial stress—for misery loves company—is a letter, written by Oliver Goldsmith to Doctor Johnson, trying to borrow three pounds, which he promises will be repaid as soon as *The Traveller* shall be published. The letter is probably worth twelve hundred dollars to-day!

Gifts flow into such a place, some appropriate and some ridiculous. The costumes of Edwin Booth, for instance, are of great interest to all, but the back tooth of a comedian—a molar—which the wife of one actor presented to us after his death, is not a very great treasure. But there it is in a glass case by day, and locked up in a steel safe at night along with the paste jewels of the stage.

My earlier friends are the most vivid to me—those who are now gone. Descriptions of them are futile and have been done too many times by others far better equipped in a literary way than myself. I remember them only as they came into the club—some peculiarity of looks, some small joke, some story around the long table at luncheon where we were brought together for a fleeting instant, each to depart the next moment and go his own way. The stories, the wit, and the necessity of competing with the best brains of America in The Players was an education to me.

There were the Aldriches—Louis and Thomas Bailey— no relation, except Louis was named after the writer. As a boy he was very poor, did not know where he came from, only that he was called "Louis." Having the job of running errands around a theater out west, he was accosted by the stage carpenter one day, who was a great admirer of the writing of Thomas Bailey.

"Your name from now on is Aldrich," he said, "Louis Aldrich. Don't forget it or you will catch the devil from me."

Louis Aldrich it was, and when he had made his way in the world and was successful enough to go in the same society with Thomas Bailey, he had reached the goal that the carpenter had unwittingly marked for him. The poet always rather resented his existence, however.

Thomas Bailey Aldrich wrote delightful verse and was a charming man, but little things sometimes irritated him greatly. I remember him coming into the club evidently as cross as two sticks. The publishers had had the "cheek" to refuse a poem of his. I asked why. "Oh, I suppose they found it too meter-icious." And this was long before the days of free verse.

Louis Aldrich made a fortune from the play "My Pardner," taken from the Bret Harte story called *Tennessee's Pardner*.

When Louis Aldrich was chairman of the house committee of The Players, I saw him one noon standing at the door of the dining room, talking to Walter, the head waiter. Presently, in a loud voice, he said:

"Walter, what is the lunch to-day?"

"Pork chops and sausages, sir."

"An insult to the house committee."

Then later at the table:

"Walter, bring me some of that damn Christian food."

Henry E. Dixey and Louis were in a war play together, and I heard the latter pray Harry (who had the part of a New York policeman) to spare him when he gave a long speech about the flag. I was one of the first-night audience, and at that most pathetic climax about Old Glory, etc., the policeman suddenly fell dead.

Many actors have a ready wit. Jack Wendall became quite famous for his excellent portrayal of the dog in Rostand's "Chanticleer." One of these silly, satisfied business men was a guest at The Players and, meeting Jack, insisted upon his giving an example of his bark right then and there. After much persuasion and, in order to silence the man, he did so. Whereupon the man proceeded to bark much louder and much better than Jack. The actor was worsted at his own game and by such a fatuous creature, but he turned and said, with the most cunning inference:

"It is fine, but you see, sir, *I* had to learn."

Speaking of Rostand, I *am* proud of a translation of mine of two lines of "Cyrano." Mark Smith had challenged my statement that it could be done in English verse and gave as a test:

"*Qu'est-ce qu'un baiser? C'est le point rose sur l'I du mot aimer.*"

I gave him:

"What is a kiss? The rosy dot upon the 'I' of bliss."

Mark was an actor and the son of an actor. I saw him first with Mrs. Leslie Carter. It is told of him that just before his birth his parents were in Paris. His father, being very patriotic, went to the American embassy, got some earth from the cellar, and, filling four saucers with it, placed them under the legs of the bed where his wife lay. With Old Glory over the bed, Mark was ushered into the world as near an American citizen as his father could make him.

One of the most interesting stage families of my time was the group of Hollands. E. S., whom we called "Ned," was perhaps the best known throughout the country and was a finished actor of the so-called old school. It was the father of these boys who made that immortal remark which named a house of worship and made it famous. Holland, with others, approached the pastor of a large Fifth Avenue church to get him to

read the burial service for a dead actor. The minister refused, saying that actors could not be buried from his church. Seeing their despair, he repented a trifle and suggested that they try the little church just around the corner. The elder Holland raised his hat and said:
"God bless the Little Church Around the Corner."

Joe Holland is the only member of the family alive to-day, and he retired from the stage a few years ago. He became very deaf and finally paralyzed, but he has in no way let it ruin his life. With grit and persistence to a degree that should be an example to everyone, here is this man, no longer young, learning to read and, although totally deaf, to speak a beautiful French, sailing a boat better than most professionals and becoming the commodore of the yacht club of the seaport town where he lives in the summer, leading a full life where most people would have given up the ghost long ago.

Joe used to ask one or another of us to go out for a drive with him in the evening. I often wondered what pleasure it could give him and once wrote on his paper (which he always carried), "Why do you do this?" A most pathetic look came into his face.

"I know you are all just being good to me and you can't keep it up long, but somehow, if I can get you to drive in the moonlight where you wouldn't want to talk, anyway, we are just as much companions in those moments as if I were not deaf."

Such delicacy of feeling could not help but come out in his actions, and something Joe did once impressed me very much. Frank Worthing, the actor, was going to England, and, although it was not mentioned, he was going to die. Joe bought half a dozen calendars and sent a sheet to everyone of Frank's friends, asking that they write a note, a poem, or music, and, if they were artists, make a sketch. These he collected, had beautifully bound and put in the stateroom of the steamer so that "every day when Frank wakes up, he will receive a good morning from a friend." There is something very fine about a man who thinks that way.

The Players sets aside one day a year for the ladies on Shakespeare's birthday, when the feminine friends of the members are allowed to invade the house between the hours of two and six in the afternoon. Here the stage-struck young girl may come in hopes of meeting her favorite matinee hero, but I am afraid she is often disappointed, as the young actor is generally timid and stays away that day. It is left to the older gallants to offer a substitute and, if it did not seem like boasting of my own generation, I should say that a John Drew, a Francis Wilson, or that dean of the American stage, an F. F. Mackay is still just as capable of holding his own with the modern flapper as he ever was. Every American or visiting actress of importance has been entertained at these receptions, while special days have been given, on rare occasions, to a few. There was one for Clara Louise Kellogg, one for Mrs. Forbes-Robertson, and one for the divine Sarah.

Sarah is easily the one person alive to-day who knows how to give a personal thrill to everyone with whom she comes into contact. I remember seeing her a year or two ago, driving in New York in an open carriage. I did not recognize her at first, but some subtle influence compelled me to raise my hat and bow in homage to—I know not what. I got in return a thrilling smile. When Madame Bernhardt was guest of honor at The Players, she chose the landing of the stairway upon which to hold her court of honor, thereby stopping all progress up or down. It required all the tact of Mr. Booth to get her satellites away from her and finally move her to a more remote spot. How fine to be a queen and calmly acknowledge it to the world!

Once I was standing with Stanhope Forbes, the Royal Academician, and his brother at the Victoria Station. The brother was then the head of the continental affairs of the Chatham and Dover Railway. All of a sudden an official rushed up and asked what he should do about the next train for Dover, saying that there was a lady who was stopping everything by insisting that she must have her dog with her.

"Well, she can't," said Forbes.

"But she insists, sir, and she is making an awful row."

"That's no matter. Who is she?"

"She says her name is something like Sarah Bernhard," said the man.

"Good God!" said Forbes, wilting. "Give her the train."

In my student days there were two "gags" on Sarah. One was, "Yesterday an open carriage drove up to the Théâtre Français out of which got Sarah Bernhardt." The other was a caricature of Sarah and Sarcey, the critic; she taking fattening, and he antiobesity, pills. While he is interviewing her one of his pills falls out of the box and is eaten by Sarah's pet tiger, which is crouched beside her on the floor. The tiger immediately becomes a rug. Sarah screams and gives it one of her pills; it becomes a tiger again.

Duse is a direct contrast, at least to an outside observer, to Sarah. I was walking in Union Square, approaching the place where Tiffany used to be, when out of the door came a somewhat elegant, but modest-appearing figure in black, moving swiftly toward a private carriage at the curb. Something about her seemed familiar and I recognized Duse. Then I saw, to my astonishment, that she was lame. She did not impress me at all on the street, but on the stage she is the finest woman actor I have ever seen. Just realize the physical handicap—you never see it behind the footlights.

What a marvelous quality she gets out of that deathbed scene in "Camille"—her simple nightgown, her expression while waiting for the nurse to leave the room that she might reach under the bolster and get a letter from "him," the tragedy of her face as her fingers do not find it, and the breaking of the sky after the storm. Her hand had touched it! My respect rose for the great simplicity of this Italian actress.

Duse's Armand throws everything at her when he begins to think she cares for material things alone. I was telling this in The Players, when an actor, since knighted by the British government, said when *he* was acting Armand, he threw the bag of gold at her. Imagine a "bag" of gold. In my first days in Paris I saw the effects of the woman Dumas used for the heroine of "Camille" sold at auction.

Duse seemed to me a failure in "Magda." It had a

northern humor that required a Modjeska to sense. The second meeting with the former lover, the country baron, which has always been such a tragedy to most actresses, produced in Modjeska nothing but amusement and a sense of irony. She had the most beautiful hands and arms I ever saw. I once sent her a sonnet about them, and, although it was ten years later before I met her, she remembered it, saying that I was the only man who had discovered the secret of her appeal to her public. Even when she was old and played "La Bataille des Dames," her arms spoke to the audience and expressed what she wished.

I have met few actresses and have been behind the scenes in the theater only once or twice in my lifetime. Aside from paying my respects to that superb raconteur, Madame Yvette Guilbert, painting a portrait of the fascinating Nazimova, meeting Ellen Terry at tea, and being kissed by the beautiful Maxine Elliott for saying she was a better actor than her husband, I have come into personal contact with only one other—an American.

One rainy March day, while walking down Thirty-sixth Street when The Lambs was in that delightful house that Stanford White built, a closed carriage stopped between me and a Dutch stoop and a young woman got out. She looked up in the air, annoyed, and was going to scuttle up the steps, when I stepped forward to put my umbrella over her. I would have done the same for a washerwoman. She took my arm like a thoroughbred, and I saw her to her door. I had hardly gotten back to the walk when a boy from The Lambs, opposite, came up, saying, "Some gentlemen in the club wish to see you, sir." I crossed over and went upstairs to confront a line of men drawn up in martial order. There were twenty of them at least, who saluted, chanting:

"We wish to congratulate you on your skill as a professional masher. You are the first man who has succeeded in picking up Maude Adams."

This was my first and only meeting with her, but she must represent a type that I think beautiful, for one of the figures in a decoration that I made entirely out of my head resembles her so much that I have been asked many times if she did not pose for it. Miss Adams is one of the women who have helped to bring the stage to that position among the arts which men like Booth hoped it would reach.

Besides women, who always come first—who is it who says, "A man and his wife are one, and she's the one?"—The Players have entertained many notable men, both local and foreign. I met Theodore Roosevelt there for the first time. Not long after, I was in a Broadway car, when I saw him hanging on to a strap. The talk turned to war. I had been back from Europe only a short time and argued that America was not like England, a cuttlefish with a vulnerable body needing long arms to get its food and protect itself against its enemies; but rather like China, an oyster covered by hard shell. The large navy necessary to the first was superfluous to the second. I was met with a hurricane of abuse, to the amusement of the whole car. I did not know that Roosevelt had just been made Secretary of the Navy at Washington.

He told this story to us at the club. Two young Englishmen once turned up at his office and he sent them out to visit at his home in Oyster Bay. After some Saturday night festivities, when the women had all retired from the table, one of the young men started to give his impressions of America. He had been here two weeks.

"Mr. Roosevelt," he said, "do you not feel that one arriving in a foreign country is often shocked by things that the people living there have gotten used to? Now we have been horrified by the American habit of lynching. Cowardly, you'll admit; subversive of all law and barbarous?"

"Oh yes," said T. R., "that's only natural. Now, for instance, I am always shocked, when I land in England, at your habit of knocking down your womenfolk and kicking them in the stomach. Subversive of all law, cowardly you'll admit—"

"Of course, that happens only among the lower classes," replied the young man, laughing mightily.

Roosevelt then showed all his teeth in a grin and said, "Well, I don't think you boys will be asked to meet any lynchers at dinner."

Literature and the stage meet in The Players, but the stage generally gets the better of it. Brander Matthews was talking to me once about a play by him and Bronson Howard that was to open shortly. I asked him about its possibilities. "Oh," he said, "if it goes it will be called another of Bronson's successes, but if not it will be just another failure of mine."

Tarkington was one of the successful writer-playwrights even in those days. He is one of the few who have borne out their early promise, a man if there ever was one, with a joy of life that is abounding and a tremendous interest in his fellow beings, however humble. This natural curiosity about life and living seems to me a necessity for anyone who is to do big work in the world. He was modest about his writing. I went with him to the first night of Richard Mansfield in "Monsieur Beaucaire." We were in tweeds and sat up in the "nigger heaven." On the stairs I said, "I suppose you dramatized this?"

"Oh no," he answered, "Mansfield found a coat of mine he liked the looks of and I cut it over to fit him."

Tark. thinks so artistically and so cleverly. Here is a quotation from a letter written to me in 1914. He tells about Arnold Bennett criticizing the writing of a well-known author as being "too adult," then goes on to say:

"Adults make everybody uncomfortable; they want to. Most of the surprises saved for the startling tags of stories by Guy de Maupassant and O. Henry are merely little bursts of naturalness—some boyish thing. We recognize the truth of them at sight—and are surprised for the reason that a boy or an artist always catches us off our guard."

There was a galaxy of playwrights, among them Bronson Howard and Clyde Fitch, now gone as is that dear, kindly, clever man, William Dean Howells—one ever to be missed. I dined somewhere beside a charming girl, and the conversation drifted to the usual topic —marriage. I noticed across the table, just opposite me, the head of Mr. Howells twisting to right and left and trying to follow our talk, so I said rather maliciously:

"One of our cleverest writers has said, 'Man, even after eighteen hundred years of Christianity, is only imperfectly monogamous.'"

Applause from across the table. "Oh, that is fine, Simmons! Do you remember who said it?"

"Why, I found it in a book I have just been reading, called *Indian Summer*."

He suddenly drew back behind the flowers. "Oh, really!"

A few days afterward a short figure crowded up to me in the elevator of a large building with an: "Oh, Simmons, I looked that up. I *did* say it."

Kipling was not a member of The Players, on account of his book about the United States. He was not well known when he first came here, and no one was prophet enough to guess that he was to become the greatest name in English of his time. Many of the older men would not "stand for" his criticism of America. I heard old Edward Bell burst forth to Edwin Booth:

"If that cussed young Englishman ever comes into this club, I'll boot him out of it."

"Yes," said Booth, and immediately left for his own room, as he always did if anything seriously disturbed him.

In spite of these prejudices, Kipling was a visitor and became a friend to many of the members. I met him very casually, but admired him greatly, thinking his comments upon us a little harsh, but quite fair in many ways. His classification of England, France, and America to Brander Matthews is interesting. England he claimed, would die for liberty, but had a poor idea of equality; France would die for equality, but was hazy about fraternity; the United States was hazy about both liberty and equality, but went in heart and soul for fraternity; and that was why they would pay five cents to stand up in a street car when others sit down for the same price.

Zogbaum, the artist, once took Kipling over to the Brooklyn Navy Yard to meet Commander Evans, known as "Fighting Bob." He told me that they at once squatted down together and began to "swap" stories, nor did they do anything else until it was time for Kipling to go. He was silent on the ferryboat coming home, and upon landing in New York asked for the nearest bookseller, where he bought a copy of his own *Seven Seas*. Borrowing a pencil from Zogbaum, he sat in the shop and wrote for some time, then handing the book to the clerk, he asked him to mail it to Evans at the Navy Yard. That is the way we got the poem, "Zogbaum looks after his pencil and I look after my style."

Edwin Booth was the spirit and controlling force of The Players when I joined. It was his home and he lent an atmosphere of good breeding and repose that has endured to the present day. I was made a member in '91 and had the honor of seeing quite a bit of him before his death. His memory for names was already going, and almost every day after breakfast, when he and I would be sitting together in the reading room with the morning papers, he would suddenly look over his newspaper at me in a quizzical manner and say:

"Pardon me, sir, but you remind me forcibly of a family of dear friends of mine the—the—the—actor-painter people—the—"

"The Forbes-Robertsons?" I would suggest.

"Yes, the Forbes-Robertsons. Have you ever been mistaken for them?"

"Oh yes, several times in London," I would reply. And, the ice so broken, we would talk of all sorts of matters.

One of the most amusing stories told me by Mr. Booth was about a skull, which, by the way, is one of the relics of The Players to-day. A woman in St. Louis wrote to Booth's father and told him she was the widow of a friend of his who was hanged for murder. She asked permission to send the skull to the actor, suggesting that he use it in "Hamlet"—"Alas, poor Yorick! I knew him, Horatio!" Booth's father respectfully but disgustedly declined. But the woman was not to be so easily put off. Young Edwin Booth happened to be in St. Louis years later, when he received a letter from the same woman, offering to the son the present the father had refused. The property skull happened to be in pretty bad condition at that time, and as he had no sentiment about it, he replied that he should like to own it. Then Booth said:

"I was in bed one morning when a little nigger boy called to see me. He had a covered basket on his arm. I was curious to see what it contained, so asked him to open it up. Placing the basket on the table, he removed the top and a napkin which was underneath. Before I knew it, basket, cover, napkin flew up in the air, and the most frightened nigger you ever saw was flying down the passageway, while on the floor lay a skull."

Skied at the top of the staircase and as much out of sight as possible is a horrible portrait, larger than life size, of a well-known actress which was once presented to The Players by some of her relatives. Booth told me that on one Ladies' Day he suddenly saw these same relatives coming up the stairs.

"I was between them and the portrait," he said, "and I succeeded in keeping them from seeing it. Never in my life have I attempted to hold an audience as I tried to hold them. I am certain that they saw nothing but Edwin Booth until I had turned them around and backed them down the stairway again."

In connecting me with the Forbes-Robertson family Mr. Booth's thoughts would often wander to painting and he once told me how Sargent did the portrait which hangs in the club. As I remember, he sat for it in several places until one day Sargent asked him to have a look at it and say what he thought. Booth was loath to give an opinion, saying it was not to be his, anyway, and he was not the one to be suited. But Sargent pressed him until he said, "No, to be frank, I do not think it is a characteristic expression of mine."

"Are you very tired?" asked the painter.

"No."

"Then again, if you will."

"That time," said Booth, "I did get tired. He must have kept me standing an hour. What did he do? Why, he began by scraping out the entire head, then rubbed in some blackish stuff and painted that," pointing to the portrait.

Sargent must have done that wonderful head *premier coup* in less than an hour!

When I look at the mouth in this picture, I am reminded of what physiognomists say, that it is the indication of our true character more than any other part of the face. Compare the young and old photographs of Emerson, Oliver Wendell Holmes, and Booth, and you will see that it is within the power of anyone (no matter how plain at birth) to have at least one beautiful feature before he dies. One may not change the setting of the eyeball—because it is dependent upon bone, which cannot be altered. The setting of the eye is what gives the beauty. Those of Christine Nilsson, the singer, appeared on the stage as dark, luminous patches of velvet, for the socket cast a deep shadow; but when I met her personally, they were pale blue and ineffectual. It is the same with the nose.

But the mouth has no bones. It is merely flesh under the control of many muscles. Surgeons tell me that if one opens the cheek of a man who has lived an intellectual life, it is surprising how many muscles one finds. On the other hand, the cheek of an ignorant laborer does not contain much more than a muscle for chewing, for opening and shutting the mouth, and for grinning and frowning. The muscles that give irony, humor, and sadness are not there.

One of the prominent men in America, who has a beautiful mouth, has told me that when he was a boy his family objected so to it as an unsightly thing and that for many years he had the habit of covering it with his hand whenever he expressed himself, for fear of comment. The change has been within the man himself and the mouth has echoed it.

One may train a plain mouth to express the beauty of the human mind which controls it. Mr. Emerson had a hole in his face as a boy, not a mouth. Oliver Wendell

Holmes, the plainest man that ever lived, had a sweet, tender, one might say almost beautiful mouth, before he died. At any actors' gathering, one can see a dozen mouths like Booth's at twenty-five, but you will hunt a long time before finding the mouth Booth died with.

The delicacy shown in a study of Edwin Booth's face was borne out in his life. He did the most dignified thing in the world, to apologize for an act of his family against the American nation, by retiring for a period from public life after the assassination of Lincoln.

He was a man who felt keenly, both mentally and physically. He hated to be touched by anyone and loathed to be buttonholed. I remember a well-known writer of fiction, who had the extraordinary capacity for doing the wrong thing at the wrong time, eagerly presenting Mr. Booth with a playbill of the performance of the night at Ford's Theater. He simply arose and went to bed, as he always did on such occasions. Something of the same kind happened quite by accident when Booth was visiting at Nutley, the home of Laurence Hutton, secretary of The Players and an old friend of the actor's. Booth had retired for the night, when Hutton remembered with horror that at the foot of the bed and in full view upon the wall was one of those same playbills. He knew that if Booth saw it he would pack his bag and silently depart. What to do he did not know. Finally, waiting until he hoped Booth was asleep, he stole upstairs, crept into the room, and carried off the bill.

This sensitiveness about his family was not due entirely to the unfortunate occurrence of Lincoln's assassination, for it was shown in various ways. One evening a man, who had become a member of The Players by presenting the club with a second folio of Shakespeare, brought a friend in as a guest and presented him to Mr. Booth.

"Why, Mr. Booth," were the friend's first words, "I saw your father play. I was in the theater in St. Louis when, as Hamlet, he drove Laertes off the stage and out into the alleyway."

I saw Booth's eyes grow dark and ominous, and, rising, he said:

"Sir, I do not doubt that you *think* you saw that, but of course you did not. That incident never took place. It has been told to me as having happened in four or five different cities in this Union. Good night, sir." And he was off to bed.

Booth was a superman and showed it in many ways, but there is just one incident which he told me, himself, that proves him one in my eyes. When I see another man's mind working, I compare it with my own, and when I see that mind doing things that my own could never do, I realize there are grades of mentality that I do not understand and cannot reach; so I bow down and worship. I do not remember how the subject of religion ever arose between us, but he said that the Booths had always been superstitious folk and that he himself had at one time been almost a convinced spiritualist. Having made up his mind on the subject, he was talking to his friend Kellar, the magician. Kellar explained to him how all the wonderful miracles were worked at the seances and then performed before Booth's very eyes, tricks more wonderful than any he had seen done in the spiritualistic meetings. All of these Kellar explained also.

"Then," said Mr. Booth, "Kellar performed some miracles that surpassed all of those that had gone before. I asked him how he did them. 'Mr. Booth,' he said, 'I could show you with ease, but these are professional secrets and my own personal property, the explanations of which I must divulge to none!' On reflection, I decided that my former belief in such matters was harmful to my mind and I gave it up."

I can understand, if I had the will power, giving up any physical habit which I might feel was doing my body harm, but to have a mental disease, realize it, and cure it, is to me almost inconceivable.

Booth was seemingly of a serene nature, but he was introspective, and underneath that outward calm must have been a deep passion and sense of his own being. He told me that he never stepped upon the stage for a first night that his knees did not knock together horribly, but once before the footlights, he forgot himself entirely. His sense of humor was deep, and although he was always the quiet one of the group, he was probably the most appreciative of a funny story or a witty remark. Even when he lay in bed with his last illness his thoughts were upon these things, for he was much disturbed because he could not remember the point of a clever story he had heard.

For quite a while he had been failing. His legs had been giving out, so that he used the little trunk elevator to go up to his room; then he slowly grew feebler and feebler. I don't doubt he suffered, but he never let us know it, and his death was merely a gentle going away.

I remember the doctor coming downstairs and saying that he had just closed the eyes of a man more than seventy years old. Mr. Booth had crowded into fifty-nine years of life the experiences of an old man.

The Players is changed to-day. Of course, all old things must give way to new; but there is a certain fine sentiment that remains. Perhaps the young man does not appreciate the ideas upon which the club was founded and the traditions which have kept it together, but something of the old spirit is bound to be communicated to him on Pipe Nights or Founders' Night, or on those occasions when old Joe Holland is brought up in his big armchair. Then all gather around, a fire blazes in the great fireplace, Mr. Booth's eyes gaze down serenely from the wall above, and each one vies with his neighbor in handing a drink or a smoke to Joe, or telling him the latest story. Then will come in some wit or jester of the gang, and jokes will be told that are as old as the hills, but ever new. There is always a visitor or recent member to be delighted at the old gag when Harry Dixey goes up to Joe and says:

"Lend me five dollars, Joe."

"Go around to my good ear, Harry."

With great ceremony, Harry will walk around.

"Lend me ten dollars, Joe."

"Go back to my five-dollar ear, Harry."

Chapter XIV: American Humor

A HUMPBACK stood in front of Des Miriltons, a fashionable club of Paris. Day and night his pathetic figure would be seen, a piteous expression on his face, as he made his silent appeal to the men going into the building—some to try their fortune at the gaming table. The French are a superstitious race and have a thousand little ceremonies to lure the great god Luck, one of the most efficacious being to rub the hump of an *enfant d'escalier*—one born on a staircase. I have seen gold pieces frequently change hands, as a member of this club rushed in or out, so this particular deformity proved fortunate, for the humpback died wealthy.

Now a hump, if it be a conspicuous infirmity, is never laughed at. One is born with it and it is therefore not one's fault. But deformities are not all physical. I come of five generations of parsons who talked for a living; also, at school, as I have said before, it was the habit of the teacher to give credit to the boy who shouted his lessons the loudest. This helped along the trouble, and I claim that talking too much is just as much a mental hump as a twisted back is a physical one, and, as such, should be pitied.

My brother used to say that any newcomer to the house where we lived thought at first that everyone was suffering from some throat disease. After a while however, he found that it was only hoarseness from talking too much. I remember, as a boy, the sounds in the Old Manse. With mother upstairs making beds, my sister halfway down, one aunt in the sitting room, and another in the kitchen, there was a sort of continuous rattle of words—never stopped, but only interrupted by the opening and shutting of doors: "Lizzie, when you go downtown, don't forget to buy —but she won't need—oh yes, I will if—it's forty inches wide, and that—but Sophie—well, red, if you— think blue will fade terr—in that case you'd bet— two yards are—why not you see the sleeves will take— oh, let her alone, she'll get it all ri—"

There is a story of this disease of mine that Jules Guerin is fond of telling. Of course, it never happened, but it makes a good tale. There was to be a contest between the greatest talkers in the East and West. A man from the Bohemian Club in San Francisco and myself were chosen. There was money bet; we were put in a locked room with a loaf of bread and a pitcher of water apiece. After three days the sounds of voices died down and the anxious listeners broke open the door. The Western talker was lying dead and I lay beside him, dying and *whispering* in his ear.

Sometimes this talk of mine has produced startling results. I had a dear friend, now dead, whose son was connected with a monthly magazine. One day I saw in it a botched attempt, as I thought, to tell, as his own, a wonderful story of Anatole France's. I was indignant and told everyone I would make it my business to "call that young man down." Some time after, I was sitting at the writing table at The Players when the boy came up to me, saying:

"I hear you have a bone to pick with me?"

"Yes," I said. "By what right do you take one of

the best stories of Anatole France's and give him no credit?"

"This is the first time that I've heard it *is* his," answered the youngster. "Why, Mr. Simmons, I got it from dad, who said that you had told it to him here in the club!"

Rather a stiff "come-back."

There have been so many criticisms of my talk that I like to remember the times when I have not been too much of a pest. It has always managed to put babies to sleep, and several times it has quieted nervous, distracted invalids. There is a hypnotic quality about it, if used consciously. Once, when quite young, I amused myself by *willing* my mother to lift her hand. She obeyed, and her giggling frightened me terribly. Another time, much later, I succeeded in swaying a mob of people in an entirely new direction by jumping on the tail of a cart and inciting them to action. These incidents taught me to use this power cautiously, which partly accounts for my inconsequential babbling.

In the St. Botolph Club in Boston I met a very clever man named Eichberg, a musician of ability who had been a pupil of Liszt. I had just returned from a week's absence when I saw him sitting in his accustomed corner, which I had always avoided, thinking he did not care for me. This time he called me over.

"I must tell you something," he said. "When one first meets you, one feels as if one has moved to a house which gives upon a railway track and cannot sleep on account of the damnable noise; but you go, and one finds that he has really moved to a house in the country and cannot sleep for the damnable silence. I am glad to see you back."

Much as my friends may laugh at this statement, there *are* times when I have listened. Frederick Villiers was the most entrancing talker one could imagine, and I protest I was dumb in his presence lest I miss one word of his conversation. Desdemona never heard anything like what I got from him. This is at least one refutation of the statement of my dear friend Oliver Herford, who said:

"Anyone can lead Ned (meaning me) up to a pause, but no man can make him take it."

In the earliest 'nineties, Herford and I had rooms beside each other in the St. Botolph Club in Boston. In front of our doors was a card printed in scarlet, indicating the direction of the fire escape. One day, seeing his chance, Oliver took this sign into his room and, blotting out the word "fire," skillfully lettered in my name in its place and hung it up again. Shortly after that a man came rushing downstairs, boiling over with mirth, yelling for all to come up to the top story. There was the sign, as brilliantly red as ever, but reading:

"Escape in case of Simmons!"

Stories of Oliver Herford come crowding to memory, topsy-turvy, one over another, and although perhaps they should have no place here among recollections of those long since passed away, his type of wit is mellow when it is born and does not need time to soften its edge. Oliver is the child of Whimsey; the eternal Puck or the Peter Pan; he has no age and is of no age; like Topsy, I believe he just "growed." His fun is full of naïveté and childlike subterfuges; no task is too arduous for him if there be a joke at the end; and he pokes that droll mind of his into the oddest crooks and corners in the daintiest way.

I recall being with him in a restaurant when a man much the worse for liquor approached our table and almost kissed him in his desire to be friendly. Finally getting it into his drunken head that he was receiving no response to his advances, he said:

"I don't believe that you remember me, Mr. Herford."

"I don't recognize your face," said Oliver, "but your manner is damn familiar."

I was in Oliver's studio one day when a strange knock came at the door—three long ones and two short raps. "S-h-h-h!" he said, and we both kept quiet. After a sufficient time had elapsed for the person to have departed, I asked him for an explanation. It seemed that —— was in the habit of calling and boring Oliver terribly, so he told him that in the future he intended opening the door only to his special friends, to whom he would give a private knock.

It needs some uncommon quirk for a man's mind to work in this fashion. Instead of giving the private signal to his friends, he gave it to his one particular aversion, so that he could recognize it instantly and get rid of him quite neatly and without malice.

Another time, Oliver invited me to dine with him. We took a cab at the door of The Players. On the way to the restaurant he went through his pockets and found he hadn't a cent. As I was broke myself, I decided we were in a pickle. Not so Oliver. We alighted at the door of a prominent café and Oliver approached the cabman:

"Say, dear fellow," he began, and the driver, thinking he was going to be held up for the fare, was disposed to be cross. But this was too trifling a matter for Oliver to even mention.

"Say, dear fellow," he continued, in his most confiding way, "I have invited my friend here to dine and I find I have forgotten my money. Could you—now I wonder if you could be a good chap and lend me ten dollars?"

To my astonishment, the man, taken completely unawares, pulled out a roll of bills and handed Oliver one of them.

One cannot be naïve by will power; the danger in consciously striving to be childlike is that one becomes childish, and that is a very different matter. I always think of Oliver Herford when I recall what Guy De Maupassant said upon being challenged to make a new Beatitude—

"Thrice blessed are the naïve, for they shall never see *but* God."

One of the brightest and most witty men I knew in the old days was the actor, Maurice Barrymore, father of the present galaxy of stage folk of that name. A beautiful body—I was told that he had been the amateur champion middleweight of England—a face more Celtic than Saxon, Barry was the originator of *bons mots* that have gone all over the country. I do not remember much about his acting, but I remember his delightful companionship late at night (for he was a highly sensitive man who burned the candle at both ends), his brilliant conversation, his great intelligence and love of the fine things of life, his finesse, and his swiftness of thinking.

Barry and I were sitting together one night at the Lambs' Club when a big fellow came up to our table and, hammering on it, said:

"Maurice Barrymore, you are a —— —— liar!"

"Oh no," said Barry, quietly, "not if *you* say so."

Once at the old Fifth Avenue Hotel he was taking a drink with some friends, when he heard a voice mumbling behind him something about a blankety, blank actor. He immediately turned and told the man to shut up, adding a well-known phrase which indicated that he was the son, on his maternal side, of a domestic animal we all know. The man rose and came forward, swinging his arms and shouting wildly:

"You call me that? By God! I wish I had you in Louisville! You wouldn't dare to call me that in Louisville!"

Barry knew that he was not really dangerous, and, besides, he was afraid of no one, so he calmly walked up to the stranger and, putting his arm affectionately about him, said:

"Oh, if your mother's reputation is a question of geography, come and have a drink."

The extreme delicacy of Barry was shown in many ways—chiefly in his kindness to any young actor who was trying to get ahead. He was not the type to help by a lot of talk, but by little attentions quietly shown. When he was playing Rawdon Crawley with Mrs. Fiske in "Becky Sharp," there was a young countryman of his, newly come over from England, who had the part of Dobbin. Barry was notoriously careless of his appearance on the stage, but in this case he groomed himself to the eyes just to give the younger man a chance to shine by contrast. He was perfectly willing to be what in vaudeville parlance is called a "feeder," if it were for the good of the play or anyone in it.

Englishmen sometimes twitted Barry for his love of America, and he often had to stand quips from us about his British parentage. An American once stuck a coin in his eye and, in a leering manner, walked up to Barry, singing that famous song of Henry Dixey's called, "It's English, You Know." Thinking to add a little flavor and more insult, the man made a vulgar remark. Barry turned to him quietly and said:

"No, it is not the English I know."

Once a crowd of English actors started to have some fun with Barry about his long residence in America and his American marriage. Then they started on the American language.

"Why you see the way they spell over here," they cried. "Good old *humour* and *honour* have become *humor* and *honor*."

"Yes," said Barry. "You see, they don't think they have to come to you for either one of these qualities, so in such matters they leave "u" out.

Speaking of "humor," I like to think of Anatole France's brilliant illumination of the word, which, paraphrased, runs something like this: "The Angel of Humor is sent us that she may teach us to laugh at the wicked and foolish, whom, without her aid, we might have the weakness to hate." In my reading of funny stories, the really good ones have an element of sadness; also I have watched the development of the faces of the humorists I have known. As they grow older the lines of mirth are sure to be backed by signs of very deep feeling. Humor is distinct from wit (which is the joyousness of childhood) and comes after suffering, proving a man to have graduated from the cave-dweller class. Savages are bitter and yell when hurt, but a gentleman keeps quiet. Humor, to me, is the cry of a well-bred man in pain.

When we New Englanders tell stories of ourselves and our forbears, they are generally based fundamentally on the hard lives, or the characteristic qualities that resulted from the hard lives, which those first settlers on the coast of the Atlantic were forced to lead. Their sense of humor conceals an infinitude of suffering, as does that of the men who live in the hills of Kentucky. Professor Shaler of Harvard told me that he had found them very much alike in their laconicism and understatement—two parents of humor.

To illustrate what I mean—my mother's sewing woman in Concord, the dried-up individual who made my breeches, always with a mouthful of pins—was asked by the neighbors when her mother died:

"Was she willin' to go?"

"Willin'! My dear, she was obleeged."

"Did she leave anythin'?"

"Yes, she left everythin'. Didn't take nothin' with her."

A story which gives a picture of the drudgery so great that they were always careful to save themselves the smallest extra task is of the old farmer sitting with his wife beside the kitchen table in the evening. A newspaper is in his hand, a kerosene lamp illuminates the room, and his feet, incased in woolen stockings, are in the cooling oven. The grandfather's clock strikes nine.

"Time to go to bed, Maria."

"Yes, Eben."

She precedes him with the lamp, and he follows with his shoes in his hand. At the foot of the staircase he stops and says:

"Did you wipe the sink, Maria?"

"Why, of course!"

They proceed. When she is at the top and he is half way up, she leans over the balustrade, saying:

"What made you ask me that, Eben?"

"Well, I *did* feel as if I'd like a drink of water, but if you've wiped the sink I guess I'll put it off till to-morrer."

There are many stories of the Yankee thrift, but one very old one is hard to beat. A farmer, in the days when a grocer also kept a bar, drives up to the country store and says:

"How much are yer givin' fer eggs?"

"Cent apiece," says the grocer.

"My wife wants a darnin' needle. What do yer ask fer 'em?" "Cent apiece," again from the grocer.

The farmer gets off his seat, takes out a weight, ties it to the horse's head, and drops it on the road. Going to the back of the wagon, he reaches into a basket and takes out one egg, carrying it carefully into the grocery.

"I'll swap yer this fer a darnin' needle."

The grocer gives him the needle and takes the egg. The farmer lingers.

"Don't yer treat on a trade?"

The grocer looks at him curiously, swears, and then says:

"What'll yer have?"

"Guess I'll hev an egg flip."

The grocer takes the egg, which is still on the counter, breaks it into the glass, and—two yolks appear.

"Hold on!" yells the farmer, "that's a double yoker. Give me another darning needle!"

Mark Twain's mind was a treasure house of hundreds of stories of this type—his humor was so essentially American. My most vivid memory of Sam Clemens is being with him around the billiard table in The Players. He thought he could play Chicago pool, and in the earlier 'nineties used to choose me for an adversary. I was younger and a better player than he. One day, having beaten him one game, I dared to be winning another. He swore at me for some shot I had made, so I said over my shoulder:

"Don't be profane."

Simulating great anger (he was funniest when he pretended gruffness) his mustache bristled, his eyes glared, his chest stuck out, and he marched up to me, his cue banging on the floor to emphasize each word:

"Young man, you do not even know what profanity is. Profanity, sir, is the unnecessary use of profane words and, applied to you, no such use is unnecessary. Go on with your —— —— game."

Mr. Clemens was very individual in his tastes. He was fond of bread and had missed it in Europe. He used to say that the British bread was putty and the French bread all crust. His drinks were always made for him in exactly the same way. His habits were not those of a fussy old man, but rather of a monogamous person who, having fallen in love once, remained true all his life. I never saw him the least bit intoxicated, but he certainly was not an abstainer. The hottest day of summer would see him with a steaming pitcher before him from which he poured a hot punch of Scotch, always mixed in the same way.

He was a genial fellow in a crowd of people and would undoubtedly have made a wonderful politician. I was hailed by him at the Grand Central Station one day. It was in the winter and he was clothed in the pure white that he affected in his later years. With his white hair and pink face, this made him so conspicuous that we were soon the center of an interested group of people, exactly as if we had been a dog fight. This always acted a stimulant upon Clemens, and he began to hold forth in the most extravagant fashion. At last he said:

"Now I must get my train—but let me see—I have forgotten something. Oh, I know! I have forgotten my wife." Then appealing to the crowd, he called: "Does anyone here happen to know where Mrs. Clemens is?"

A dozen voices answered in the affirmative, and some one ran to fetch her. Mark Twain stood perfectly still until she was escorted to his side by an admiring bystander. I can imagine Roosevelt doing this, but Mr. Emerson or Woodrow Wilson—never.

A deep sense of civic responsibility was one of Mr.

Clemens's most marked characteristics. His idea was that every man in a community should consider himself responsible if things did not go well, and not be too lazy to raise a kick. He told me of dining in a Pullman car once where the menu stated there was a selection of roast beef or chicken. He ordered the chicken, was told there was none left, so made up his mind to be contented with the roast beef. Before he had finished, the conductor of the car came in and the negro waiter served him with chicken.

"He was a servant of the company and I was a patron," Clemens said, "and I rose and proclaimed that that was my roast chicken. I did not get it, but when I arrived home I wrote to the company president and received an apology. If you have a complaint, do not write to a small official, for it will never penetrate upward, but if you write to the highest, it may leak down."

Another time, coming from Hartford with his daughter, he took a green car at the station. It was very crowded and they had to stand. Mr. Clemens protested at the conductor pushing them about and punching his daughter in the ribs as he collected the fares. Whereupon he said:

"Jesus Christ! Do you think you own this car?"

"*I* don't mind being called that," said the humorist, "but my daughter lives in Hartford and is not used to such language. Her feelings were hurt."

They got off at the car barn and, looking about for some one with whom to register a "kick," met Billy Laffan (part owner and editor of the *Sun*), who advised them to let the newspaper do the kicking.

Sam wrote his troubles to the *Sun*. The next day the *Tribune* (it was an august sheet in those days) came out with an editorial saying that it was bad taste on the part of Mark Twain to make fun of the Holy Name; that they had looked up the matter and found that it was all a figment of his imagination. This was answered, the following day, with a letter from the president of the car line, saying that the story *was* true, that the offending conductor had been discharged, and that he (the president) wished to thank Mr. Clemens publicly for having helped them in the matter.

The sequel to the occurrence was told me by Mr. Clemens himself.

"Some time after, I was at my home in Hartford, when my maid came into my study to say that there was a man calling upon me. She showed in a fellow I did not recognize. He began by saying:

"'Mr. Clemens, I am the man who called you Jesus Christ.'"

"'Admit your mistake?' I asked."

"'Yes, and I have come to ask a favor. Don't you think the public is as much to blame as I am? When I get tired I begin to get hasty, and I have never been called down before. If the public had done its duty in the beginning, I would not have gotten into trouble. I have a wife and four children to support and the president of the company will not take me back unless you write a letter and ask him.'

"Of course, I wrote the letter."

I often heard Mr. Clemens expatiate on his well-known subject—the Almighty Dollar. He had been out West where gold was struck in abundance, and he could not see any difference between the nationalities in the scramble to get there first. The English were always twitting us about our love of money, but, as he said:

"I admit we are hunting for the almighty dollar, but the Englishman is hunting just as hard for the almighty penny."

As to fear, Roosevelt was talking in the club shortly after the Spanish War, saying that every man's experience is the same, that he is always horribly afraid before his first battle, but that it wears off. Then he appealed to Clemens, asking him if it were not his feeling during the Civil War.

"Yes," Clemens answered, "I was scared to death at my first battle, but it seems to have been different with you. Yours wore off. My fear stuck to me during the whole war."

Whatever his physical fear, his mental bravery was phenomenal. It requires a particular kind of courage for a man to start all over again, as he did, in his later years. After losing all his money in the publishing business, he picked up the pieces and traveled about the world, lecturing, to get the money to pay back his indebtedness, sixty per cent of which was to his wife. This made no difference to a gentleman, and he treated her exactly as if she were a strange creditor. He used to come to The Players while he was going through his bankruptcy proceedings. It seemed to be a good place to get rid of his troubles. When he wasn't being funny, he pretended to be cross; but when he was quiet, I noticed his face was very sad.

He was an intensely American type in looks, and it was hard to get beyond the barrier he made for himself; but once he chose to let you in, his eyes said, "Down to you, sir," and you saw the superman.

It was more his manner of saying than what he said that made Mr. Clemens so amusing. I was told he sat at a dinner table and talked for twenty minutes upon the name Brander Matthews, with everyone exploding in laughter. He spoke through his nose slowly and with curious drawl, and repeated his thoughts many times, each variation being funnier than the preceding one, until he worked up to a screaming climax.

But when he wanted to be serious he made you feel (as Priam says of Ulysses), "Words, like winter snowflakes, fell from his mouth. Then might no man compare with Ulysses." One afternoon a crowd of us were in the club, drinking and making frivolous talk. Clemens was doing more than holding his own with the best of us, when suddenly a thought seemed to strike him. He left for a moment, and when he returned, the expression of his eyes was changed. He had a book in his hand and he sat down, saying:

"I will now read you the greatest piece of prose since the days of Marlowe."

And then, his nasal twang gone, his voice attaining a beautiful sonority, he read, as no one else could have done it—the Gettysburg Speech. It was one of the big moments of my life.

I remember well a comment he made afterward:

"If any one of you men ever have a class in English," he said, "give them this. Let them try to put an adverb after the word *here*. No one but Lincoln could have thought of using, 'That we here *highly* resolve.' No! No! No one!"

The last time I saw Mark Twain was at a luncheon at Delmonico's, given by one of my friends in honor of a British army attaché. I got there rather early and my host was worried for fear his guest of honor would be disappointed in Mr. Clemens. He was getting old and did not perform readily. I said:

"Will you leave it to me? I'll make him show off; but you must promise not to be surprised at anything and to back me up, however foolish I may act."

He promised.

I went to the butler and asked him to see that there was a man behind Mr. Clemens to refill his glass as soon as he took a sip. He did not drink much in those days, so it was important he must not be given a chance to refuse. Before the chill of the beginning of the lunch had passed off, I rose and said to my host:

"I want to tell a story."

Derision from the others: "He talks all the time!" "Shut up!" They even threw bread at me to keep me quiet. But I insisted in a silly way, as if I were drunk, and my host backed me up. Then I began to tell one of Mr. Clemens's pet stories in such a manner that no one but he would recognize it. I mixed it all up and finally missed the point altogether, sitting down with a fatuous grin.

He couldn't stand it. His face grew red, he bristled and glared, reached for his cocktail, downed it, and rose.

"That was a good story," he said, indignantly, "but *he* can't tell it. This is the way it should go." And he told it in his inimitable way.

After that nothing could stop him. He was witty, clever, and the life of the lunch. The old Clemens girded on his armor and went out again arrayed for battle; but I often wonder if he went to his grave thinking I was as much of an ass as I appeared that day.

Chapter XV: Paint and Painters

AN old college friend of mine once wrote to me and asked what he should do about his son, who was in Harvard, but wished to give up college and become a painter. I answered and said: "Discourage him; discourage him to the point of starvation, for if he be sincere in his love of the fine arts, he will pay no attention to you. No man is a real artist unless he finds the impetus toward it so great that he sticks to it in spite of every deprivation." I do not know whether my friend took my advice or not, but at any rate his son, Barry Faulkner, has become, with or without discouragements, one of our foremost younger decorative painters.

Emerson understood, perhaps better than anyone, as he tells us in his

To An Artist

Forget the hut and seek the palace,
Reck not what the people say,
For where'er the trees grow biggest
Huntsmen find the easiest Way.

George Lathrop told me that shortly after his marriage with one of the daughters of Nathaniel Hawthorne he was very much surprised at receiving a formal visit from Mr. Emerson one afternoon. The poet was old then and was not in the habit of going about much, so the call portended something of importance. After the usual conversation, Emerson said, pointedly:

"Mr. Lathrop, I understand that you have chosen words as a means of livelihood?"

"Yes, sir," said Lathrop.

"And have married?" continued Emerson. "An added insanity?"

Poverty is one of the strongest enemies that the artist has to fight. We should each one have a Mæcenas to keep us; I know of but one or two cases in this country where men have succeeded in gaining membership in the first rank in the opinion of other artists (for they are his peers and deciding fact) without money behind them. They inherit it, they marry it, or they are backed by some one so that they may have a security of rental, food, and materials. There is not enough market for the fine arts that a man may live by them alone.

After all, it is as it should be. We are a young nation, really in our infancy, and babies do not need art until they have been fed and kept warm. It takes many generations of growing wheat until the body is ready for something finer. So far, the fine arts have been an indication of the coming death of the country that produced them—like a bush or vine, a nation flowers and then dies. Only the seeds grow, and those in another place. If I were asked to give my opinion, I would vote against forcing the people to accept the fine arts, as I would vote against giving a baby tobacco or alcohol, which would most assuredly stop its growth. (However, Emerson says, "America has a genius for making new law," and it may be that we can change this. I sincerely hope so.)

All this is hard for the artist whose only desire is to catch and keep some of the beauty that he finds about him, and if he is forced to depend upon the sale of these dreams to provide him with bread and butter, he is quite liable to starvation or cynicism. The ordinary person cannot possibly realize how close to the wind an idealist often gets. To say that you are "broke" means nothing to the business man. I once heard one of them tell a painter friend of mine that it was all wrong for him to owe his washerwoman, that he should do, as all practical folk did, go down and hypothecate a bond! It is unethical for an artist (as it is for a professional man) to go into the courts-or to advertise. He must not ask for work or show that he is hard up in any way, and, like the stage folk, he must hold his work at a high price. The distance between the price of a work of art and the money one can obtain for it is a long road, however. I was astonished to read in a newspaper, not long ago, that a picture of mine, bought by a well-known millionaire, was appraised, at his death, for exactly ten times the amount I had received for it not more than ten years before.

If a man dies or goes crazy—so that the source of supply is definitely cut off—his work immediately jumps in value. I often think of John Twachtman, struggling along without any particular recognition, selling his pictures for little or nothing, and almost bankrupt when he died. His brother painters knew the value of his work and resolved to make the public see it. The dealers fought shy of it, as he had not been a popular seller when alive. Choosing the right week in February and the proper gallery (the American Art Association) such men as Thomas Dewing and Alden Weir, who commanded a position in the fine arts in this country, were joined by one of the unusual people in America—a man with a strange combination of business ability, overwhelmed by a love of beauty—Thomas W. Clarke. Twachtman's pictures, of which there were a great many, were properly placed before the public, with the result that his bills were paid and a substantial sum realized for his widow. A number of his best canvases were reserved so that Mrs. Twachtman might have them for a nest egg.

What a contrast while he was alive! One friend of his has in his possession to-day many exquisite sketches which he purchased from time to time for twenty-five dollars apiece. They are now worth thousands. I remember walking wearily up and down Fifth Avenue all of one afternoon with Twachtman, each of us with one of his unframed landscapes under his arm, visiting dealer after dealer in a vain effort to sell one of them for twenty-five dollars in order that he might obtain enough money to remain a member of The Players. In one gallery we were offered fifteen dollars. By that time we were quite tired, and I had to restrain John from striking the man. In sadness we returned to the club and placing the canvases in the cloak room, went downstairs to cheer ourselves with a drink, where I (talking as usual) told our afternoon's experience to a limited number of friends. I had hardly finished when the clerk reached out through the side window and handed John a receipted bill for his dues. Stanford White had heard the story and paid them.

As a sequel to this tale: a year or two ago at a picture shop of the second rate—the kind that is hung

with framed canvases to the ceiling—I saw in the
window, in a gorgeous and very vulgar frame, one of
those pictures that we had carried unsuccessfully
along the Avenue so long ago. On a card in large
letters was printed, "One of the greatest landscapes
of John Twachtman." I went in and inquired the
price. It was thirty-five hundred dollars!

Twachtman painted such exquisite small things.
It made no difference to him—the size, shape, or
texture of his material—he could always conjure up
an idea that fitted it perfectly. Whenever I was working at a large decoration he would come up to my
studio and carry away the triangular pieces of canvas
that inevitably come off a work of this kind. I suppose
the pictures he made on them have sold for more,
since he died, than all of my decorations put together.

He looked like a faun; one would expect, upon
moving back his hair, to find some furry ears. He
had the nature of a faun. There was no place for him
in the nineteenth century; he would have been a
normal creature in the Golden Age. His simplicity
of mind showed in his work. I have stood before one of
his landscapes and thought: "How *did* you do it?
How *could* you see the thing so simply?" My mind is
always cluttered up with details, but, for him, they just
did not exist. I cannot imagine John in an airplane;
it would have been incongruous. His place was in the
fields, living on berries and herbs, refreshing himself
at the brooks and streams, as he went his merry way,
here and there catching and keeping for the world
a fleeting glimpse of Nature as she showed her secret
self to him. John Twachtman is as good an example

as I know, of my own definition of an artist—"*one who shall show you the stars during the daytime.*"

All the world is striving to manufacture what the people want, but an artist is in an entirely different position. There is no value to a picture at the pawnbroker's. You can borrow practically nothing on a Corot; you can get more on the frame than on the canvas.

One day when I was very hard up, a young architect from Paris who was building the New Amsterdam Theater here telephoned me that Mr. Finn had recommended me to do some work for him. It appears that he had made a contract with a certain painter for a series of panels representing the development of the North River. Although the contract had been running two years and the theater was to open in two weeks, the painter had only half finished the work. There was nothing to do, as the theater *must* open, and Mr. Finn had told him I was the only man who could do them in a hurry, but he would have to pay a stiff price. I asked him what I thought was fair (I never know what my work is worth), and choosing the subjects, running from Eric the Red to the last international yacht race, I began.

I was living at that time in a studio which had formerly been a stable, with a cement floor graded to the central hole, where there was an outlet to the sewer. Just before this the sewer had become stopped up and, as it had rained heavily, the water had gathered on the studio floor. There was no time to fix it; I had only two weeks to do six panels, each one more than five feet long, and could not have the plumbers messing around. Of course, I had no money to hire another place to work. I had a time! Every morning I raced to the Library to look up the historical facts, and then came home to make my compositions. All this while there were four inches of water on a level all over the floor, a line of bricks to walk from my easel to my painting table, and another line from the table back to where I could get a point of view of my work. Of necessity, from the door to the bed was a third brick pathway. Every now and then, in the excitement of creation, I would fall off of my improvised bridges and drench my feet. But youth is lucky and I escaped pneumonia—also I finished the panels in time.

At another time in my life, I found myself with a lot of pictures and no money. There were four people depending upon me, no work, and nothing I could realize upon. On awakening one morning I discovered that the entire capital of the group was one nickel, which I found in a baby's bank. This had been robbed sundry times before, but the little coin had somehow been missed. It was necessary to do something, and that immediately. A friend who had dined with us the evening before upon a stew made of thirty-five cents' worth of beef neck and some potatoes had suggested that a certain elderly banker, the silent partner of a well-known financier, had just "turned down" a proposition made to him for an overmantel decoration. The artist had asked too much and my friend suggested that I go and make a bid.

The banker's office was away downtown, and, arrayed in white shoes and hat and my best white serge suit from London (it was one of the hottest days of the year), I marched out with my nickel in my pocket. At that time I was living up on Ninety-sixth Street, so I sauntered casually over to the subway station, pushed the coin nonchalantly through the grating of the ticket office. The man promptly shoved it back with the curt remark, "No good." I let it fall on the floor; it dropped with a dull thud and I threw it angrily away, not thinking so much of my own disappointment, but disgusted with the person who had been so cruel as to cheat a baby by putting a lead nickel into its bank.

However, I still had a journey to make, and gazed about, looking for an idea. My eye fell upon the shop of my barber where I was in the habit of having my hair cut. Going in, I asked him to lend me some change. My clothes and my manner must have deceived him, for he pressed me to take a dollar, although I asked only for a dime and said that I would not be responsible for returning more. Armed with the ten cents, I was on my way.

Mr. Lungren, for it was he, was in his office, received my proposal with enthusiasm, and I got my order. He was just about to dismiss me politely, when I said I must have one third cash on the spot. He asked why, evidently thinking I did not trust him, but I replied with Bill Nye's well-known story of going into a shabby little restaurant, ordering two boiled eggs, and receiving a check for one dollar. Upon a demand for the reason for such an exorbitant charge, the proprietor replies:

"Look around you. I need the money."

Mr. Lungren laughed and started to make out a

check, but I insisted upon currency, saying that a check was only a promise to pay and no good to a drowning man. Then I added, "I want it in small bills, please." I got it in twenties and tens.

On the way home, I stopped at every subway station, went up to the surface, and bought a drink and broke one of the bills. By the time I had traveled from Wall Street to Ninety-sixth Street my mind was in a very mellow condition and my pockets bulging in every direction. Marching into the house, I yelled for the startled members of my family and, emptying my pockets, hurled the bills into the air so that they flew into every part of the room. These high spots in a man's life are worth all the years of poverty and struggle.

In spite of the fact of the manner of my receiving the order, I think I made a pretty good representation of "Hospitality" for Mr. Lungren.

During these periods of "hardupness" in my life, I was constantly having the strangest things happen— things that almost made me believe in miracles. I am often criticized for being too optimistic, but my experience has made me so. Luck has always come to me out of the empty air. The telephone, the mail, a chance meeting with a friend, any one of a thousand occurrences may happen to change the tide of affairs at any moment. Oftentimes, in Europe, would come a letter from mother with a wholly unexpected check. Mothers seem to have a seventh sense which tells them when their children need help, and I always felt that there was an especial bond of sympathy between my mother and myself. She probably knew that I was rather an outcast and needed her more than the others, and I am sure that I understood her better than anyone else. For example, when I painted mother's portrait, everyone criticized me because I did not have her knitting. I never saw my mother knit; she did not have time. Whenever she had a moment's leisure to sit down, she had some sewing in her hand, so I made her mending a stocking.

This was a time of portraits—I did President Hill of Harvard, Mr. Sayre of Bethlehem, and many others —and small decorations, including several overmantels and ceilings, but finally, out of the clear sky came along one of the largest orders that I ever received—to help do the Capitol of the state of Minnesota, at St. Paul.

It was rather a big idea for a state to decorate its building so extensively, and Cass Gilbert, the architect, deserves a great deal of credit for the venture. I was given four huge panels below the dome of the rotunda. They were about twenty-eight feet long and thirteen in height. Placed ninety feet from the ground, they looked like postage stamps when finished. The two rooms where the Supreme Court and the House of Representatives met were given to Blashfield and La Farge.

The subject chosen was the Settling of the West. The first panel represents the Young Man Leaving Home; the second, the Cleaning Up of the Land; the third, Breaking the Soil, which he does by lifting a great stone out of a hole from which issues a young girl bearing maize; and the last, the Young Man Is Crowned and sends the Four Winds to the Four Quarters of the globe bearing the gifts of Min-

"CLEANSING THE SOIL OF THE BAD ELEMENTS"
Panel by Edward Simmons, Minnesota State Capitol, St. Paul
Copyright by Edward Simmons; from a Copley Print, copyright by Curtis & Cameron, Publishers, Boston

nesota. In every panel he is accompanied by Hope and Minerva.

There were several guides in the Capitol employed to show the visitors around and explain the sights to them. I thought it would be splendid for me to give them special instructions about my work, so that they would not make the usual ludicrous mistakes. But guides seem to be a different breed of animal chosen for the wide range of their imaginations. I supposed everything was going all right, when one day a particularly loquacious one came to me and showed me a miniature palette in his buttonhole, telling me he was an artist himself and belonged to a club of artists. He knew all about the ladies in my decoration—the one veiled in chiffon (which I had made for Hope) he called Sin, entirely neglecting the nude woman in the foreground (Sin) clinging to a grizzly (Savagery). He had probably received his early education in and about a Burlesque show.

It was in St. Paul that I saw the most wonderful collection of paintings ever gathered together (as far as I know) by a private individual. Mr. J. J. Hill had built a special room, especially lighted with everything adequate to show them to the best advantage. And such pictures! He had numbers of Corots—one of the nude Magdelen—Millet's "Goose Girl," and beautiful Daubignys. One Corot (of Biblis) was stunning. I could have lain on my back under the trees of the landscape and gone miles and miles through the distances between the clouds.

There were capitals and capitols to decorate after St. Paul, but none of them such a large order. In the Law

Courts of Mercer, Pennsylvania, I put figures representing the different characteristics of the law; at Des Moines, Iowa, I was given a long and narrow half-moon panel, twenty-five or thirty feet in length and only about five feet in width at the center, and they *would* have for a subject, the Presentation of the Flag to the First Regiment that went to the Civil War. Of course, I couldn't get in a human figure and a flag in the proper way, so I made an awkward girl holding it and letting it sag to the ground.

In the Capitol of Pierre, South Dakota, I painted a panel of the Lewis and Clark expedition which camped at about this place. I made the river and the bluffs, with a voyageur in a coonskin cap sitting on an overturned canoe and bargaining with an Indian who is showing him a buffalo pelt. An amusing incident, which my friends would say shows how "Simmy always falls on his feet," is the way I painted the Indian. The librarian of the building was a great expert on Indian lore and had ferreted out much obscure knowledge, much to the annoyance of some of the painters, who were constantly having to change their figures to agree with his statements. I made an Indian with two braids of hair, but later added another, as he had his back turned and it suited my composition. This librarian wrote me an enthusiastic letter saying that he had supposed himself the only man in existence who knew that the tribe of Sioux Indians that lived in South Dakota were the only ones who wore their hair in three braids.

About this time (I was sixty years old) I thought it wise to stop and take cognizance of myself. My work was too literal, too full of details, and I wondered what the causes could be. First, there was my natural timidity. As a boy, I was taught not to fight. Surrounded by women all my childhood, with natural tendencies to stay in the house and read or draw, the baby of the family and always ailing—all these circumstances kept me away from a rough-and-tumble boy's life. I can remember only one real fight in my young days. It was when I was seven years old.

I had a little spotted overcoat which in the opinion of the authorities had gotten too shabby. It must have been very old, for it was given to the small son of our washerwoman, a boy about my age. In front of the schoolhouse one day, we were coasting, when some one put a stick on the coast. I hit it and was thrown off my sled. It happened again, and I realized that it had been intentional. I lost my temper and threatened all sorts of things happening to the boy who did it, and dared him to do it again.

It happened again. I was furious and told the offending boy to step out. Lo! my washerwoman's son with my overcoat on! Of course, I was badly pummeled, but I can remember the mystic feeling of striking my spotty overcoat. Though I really was worsted in the battle, I bore but few signs of it, and as he got a black eye, when asked who won I very meanly pointed to the evidence and left the questioner to his own inference.

This quality of timidity has always been accompanied in my nature by a great love of heroic deeds, and I find that it is so of many persons of my type. My brother told me of meeting Charles Reade when he went to England with the Harvard crew to row a match with

Oxford. Mr. Reade lived close by, on the Thames, and he dined and wined the boys. In return they invited the author to go out in the launch to see them get into their shell. This very tall man, whose stories redounded with feats of bravery, walked down the fixed steps which led to the float, but when he felt the raft moving under his feet, he drew back and would go no further.

Reade was also overwhelmed by love of facts and could always produce the proof of any statement he made. (I see a lot of myself in this.) The great joke among the Harvard boys was when he declared, after a long recital of something that he thought had occurred in America:

"I found the statement in one of the reputable journals of your country"—and he produced the *Police Gazette!*

Other faults in my work were caused by my early New England environment and education. To me, modern education is like a puddle in the road—very broad, but only two inches deep—and one must remember that truth has never been said to come from a puddle. In pictures, truth dwells in deep places. There is a painting in France of "Truth Arising from a Well" and the scandalized burghers fleeing in every direction. It isn't considered decent, even in New York, to listen to naked truth, hence the crucifixion of all geniuses, from Christ to Whistler.

It is so strange to see mothers teaching their girls; for example, to take care of babies by giving them dolls, but as to the method of procuring these babies—no! My early ignorance had driven me in the opposite direction later in life. In my desire to be truthful, I went too far and filled my work with a mass of unimportant details.

The subject of education reminds me of an experience I once had with a man of high authority, in the question of the teaching of youth. In fact, he was the president of the board of education of the largest city of the country. Also, he was in the "art" business—that is, he made what were supposed to be the most artistic calendars and pictures used by large firms for advertising purposes. During my hard-up days a friend of mine suggested that I send him a canvas of a girl's head that I had done out of pure *chic*, thinking it was the style of thing he could use. I have never been successful with illustration (it needs a special talent), and I would have been surprised if he had accepted it, but I was surely not prepared for this statement from a man occupying so prominent a position in the educational world as he.

"Too much character in the face, Mr. Simmons, too much character. We mustn't have any at all."

And this man's productions go all over the United States, in many obscure and out-of-the-way places. They are the only specimens (besides those atrocities—the Sunday colored supplements) that the people have upon which to form an artistic taste.

Then there is that tendency to "follow de crowd." We all have it, and in attempting to get away from it resort to the other extreme, resulting in so-called Cubism and Futurism, etc. We are like the sheep I saw on Scott's ranch in California. Although for two generations the rail fence leading from one field to another had not existed, these creatures still skipped in the empty air, just as did their grandfathers long ago. We are the same, else why do sculptors make statues in marble when there is an abundance of wonderful jasper in this country? Tradition and the Greeks say so. I have no quarrel with the man who goes to the other extreme, provided he first learns what the world has found out, up to his time, about his art, and then chooses to differ. He may possibly add something. But if he insists upon being ignorant, it is like the Sultan's order to his general to burn the library at Alexandria. "If the books agree with the Koran, they are needless; if they disagree, they are wicked. Burn them."

We speak of Realism and Idealism—it seems to me that we just go around in circles and all such discussion is futile. First, we dig with our noses, like the ground hog, producing Realism; then we gradually climb up, going through all the stages of Idealism, Superidealism, Æstheticism, and Euphuism. Then bang! we drop back again to the ground hog and dig for the truth.

Kenyon Cox gave us the best idea of this question that I know of. He said (to paraphrase): "Every honest worker is striving to realize his ideal. He maintains, if he succeeds, that he has produced Realism, but it is not the way we outsiders see it. To us it is Idealism."

Hawkins told me about following Corot in the fields when he was painting. One day when the master had made a particularly beautiful landscape, with cows browsing in the foreground, Hawkins objected to the fact that Corot had painted in a pond when there was really none in sight.

"My cows will be in my picture for a thousand years," he answered, "and I put in the pond to give them some water."

In 1913, the order for the Panama Pacific International Exposition at San Francisco came along, and in order to free my mind of old ties and get a new point of view, I took a boat to the Barbadoes, before starting my compositions.

If any man wishes to find a perfect figure with purely Greek movement, let him go the Barbadoes. The black women walking past his window will give him the sensation of Greek statues in motion. I was not long enough there to see much of the islands, as recovered health and spirits and a great new urge for work drove me home long before I had planned. On going to the steamship office, I found that my return ticket could not be used for more than two months, no berth being free until then, but I resolved to go home, and when I make up my mind to a thing I generally succeed.

A steamer came in three days, of course full, and I made a bet with a friend that I could return by it. So, getting my duds together and arranging with a boatman to do just as I told him, I set out for the steamer in the harbor. I chose the hour when most of the officers would be on shore, dining, sent the men up ahead of me with my baggage, to be deposited in a corner of the deck, following it with my return ticket. Then I hid behind a fresh-air funnel. When the ship was well away and the pilot dropped, I emerged, sought the smoking-room and the steward.

"When does this room close?"
"At midnight."

"Could you make me up a bed there?" tipping him.
"It's against the rules, but I could."

I then sought the purser. A big fight, but I won out, and all during one of the pleasantest voyages I ever made I slept upon a mattress placed upon four chairs in the smoking room.

It was the delight of my life to be able to carry out, in the San Francisco work, an idea that I had been mulling over for years—namely, that of doing a large panel with only three pots of color—red, yellow, and blue—and three brushes. Somehow, I felt that this would simplify my work, and I think I was right. The canvases, forty-six feet long, were to be placed high in the open air, and needed a certain boldness of treatment which I meant to acquire, so I made a flesh-color sky, white drapery, pink roses, black hair, etc., all with three colors, crisscross, using red, white, and blue stripes about as wide as my finger, for the entire composition. I was in doubt as to whether I could express form in this way, but found that I could, and there is not a single outline in the two panels.

I was, as I have been in many other cases, forbidden to use the nude, the idea being that the Westerners would not stand for it. As usual, I paid no attention to the order and painted a nude female figure nine feet tall, directly facing one, for the Fine Arts. No one seemed to notice it, as I heard no objections raised. As Thomas Dewing says, "Vulgarity is in every human being and will out. With some it shows in their acts or talk, and with some in their work. It would seem wiser to have it come out in some less permanent way than work."

The two panels were painted in my studio with the help of my assistant, Ira Remsen, and in 1914, before the fair opened, all of the artists assembled in San Francisco to add the finishing touches and see their work placed. It was my second visit to the Coast, and my earlier memories of the good times, hospitality, and generosity were repeated. Childe Hassam and Robert Reid were among those who helped beautify the buildings, Hassam proving that he was a decorator as well as a picture painter, and Reid making one of the hits of the fair by those fine things in the Fine Arts Building which the city of San Francisco has seen fit to preserve for all time.

Our membership in the Lambs' Club gave us the privilege of enjoying the Bohemian Club, with whom courtesies are exchanged, and in the summer we made the trip to the Bohemian Grove to see the annual play produced. Here in the Outdoor Theater, with the giant redwoods forming a background, one gets a unique impression, if not purely artistic. The proscenium is two hundred feet high and the stage too large for the human animal, making an effect (as the play which I saw was based on purely modern ideas, fit only for an intimate audience) rather disappointing. Like everything else in California, however, it is overwhelming.

Over in the Greek Theater in Berkeley, during this summer, it was my good fortune to see Gilbert and Sullivan in the right setting for the first time. The idea of "Trial by Jury" (with the inimitable DeWolf Hopper), played in this theater which has been copied from one of classic times, seemed rather incongruous. But to my surprise it was as Greek as Aristophanes.

One is always having surprises out West. I saw one of the three or four best decorations in America, painted by a Californian and totally unknown. They say that a prophet is never respected in his own land, so, instead of giving Charley Dickman, the artist, one of the important jobs at the Exposition, the committee came east to New York and even went to Europe for painters.

The decoration that I speak of is across the bay from San Francisco in Oakland, in the office of a Borax company. Dickman has given a picture of the desert, where the product is found, using that Corot gray of Death Valley as a basic color harmony, making the figures and a horse, all of the same tone, chime in with no discord. It shows an unusual ease of treatment of a very difficult question. Again he has managed to turn two corners (which is supposed to be against all laws of decoration) so successfully that one is unaware of the fact. To me, it was a remarkable work of art, but no one in town seemed to know about it.

I had hoped to stay in California; every one dreams of dying there, I suppose, but I found it would be impossible to make a living. They will not purchase anything that has not already been hallmarked by New York or European approval. Then, too, the climate produces a strange effect upon the Eastern temperament. I saw an apple tree with fruit larger and different from any I had ever eaten. The farmer assured me, upon his word of honor, that he had brought it from New England as a young tree and that it had been a true Eastern russet.

After my return to New York I carried out two

EDWARD SIMMONS
At the age of seventy

ceilings for Mr. Rockefeller, which were placed in the tea houses at the entrance to his Tarrytown home; I made a decoration for a lumber man down in Mississippi, and then came the War. I was too old to go; they even refused me in the Camouflage section, although I insist I would have been of use.

Although I was not allowed to take part in the War, my whole world changed. The color of everything—we were enmeshed in khaki. To eyes accustomed to riotous shades, this deadening of the whole tone of things was tremendously depressing. And then the strides—machine guns, tanks, bombs, poison gas, everything came tumbling and tossing, one over the other, in a mad strife for something to end it all. But all the time they were only getting farther involved. I wanted to keep step, and felt as if I were marching, marching, marching—until I would suddenly become conscious that I was only sitting still. I had never found the necessity of realizing the meaning of the old saying, "He also serves——" For the first time I was forced to acknowledge that it was the age of the young. I saw a picture of myself as the perfect Uncle Sam, his long legs stiff, his gray hair flying in the wind, his coat tails standing out farther than they had ever done, struggling to keep his footing; while all about him, over him, and under him were a mass of young men and boys in uniforms of tan, bearing the modern equipment of war and heeding not at all this old-fashioned figure who was gradually being left behind.

Chapter XVI: In Retrospect

I ONCE started a sonnet to "My Soul," but, having written one line, I found that I had said all—

Cross-hatched with many a shameful scar.

It is doubtful if I have a soul, but if so, I am sure that if it shows scars of victory, they are the results of battles that should not have been fought.

We have never been a religious family, as I look back. The future? For me it is here. My mother understood. Think of the agony of a woman who had never had a hand laid upon her since she was a child, lying completely helpless, paralyzed for six years! The last time I saw her, I said:

"Mother, you and I know what we believe about a future life?"

She nodded feebly.

"You are unhappy here?"

Again the nod, with a pathetic look in her eyes. I leaned over and whispered in her ear.

"Mother, I hope you die to-night."

No one knew of our conversation, but I was told afterward that she wrote on her slate that evening, "Edward has cheered me up greatly."

I see that I have always felt this way and have tried to live the fullest life possible. When I think of the progress of mankind during my seventy years—from lamps to electricity, from horses to gasoline, from slow mails to wireless, and the aeroplane bringing the other continent as near to us to-day as the next town was in my boyhood—I marvel at those who say that the world is going backward.

The advance of one human being is comparable to the advance of the whole race—it is the resultant force of a spiral spring. At the bottom of the coil is Realism; at the top, Idealism and, although we are a long time in getting around the circle, the progress is as certain as the air we breathe.

All these changes should make me feel old, but they don't. Like Barton Hill, who went to call upon an old friend and mistaking the daughter (who came to greet him) for her mother, said:

> "Now I solve the wondrous question,
> Now I find what I did lack.
> You've stolen some years from your mother
> And forgot to give them back."

I do not wish to belong to my own generation. "Whom the gods love, die young" does not mean that they die when they *are* young, but that they are *young* when they die, and I could not ask anything finer from a generous Creator.

I have been happy from the time I was born. It may be that time covers with an ivy of forgetfulness the early wounds and renders them less hideous, but I do not think so in my own case. I am a lover; I am happy because I love all things. I feel like our Irish cook who brought in a fish from the river, cooked it, and proceeded to consume it all, clutching it at the tail and eating all the way up, saying,

"It's all very swate; it's all very swate."

Since a boy, I have been able to take an interest in

the crack in a granite stone and wonder "why"; in the lichen that grows upon it, and "why"; in the blackberry bushes around it, and "why"; in the earth underneath through its change into sand; in the weather and in the life of all the little things. After death, to furnish the manure for all these is enough of a future life for me.

Meanwhile, there is still beauty in the curve of a wave or a woman's breast, there is liberty and there are friends. But best of all there is hope. I am still an optimist.

THE END